Dana
M

GRANADA
SEVILLE
CORDOBA

'There are spots around the Mediterranean
where the presence of past glories becomes
almost tangible, a mixture of mythic
antiquity, lost power and dissipated energy
that broods over a place like a ghost.'

CADOGANguides

Contents

About the authors

Dana Facaros and **Michael Pauls** have written over 30 books for Cadogan Guides, including the entire Spain series. They have lived all over Europe but have recently hung up their castanets in a farmhouse surrounded by vineyards in the Lot valley.

About the updater

Adam Coulter's first memory of Andalucía is of standing outside a tapas bar in Seville on a warm October night in 1989. He moved to Spain two years later, living in Oviedo and Madrid but frequently visiting the south. He now lives in London but returns to Spain whenever he can find a suitable excuse.

Cadogan Guides
Network House, 1 Ariel Way, London W12 7SL
cadoganguides@morrispub.co.uk
www.cadoganguides.com

The Globe Pequot Press
246 Goose Lane, PO Box 480, Guilford,
Connecticut 06437–0480

Copyright © Dana Facaros and Michael Pauls
    1991, 1994, 1996, 1999, 2001
Updated by Adam Coulter 2001

Cover and photo essay design by Kicca Tommasi
Book design by Andrew Barker
Cover photographs by John Ferro Sims
Maps © Cadogan Guides,
    drawn by Map Creation Ltd
Editorial Director: Vicki Ingle
Series Editor: Linda McQueen
Editor: Linda McQueen
Layout: Sarah Rianhard-Gardner
Indexing: Judith Wardman
Production: Book Production Services

Printed in the UK by Cambridge University Press
A catalogue record for this book is available
    from the British Library
ISBN 1-86011-826-7

Granada Seville
Cordoba
a photo essay

by John Ferro Sims

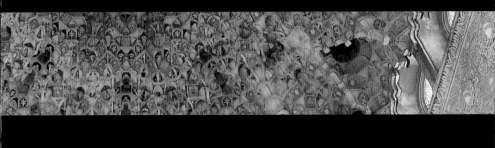

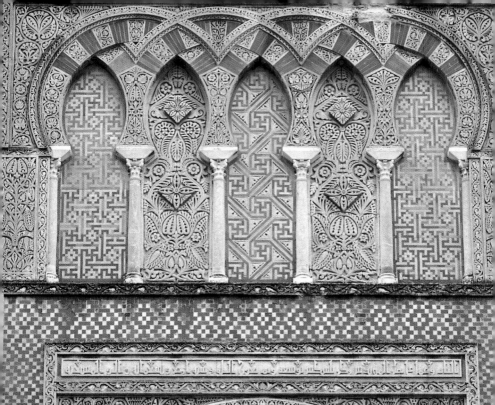

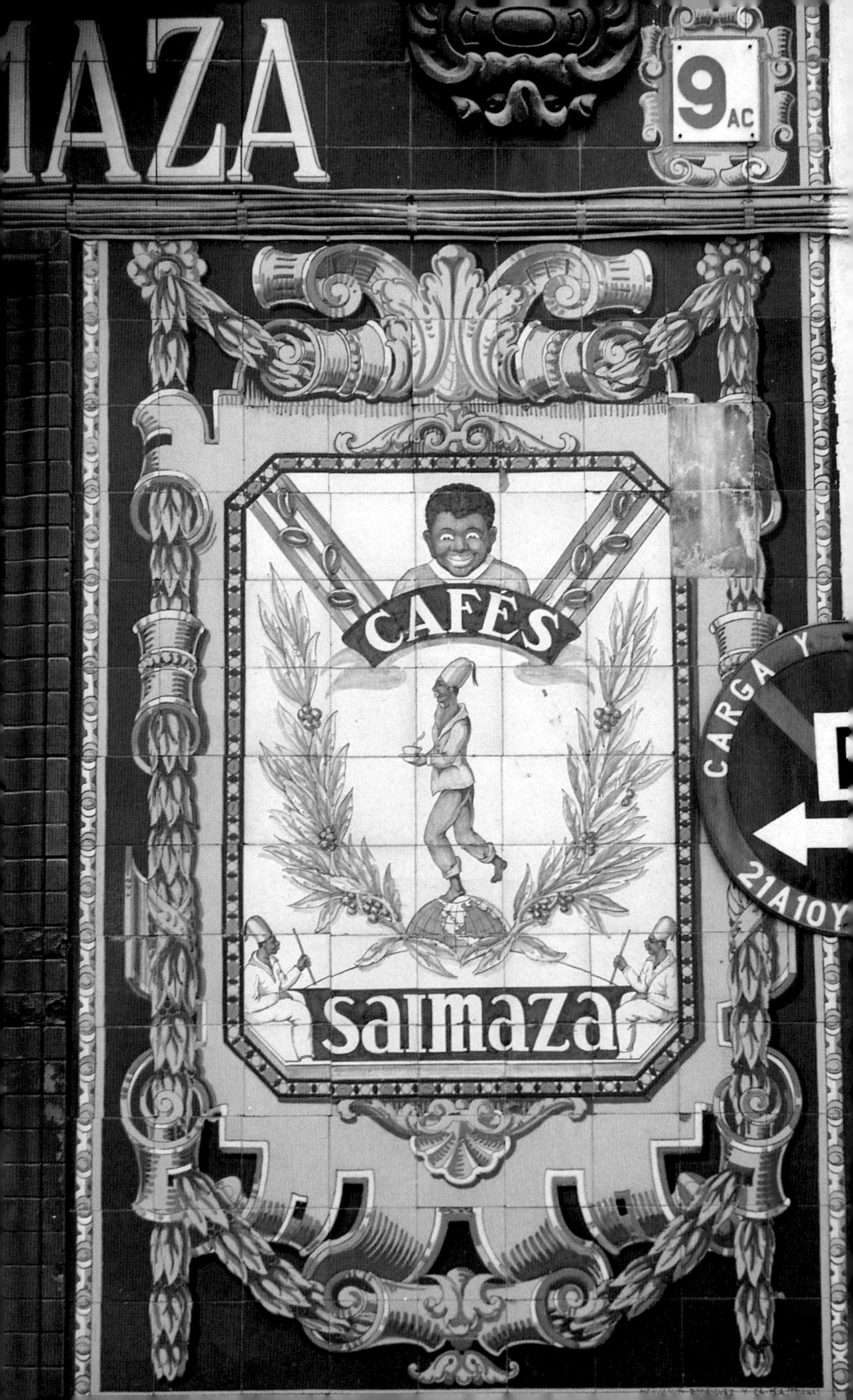

MAZA
9 AC
CAFÉS
salmaza
CARGA Y
21 A 10 Y

Granada,
Alhambra,

Cordoba,
flamenco festival

Seville window

Seville,
Semana Santa procession

Seville, Feria

Cordoba,
La Mezquita

Granada,
Alhambra,

Seville, Alcázar

Granada

Seville

Cordoba

Seville, azulejo tiles

Granada.
Alhambra

Granada

About the photographer

John Ferro Sims was born of Anglo-Italian parents in Udine, Italy. He worked successfully for five years as an investment analyst before quitting the world of money for a career as a professional photographer which has taken him around the world. He has published 9 books.

Introduction

You don't often see Andalucíans going off on picnics in the country. The ground is dry, vegetation sparse, and the sun can seem like a death-ray even in winter. The climate has always forced people here to seek their pleasure elsewhere; it is the impetus behind their exquisite gardens, and it has made of them the most resolutely urban people in Europe. In city centres the air is electric, a cocktail of motion, colour, and fragrances that goes to your head like the best *manzanilla*. But the cities of the south didn't get this way overnight.

Nearly everything that is special about modern Andalucía got its start in the charmed lost world of al-Andalus. When the Arab raiders settled in these towns after their conquest, they rather quickly went mad for gardens and poetry, for fountains and fairytales. A thousand years ago, when the Christian kings of Europe were sleeping on rushes and learning to write their names, a caliph of Cordoba was holding court in a garden pavilion with walls made of falling water, around a reflecting pool of liquid mercury. The Moors brought the first oranges, and the first roses (both from Persia). They brought Ziryab, the Blackbird, greatest musician of his day, from Baghdad, and he added a fifth string to the local version of the lute to create the Spanish guitar – when he played it, the audience would cry 'Allah!', which their modern counterparts have turned into '*Olé!*'

And as a special gift to these three cities, the Moors left each one a magic building, something unique in all the world, to serve as the city's symbol and mould its destiny through the centuries to come.

Seville got La Giralda, still the tallest tower in Spain and by far the showiest. To live up to this symbol Seville after the Moors became the capital of all the finest Spanish stereotypes: the home of roses and passion, *mantillas* and bulls and flamenco. Aristocrat Seville is the compulsive exhibitionist among these three cities, and she keeps herself on permanent display even when she is not putting on another World's Fair.

Cordoba got the Great Mosque. This city is strong for *los toros* too, and all the rest of the Andalucían shibboleths, but, being home to such a magnificently subtle and philosophical monument, Cordoba has become a much more quiet and introspective city than its neighbour down the Guadalquivir. Besides the mosque, Cordoba's beau-ties are the flower-strewn patios hidden behind the walls of its houses. They leave the gates open so you can have just a peek.

Granada's gift was the Alhambra, by common consent the loveliest palace in the world, in the loveliest setting, underneath the snowcapped Sierra Nevada. Such a past, combined with the rather gloomy history that followed, makes Granada the most wistful and melancholy of these cities; how you see it may depend on the mood you're in when you come.

Even on a rare cloudy day, though, melancholy will never set in too deeply. You'll find that all three of these towns have thrived in the 'New Spain' of the last twenty years. And they all seem to be full of noisy, happy folk who care only to remember the fun parts of their past, while getting along with the important things of life – seafood and sherry, music and dancing. You won't be bored.

A Guide to the Guide

The first three chapters offer an anthropological background. **History** begins in the caves around Gibraltar, and then develops over 50,000 years to rest awhile in the pavilions of Seville. **Art and Architecture** follows through the design of Spanish buildings. **Snapshots of Andalucía** provides a random glimpse of the region's culture in a potpourri of short essays. **Food and Drink** gives you the background to southern Spain's gourmet and street cuisine, and includes a Spanish menu reader to help you choose from the vast array of possibilities.

For many Hispanophiles with little time to spare, combining visits to two or three cities is the best option; indeed many tour operators (including those listed on p.75) offer such holidays tailor-made. If you prefer to draw up your own itinerary and choose your own accommodation, the **Travel** and **Practical A–Z** chapters are packed with information to help you plan your journey, travel between cities, and select a place to stay.

The three dazzling cities of **Granada**, **Seville** (Sevilla) and **Cordoba** (Córdoba) are then covered in detail, each with its own background of history and art, and all the sights you might choose to visit: museums, art galleries, mosques and cathedrals, marketplaces, squares, or simply those atmoospheric streets that are a pleasure just to wander around. Each chapter opens with a practical guide to where to stay and eating out, shopping and nightlife, flamenco and tapas bars. Finally there are suggestions for **day trips** out of each city that can be made by car, or by local bus or train.

The book concludes with **Language**, a **Glossary** of historical, political, artistic and architectural terms used in the guide, suggestions for **Further Reading** that might enlighten you, and a **Chronology**.

Geography of the Region

Andalucía covers the southern fifth of the Iberian peninsula, occupying an expanse equivalent to slightly more than half the area of Portugal. Its natural border to the north is the rugged **Sierra Morena** mountain chain; the wild Atlantic batters its western shores and the timid Mediterranean laps its southern coast. The Sierra Morena mountains, although reaching barely 4,000ft, were for a long time a deterrent to northern invaders. The only natural interruption is the **Pass of Despeñaperros**, or the 'gateway to Andalucía'. Numerous early travellers spoke with awe of the first time they traversed this pine-clad gorge; the frontier that separated 'the land of men from the land of gods'. Arriving in Andalucía at this point provides a strong contrast indeed from the barren plains of La Mancha to the north. These peaks, rich in minerals, sweep down to the fertile **Guadalquivir** plain, widening towards the western coast to form broad salt marshes and mud flats – including the **Coto Doñana National Park**. From here, the coast as far as the Portuguese border is virtually one long sandy beach.

South of the Guadalquivir valley the land rises again to form the craggy, spectacular **Serranía de Ronda** mountain range, home to bandits and smugglers for centuries;

the terrain then descends sharply to meet the balmy palm-lined shores of the Mediterranean, with Tarifa, the furthest south you can go on mainland Europe, and a mere 12km from the African coast, and Gibraltar, that geological oddity of a rock. From the Serranía de Ronda the land dips and rises as it goes east till it joins the heights of the snow-capped **Sierra Nevada**, the highest peaks on mainland Spain, below which lie long beaches, tiny coves and crystal-clear water.

Dry as it is, Andalucía when properly tended has been the garden of Spain. The soil in most areas, *argiles de montmorillionite*, holds water like a sponge. The Romans first discovered how to irrigate it; the Moors perfected the system, and also introduced the palm and such crops as cotton, rice, oranges and sugar. Today most of the inhabitants of the region live in cities – it's traditionally one of the most urbanized regions in Europe – but its farmers have discovered the modern delights of tractors and of owning their own land. Unless the Habsburgs or the Francoists come back, the region will have no excuse for not making a good living. Between the towns, spaces seem vast and empty, endless hillsides of olives, vineyards, wheat and sunflowers. Come in the spring, when the almond trees are in blossom, the oranges turn orange and wild flowers surge up along the roadsides – the unforgettable splash of colour that characterizes cheerful Andalucía and its warm, vibrant people.

Animal Magic: Wildlife Reserves

There are over 20 important wildlife reserves in Andalucía – the coast, the wetlands behind it, the scrub deserts of Almería and the mountain slopes of the Sierra Nevada, and many of them are accessible as day trips from Granada, Seville and Cordoba. They are given different names, depending on their importance. **Reservas Naturales** are usually small sites of specific scientific interest such as lagoons or copses. **Parques Naturales** are larger and permit traditional land use within their borders. **Parques Nacionales** are of international importance with restricted access.

Most famous and most spectacular of all is the **Coto Doñana**, on the Cadiz coast west of Seville, southern Spain's only Parque Nacional. Though the terrain may appear flat and monotonous at first sight, it consists of a range of different and distinct habitats including cork oak forest, scrubland, swamp, raised flooded areas and reedy channels filled by the Guadalquivir as it reaches the coast. These are a haven for hundreds of species of native and migratory birds including the largest population of Spanish imperial eagles in the world. These share the wetlands with pardel lynx, wild boar and 50 other species of mammals, reptiles and amphibians.

The **Sierra Nevada Parque Natural**, south of Granada, which peaks at 3,482m, is famous for its alpine flowers, which include 70 endemic species and its butterflies. Spanish Ibex, rescued from the brink of extinction in the 1940s, also live here. They are seen most easily in the evening on the lower peaks. The lower slopes, known locally as '*zona erizo*' (hedgehog zone) are shrouded in prickly scrub, and below them the valleys of the Alpujarras are filled with birdsong, butterflies and semi-tropical fruits – even custard apples grow here.

History

03

Prehistory

Southern Spain has been inhabited since the remotest antiquity. The area around Huelva is only one of the places in Spain where remains from the early Pleistocene have been found, and some finds on the peninsula suggest somebody was poking about as far back as one million years ago. Only 250,000 years ago, they were making tools out of elephant tusks, when they were lucky enough to catch one. A site near – of all places – the centre of Marbella is currently being excavated for its Middle-Palaeolithic remains. Neanderthal man wandered all over Spain some 50,000 years ago, and Gibraltar seems to have been one of his favourite locations. Later people, the devious and quarrelsome *homo sapiens*, contributed the simple cave paintings in the Cueva de la Pileta and some other sites near Ronda *c.* 25,000 BC – nothing as elaborate as the famous paintings at Altamira and other sites in northern Spain, though they date from about the same time.

The great revolution in human affairs known as the **Neolithic Revolution**, including the beginnings of agriculture and husbandry, began to appear around the Iberian coasts *c.* 6000 BC. By the 4th millennium BC, the Neolithic people had developed an advanced culture, building dolmens, stone circles and burial mounds all along the fringes of western Europe – Newgrange, Avebury, Stonehenge, Carnac. In southern Spain, they left the huge tumuli at Antequera called the Cueva de Romeral and the Cueva de Menga. By *c.* 3200 BC, they had learned to make use of copper, and a metal-working nation created the great complex at Los Millares near Almería, a veritable Neolithic city with fortifications, outer citadels and a huge tumulus surrounded by circles of standing stones. Los Millares and sites associated with it began to decline about 2500 BC, and most of them were abandoned by 2000 BC, replaced by different, bronze-working peoples who often founded their settlements on the same old sites.

1100–201 BC

The native Iberians learn that if you've got a silver mine in your backyard, you'll never be lonely

In the 2nd millennium BC, while early civilizations rose and fell in the Middle East and eastern Mediterranean, the west remained a backwater – southern Spain in particular found nothing to disturb its dreams until the arrival of the **Phoenicians**, who 'discovered' Spain perhaps as early as 1100 BC (that is the traditional date; many archaeologists suspect they didn't appear until 900 or 800). As a base for trading, they founded Gades (Cadiz), claimed to be the oldest city in western Europe, and from there they slowly expanded into a string of colonies along the coast. The Phoenicians were after Spain's mineral resources – copper, tin, gold, silver and mercury, all in short supply in the Middle East at this time – and their trade with the native Iberians made the Phoenicians the economic masters of the Mediterranean (the flood of Andalucían silver from the Río Tinto mines into the Middle East caused one of history's first recorded spells of inflation, in the Assyrian Empire). Such wealth eventually attracted the Phoenicians' bitter rivals, the **Greeks**, who arrived in 636 BC and founded a trading post at Mainake near Malaga, though they were never to be a real force in the region.

The great mystery of this era is the fabled kingdom of **Tartessos**, which covered all or part of Andalucía; the name seems to come from Tertis, an ancient name of the Guadalquivir River. Phoenician records mention it, as does Herodotus, and it may be the legendary 'Tarshish' mentioned in the Book of Kings, its great navy bringing wares of Spain and Africa to trade with King Solomon. With great wealth from the mines of the Río Tinto and the Sierra Morena, Tartessos may have appeared about 800–700 BC. Very little is known of the real story behind the legends of Tartessos, but they reflect the fact that Iberian communities throughout the peninsula were rapidly gaining in wealth and sophistication. Archaeologists refer to the 7th and 6th centuries as the 'orientalizing period' of Iberian culture, when the people of Spain were adopting wholesale elements of life and art from the Phoenicians and Greeks. Iberians imported Greek and Phoenician art, and learned to copy its themes and techniques for themselves. They developed an adaptation of the Phoenician alphabet, and began an agricultural revolution that has shaped the land up to this day with two new crops their eastern visitors brought them – the grape and the olive.

By the 6th century, the Phoenicians of the Levant were under Babylonian rule, and **Carthage**, their western branch office, was building an empire out of their occupied coasts in Spain, Sicily and North Africa. About 500 BC, the Carthaginians gobbled up the last remains of Tartessos and other coastal areas and stopped the Greek infiltration. The Carthaginians maintained the status quo until 264–241 BC, when Rome drubbed them in the First Punic War.

Before that, Carthage had been largely a sea power. After Rome built itself a navy and beat them, the Carthaginians changed tack and rebuilt their empire as a land power, based on the resources and manpower of Spain. Beginning in 237, they established military control throughout most of the peninsula under **Hamilcar Barca**. This, along with other factors, alarmed Rome enough to reopen hostilities. In the rematch, the **Second Punic War** (218–201 BC), Hamilcar's son **Hannibal** marched off to Italy with his elephants and a largely Spanish army. Meanwhile the Romans under **Scipio Africanus** entered Spain by sea. At first, Scipio's intention was merely to cut off Hannibal's supply routes to Italy. But it was a brilliant stroke, and under Scipio's able command the Romans were able to eventually gain control of all Iberia, winning important battles at Bailén in 208, and Alcalá del Rio, near Seville, the following year. After that, Scipio was able to use Spain as a base to attack Carthage itself, forcing Hannibal to evacuate Italy and leading to total victory for Rome.

201 BC–AD 409
The Romans muscle in, and do the Spaniards the way the Spaniards would one day do the Mexicans

Unlike their predecessors, the Romans were never content to hold just a part of Spain. Relentlessly, they slogged over the peninsula, subjugating one Celtic or Iberian tribe after another, a job that was not entirely completed in northern Spain until AD 220. Even then, rebellions against Rome were frequent and bloody, including a major one in Andalucía in 195. Rome had to send its best – Cato, Pompey, Julius Caesar and Octavian (Augustus) were all commanders in the Spanish conquest. Caesar, in fact, was briefly governor in Andalucía, the most prosperous part of the peninsula, and the one that adapted most easily to Roman rule and culture.

Not that Roman rule was much of a blessing. Iberia, caught in the middle of a huge geopolitical struggle between two powerful neighbours, had simply exchanged one colonial overlord for another. Both were efficiently rapacious in the exploitation of the all-important mines, keeping the profits for themselves alone. As in every land conquered by the legions, most of the best land was collected together into huge estates owned by the Roman élite, on which the former inhabitants were enslaved or reduced to the status of tenant farmers. The Iberians had reasons to resist as strongly as they did.

At first the Romans called Andalucía simply 'Further Spain', but eventually it settled in as **Baetica**, from the Bætis, another ancient name for the Guadalquivir river. During the first three centuries AD, when the empire was at its height, Baetica became a prosperous, contented place – by grace of its great mineral and agricultural wealth the richest part of the empire west of Italy and Tunisia. Baetica poured out oceans of plonk for the empire; the Romans sniffed at its quality but they were never shy about ordering more. In Rome today you can see a 160ft-high hill called Monte Testaccio, made entirely of broken amphorae – most of them from Spain. Besides wine, oil and metals, another export was dancing girls; Baetica's girls were reputed to be the hottest in the empire. And for the choicer Roman banquets, there was *garum*, a highly prized condiment made of fish guts. Modern gourmets have been trying to guess the recipe for centuries.

New cities grew up to join Cadiz, Itálica and Malaga. Of these, the most important were **Hispalis** (Seville) and **Corduba** (Cordoba), which became Baetica's capital. Other towns owe their beginnings to the common Roman policy of establishing colonies populated by army veterans, such as Colonia Genetiva Iulia Ursa – modern Osuna. Among the cosmopolitan population were Iberians, Celts, Phoenicians, Italians, and a sizeable minority of **Jews**. During the Diaspora, Rome settled them here in great numbers, as far from home as they could possibly put them; they would play an important and constructive role in Spanish life for the next 1,500 years. The province also had a talent for keeping in the mainstream of imperial politics and culture. Vespasian had been governor here, and Baetica gave birth to three of Rome's best emperors: Trajan, Hadrian and Theodosius. It also contributed almost all the great figures of the 'silver age' of Latin literature – Lucan, both Senecas, Martial and Quintilian. None of these, of course, were really 'Andalucíans' except by birth; all were part of the thin veneer of élite Roman families that owned nearly everything, and monopolized colonial Spain's political and cultural life. Concerning the other 99 per cent of the population, we know very little.

409–711

Finally rid of its Roman bosses, Spain hasn't a minute before some malodorous blue-eyed Teutons come to take their place

By the 4th century, the crushing burden of maintaining the defence budget and the government bureaucracy sent Spain's economy, along with the rest of the Empire's, into a permanent depression. Cities declined, and in the countryside the landowners gradually squeezed the majority of the population into serfdom or outright slavery. Thus when the bloody, anarchic **Vandals** arrived in Spain in 409, they found bands of rural guerrillas, or *bagaudae*, to help them in smashing up the remnants of the Roman system. The Vandals moved on to Africa in 428, leaving nothing behind but, maybe, the name Andalucía – some believe it was originally Vandalusia.

The next uninvited guests were the **Visigoths**, a ne'er-do-well Germanic folk who had caused little trouble for anyone until they were pushed westwards by the Huns. After making a name for themselves by sacking Rome under their chief Alaric in 410, they found their way into Spain four years later, looking for food. By 478 they had conquered most of it, including Andalucía, and they established an independent kingdom stretching from the Atlantic to the Rhône. The Visigoths were illiterate, selfish and bloody-minded, but persistent enough to endure, despite endless dynastic and religious quarrels; like most Germans, they were Arian heretics. There weren't many of them; estimates of the original invading horde range up to some 200,000, and for the next three centuries they would remain a warrior élite that never formed more than a small fraction of the population. For support they depended on the landowners, who were making the slow but logical transition from Roman *senatores* to feudal lords. An interruption to their rule, at least in the south, came in 553; Justinian's reviving Eastern Empire, having already reclaimed Italy and Africa, tried for Spain too. Byzantine resources proved just enough to wrest Andalucía from the Visigoths, but the overextended Empire was hardly able to hold all its far-flung conquests for very long. Over the following decades the Visigoths gradually pushed them back, though some coastal bases remained in Byzantine hands as late as the Arab invasion.

Despite all the troubles, Andalucía at least seems to have been doing well – probably better than anywhere else in western Europe – and there was even a modest revival of learning in the 7th century, the age of St Isidore (*c.* 560–636), famous scholar of Seville. King Leovigild (573–86) was an able leader; his son Reccared converted to orthodox Catholicism in 589; both helped bring their state to the height of its power as much by internal reform as military victories. Allowing the grasping Church a share of power, however, proved fatal to the Visigoths. The Church's depredations against the populace and its persecutions of Jews and heretics made the Visigothic state as many enemies within as it ever had beyond its borders. By the time of King Roderick, a Duke of Baetica who had usurped the throne in one of the kingdom's periods of political turbulence, Visigothic Spain was in serious disarray.

711–756
The Spaniards are conquered by a people they had never before heard of

The great wave of Muslim Arab expansion that began in Mohammed's lifetime was bound to wash up on Spain's shores sooner or later. A small Arab force arrived in Spain in 710, led by **Tarif**, who gave his name to today's Tarifa on the straits. The following year brought a larger army – still only about 7,000 men – under **Tariq ibn-Ziyad**, with the assistance of dissident Visigoths opposed to Roderick, and a certain Count Julian, Byzantine ruler of Ceuta, who supplied the ships to ferry over the Arab-Berber army; Tariq quickly defeated the Visigoths near Barbate, a battle in which Roderick was killed. Toledo, the Visigothic capital, fell soon after, and a collection of Visigothic nobles were on their way to Baghdad in chains as presents to the Caliph. Within five years, the Arabs had conquered most of the peninsula, and they were crossing the Pyrenees into France.

The ease of the conquest is not difficult to explain. The majority of the population was delighted to welcome the Arabs and their Berber allies. The overtaxed peasants and persecuted Jews supported them from the first. Religious tolerance was guaranteed under the new rule; since the largest share of taxes fell on non-believers, the Arabs were happy to refrain from forced conversions. The conquest, however, was never completed. A small Christian enclave in the northwest, the kingdom of Asturias, survived following an obscure but symbolic victory over the Moors at Covadonga in 718. At the time, the Arabs would barely have noticed; Muslim control of most of Spain was solid, but hampered almost from the start by dissension between the Arabs, the neglected Berbers, the large numbers of Syrians who arrived later, in another army sent from the east, and among the various tribes of the Arabs themselves. The Berbers had the biggest grudge. Not only did the Arabs look down on them, but in the distribution of confiscated lands they were not given their promised fair share. The result was a massive **Berber revolt** in 740. This was put down with some difficulty, but it was only one of a number of troubles, as fighting between the various Arab princes kept Spain in an almost continuous state of civil war. Between the feuding invaders, Spain suffered through one of the darkest centuries in its history.

756–929
Spain becomes al-Andalus, and things are looking up

Far away in Damascus, the political struggles of the caliphate were being resolved by a general massacre of the princes of the Umayyad dynasty, successors of Mohammed; a new dynasty, the Abbasids, replaced them. One young Umayyad escaped – **Abd ar-Rahman**; he fled to Cordoba, and took power with the support of Umayyad loyalists there. After a victory in May 756, he proclaimed himself emir, the first leader of an independent emirate of al-Andalus. At first, Abd ar-Rahman was only one of the contending petty princes fighting over a ruined, exhausted country.

Eventually he prevailed over them all, though the chronicles of the time are too thin to tell us whether he owed his ascendence to military talent, good fortune or just simple tenacity. It took him over thirty years of fighting to do the job, and besides rival Arabs he had to contend with invading Christian armies sent by Charlemagne in the 770s – a campaign that, though unsuccessful, left us the legend of Roland at Roncesvalles, source of the medieval epic *Chanson de Roland*.

Under this new government, Muslim Spain gradually recovered its strength and prosperity. Political unity was maintained only with great difficulty, but trade, urban life and culture flourished. Though their domains stretched as far as the Pyrenees, the Umayyad emirs referred to it all as **al-Andalus**. Andalucía was its heartland and Cordoba, Seville, and Malaga its greatest cities, unmatched by any others in western Europe. Abd ar-Rahman kept his capital at Cordoba and began the Great Mosque there, a brilliant and unexpected start to the culture of the new state.

After Abd ar-Rahman, the succession passed without difficulty through Hisham I (788–96), Al-Hakim I (796–822), and Abd ar-Rahman II (822–52), all of them sound military men, defenders of the faith and patrons of musicians and poets. Abd ar-Rahman I's innovations, the creation of a professional army and palace secretariat, helped considerably in maintaining stability. The latter, called the *Saqaliba*, a civil service of imported slaves, was made up largely of Slavs and black Africans. The new dynasty seems also to have worked sincerely to establish justice and balance among the various contentious ethnic groups. In the days of Abd ar-Rahman I, only a fifth of al-Andalus's population was Muslim. This figure would rise steadily throughout the existence of al-Andalus, finally reaching 90 per cent in the 1100s, but emirs would always have to deal with the concerns of a very cosmopolitan population that included haughty Arab aristocrats prone to factionalism, leftover Roman and Visigothic barons, who might be Christians or *muwallads* (converts to Islam), Iraqis, Syrians, Yemenites, and various other peoples from the eastern Muslim world, Berbers (who made up the bulk of the army), Jews, slaves from the furthest corners of three continents and all the old native Iberian population.

One weakness, shared with most early Islamic states, was the personal, non-institutional nature of rule. Individuals and groups could address their grievances only to the emir, while governors in distant towns had so much authority that they often began to think of themselves as independent potentates – a cause of frequent rebellions in the reigns of Mohammed I (852–86) and Abd Allah (888–912). Closer to home, discontented *muwallads* in the heart of Andalucía coalesced around the rather mysterious figure of **Umar ibn-Hafsun**. After his rebel army was defeated in 891, he and his followers took refuge in the impregnable fortress of Bobastro, in the mountains near Antequera, carrying on a kind of guerrilla war against the emirs. Later Christian propagandists claimed ibn-Hafsun as a Christian. Though this is unlikely, a church can still be seen among the ruins of Bobastro. After ibn-Hafsun's death, his sons held out until Bobastro was finally taken in 928.

A less serious problem, though a bothersome one, was the **Vikings**, who raided Spain's coasts just as they did all others within the reach of their longboats. Even though their raids took them as far as Seville, al-Andalus was better able to fight off the Northmen than any of the Christian states of Europe; under the reign of **Abd ar-Rahman II**, al-Andalus made itself into a seapower, with bases on both the Mediterranean and the Atlantic. In those days, interestingly enough, al-Andalus held on to two key port towns in North Africa, Ceuta and Melilla, to guard its southern flank – just as Spain does today. The pirates of Fraxinetum, La Garde-Freinet in southern France, made life miserable for the Provenceaux and helped keep the western Mediterranean a Muslim lake; they too acknowledged the sovereignty of Abd ar-Rahman.

929–1008
A Caliph rises in the west, and a great civilization reaches its noonday

In the tenth century, al-Andalus enjoyed its golden age. **Abd ar-Rahman III** (912–61) and **al-Hakim II** (961–76) collected tribute from the Christian kingdoms of the north, and from North African states as far as Algiers. In 929, Abd ar-Rahman III assumed the title of caliph, declaring al-Andalus entirely independent of any higher political or religious authority. Umayyad al-Andalus was in fact cooperating closely with the Abbasid Caliphate in Baghdad, but Shiite heretics in North Africa had declared their own caliph at Tunis, and Abd ar-Rahman, who like all the emirs was orthodox in religion, was not about to let himself be outranked by an upstart neighbour. After the peaceful reign of al-Hakim II, a boy caliph, Hisham II, came to the throne in 976. In a fateful turn of events, effective power was seized by his minister Abu Amir al-Ma'afiri, better known by the title he assumed, **al-Mansur** ('the Victorious', known to the Christians as Almanzor). Though an iron-willed dictator with a penchant for bloody slaughters of anyone suspected of opposing him, al-Mansur was also a brilliant military leader, one who resumed the offensive against the growing Christian kingdoms of the north. He recaptured León, Pamplona and Barcelona, sacked almost every Christian city at least once, and even raided the great pilgrimage shrine at Santiago de Compostela in Galicia, stealing its bells to hang up as trophies in the Great Mosque of Cordoba.

A more resounding al-Andalus accomplishment was keeping in balance its diverse and increasingly sophisticated population, all the while accommodating three religions and ensuring mutual tolerance. At the same time, they made it pay. Al-Andalus cities thrived, far more than any of their neighbours, Muslim or Christian, and the countryside was more prosperous than it has been before or since. The Arabs introduced cotton, rice, dates, sugar, oranges, artichokes and much else. Irrigation, begun under the Romans, was perfected; contemporary observers counted over 200 *nurias*, or water wheels, along the length of the Guadalquivir, and even parched Almería became a garden. It was this 'agricultural revolution', the application of eastern crops and techniques to a land perfectly adapted for them, that made all the rest possible. It meant greater wealth and an increased population, and permitted the growth of manufacturers and commerce far in advance of anything else in western Europe.

At the height of its fortunes, al-Andalus was one of the world's great civilizations. Its wealth and stability sustained an impressive artistic flowering – obvious today, even from the relatively few monuments that survived the Reconquista. Cordoba, with al-Hakim's great library, became a centre of learning; Malaga was renowned for its singers, and Seville for the making of musical instruments. Art and life were also growing closer. About 822, the famous **Ziryab** had arrived in Cordoba from Baghdad. A great musician and poet, mentioned often in the tales of the *Thousand and One Nights*, Ziryab also revolutionized the manners of the Arabs, introducing eastern fashions, poetic courtesies, and the proper way to arrange the courses of a meal. It wasn't long before the élite of al-Andalus became more interested in the latest graft of Shiraz roses than in riding across La Mancha to cross swords with the barbaric Asturians.

When Christian Europe was just beginning to blossom, al-Andalus and Byzantium were its exemplars and schoolmasters. Religious partisanship and western pride have always obscured the relationship; how much we really owe al-Andalus in scholarship – especially the transmission of Greek and Arab science – in art and architecture, in technology, and in poetry and the other delights of civilization, has never been completely explored. Contacts were more common than is generally assumed. Christian students often found their way to Toledo or Cordoba – like the French monk, one of the most learned Christians of his day, who became Pope Sylvester II in 997.

Throughout the 10th century, the military superiority of al-Andalus was great enough to have finally erased the Christian kingdoms, had the caliphs cared to do so; it may have been a simple lack of aggressiveness and determination that held them back, or perhaps simply a constitutional inability of the Arab leaders to deal with the green, chilly, rainy world of the northern mountains. The Muslim–Christian wars of this period cannot be understood as a prelude to the Crusades, or to the bigotry of Ferdinand and Isabella. Pious fanaticism, in fact, was conspicuously lacking on both sides, and if the chronicles detail endless wars and raids, they were always about booty, not religion. Al-Andalus had its ambassadors among the Franks, the Italians, the Byzantines and the Ottonian Holy Roman Empire, and it usually found no problem reaching understandings with any of them. In Spain itself, dynastic marriages between Muslims and Christians were common, and frontier chiefs could switch sides more than once without switching religions. The famous **El Cid** would spend more time working for Muslim rulers than Christians, and all the kings of León had some Moorish blood. Abd ar-Rahman III himself had blue eyes and red hair (which he dyed black to keep in fashion); his mother was a Basque princess from Navarre.

1008–1085
Disaster, disarray. Al-Andalus breaks into pieces

It is said that the great astronomer Maslama of Madrid, who was also court astrologer at Cordoba, foretold the end of the caliphate just before his death in 1007. A little political sense, more than knowledge of the stars, would have sufficed to demonstrate that al-Andalus was approaching a crisis. After the death of al-Mansur in 1002, the political situation began to change dramatically. His son, Abd al-Malik al-Muzaffar, inherited his position as vizier and *de facto* ruler and held the state together until his death in 1008, despite increasing tensions. All the while, Hisham II remained a pampered prisoner in the sumptuous palace-city of **Medinat az-Zahra**, outside Cordoba. The lack of political legitimacy in this ministerial dictatorship, and the increasing distance between government and people symbolized by Medinat az-Zahra, contributed to the troubles that began in 1008. Historians suggest that the great wealth of al-Andalus had made the nation a bit jaded and selfish, that the rich and powerful were scarcely inclined to compromise or sacrifice for the good of the whole. The old Arab aristocracy, in fact, was the most disaffected group of all. Al-Mansur's conquests had been delivered by a kind of new model army, manned by Berber mercenaries. With their military function gone, the nobles saw their status and privilege steadily eroding.

Whatever the reason, the caliphate disintegrated with startling suddenness after 1008. Nine caliphs ruled between that year and 1031, most of them puppets of the Berbers, the Saqaliba or other factions. Civil wars and city riots became endemic. Al-Mansur's own Berber troops, who felt no loyalty to any caliph, caused the worst of the troubles. They destroyed Medinat az-Zahra, and sacked Cordoba itself in 1013. By 1031, when the caliphate was formally abolished, an exhausted al-Andalus had split into at least 30 squabbling states, run by Arab princes, Berber officers or even former slaves. Almost overnight, the balance of power between Muslim and Christian had reversed itself. In 999, al-Mansur had been sacking the towns of the north as far as Pamplona. Only a decade later, the Counts of Castile and Barcelona were sending armies deep into the heart of al-Andalus, intervening by request of one party or the other.

The years after 1031 are known as the **age of the *taifas*,** or of the 'Party Kings' (*muluk al tawa'if*), so-called because most of them owed their position to one of the political factions. Few of these self-made rulers slept easily, in an era of constant intrigues and revolts, shifting alliances and pointless wars. The only relatively strong state was that of Seville, founded by former governor **Mohammed ibn-Abbad**, who was also the richest landowner in the area. For political legitimacy he claimed to rule in the name of the last caliph, who had disappeared in the sack of Medinat az-Zahra, and miracu-lously reappeared (ibn-Abbad's enemies claimed the 'caliph' was really a lookalike mat weaver from Calatrava). Ibn-Abbad was unscrupulous, but effective; his successes were continued by his sons, who managed to annexe Cordoba and several other towns. Under their rule Seville replaced stricken Cordoba as the largest and most important city of al-Andalus.

1085–1212
Moroccan zealots come to Spain's defence, if only for a while

The total inability of the 'Party Kings' to work together made the 11th century a party for the Christians. Nearly all the little states were forced to pay heavy tribute to Christian kings; that, and the expenses of their lavish courts and wars against each other, led to sharply higher taxes and helped put an end to a 200-year run of economic expansion. **Alfonso VI**, King of Castile and León, collected tribute from most of the *taifas*, including even Seville. In 1085, with the help of the legendary warrior El Cid, he captured Toledo. The loss of this key fortress-city alarmed the *taifas* enough for them to request assistance from the **Almoravids** (*al-Murabitun*, the 'warrior monks') of North Africa, a fanatical fundamentalist movement of the Berbers which had recently established an empire stretching from Morocco to Senegal, with its capital at the newly-founded city of Marrakech.

The Almoravid leader, **Yusuf ibn-Tashufin**, crossed the straits and defeated Alfonso in 1086. Yusuf liked al-Andalus so much that he decided to keep it; by 1110 the Almoravids had gobbled up the last of the surviving *taifas* and had reimposed Muslim rule as far as Saragossa. Under their rule, al-Andalus became more of a consciously Islamic state than it had ever been before, uncomfortable for the Christians and even for the cultured Arab aristocrats, with their gardens and their poetry (and their long-established custom of dropping in on Christian monasteries for a forbidden glass of wine). The chronicles give some evidence of Almoravid oppression directed against Christian communities, and even deportations; religious prejudices were hardening on both sides, especially since the Christians evolved their crusading ethos in the 1100s, but the Almoravids did their best to help bigotry along.

Popular rebellions against the Almoravids in the Andalucian cities were a problem from the start, and a series of big ones put an end to their rule in 1145; al-Andalus rapidly dissolved into confusion and a second era of 'Party Kings'. Two years later Almoravid power in Africa was defeated and replaced by that of the **Almohads**, a nearly identical military-religious state. The Almohads (*al-Muwahhidun*, 'upholders of divine unity') began with a Sufi preacher named ibn-Tumart, proselytizing and proclaiming *jihad* among the tribes of the Atlas mountains of Morocco. By 1172 the Almohads had control of most of southern Spain. Somewhat more tolerant and civilized than the Almoravids, their rule coincided with a cultural reawakening in al-Andalus, a period that saw the building of La Giralda in Seville. Literature and art flourished, and in Cordoba lived two of the greatest philosophers of the Middle Ages: the Arab, Ibn Rushd (Averroës), and the Jew, Moses Maimonides. The Almohads nevertheless shared many of the Almoravids' limitations. Essentially a military regime, with no deep support from any part of the population, they could win victories over the Christians (as at Alarcos in 1195) but were never able to take advantage of them.

1212–1492
Al-Andalus falls to the eaters of pork; one small corner remains to the faithful

At the same time, the Christian Spaniards were growing stronger and gaining a new sense of unity and national consciousness. The end for the Almohads, and for al-Andalus, came with the **Battle of Las Navas de Tolosa** in 1212, fought near the traditional site for climactic battles in Spain – the Despeñaperros pass, gateway to

Andalucía. Here, an army from all the states of Christian Spain under Alfonso VII (1126–57) destroyed Almohad power for ever. Alfonso's son, **Fernando III** (1217–52), captured Cordoba (1236) and Seville (1248), and was made a saint for his trouble. The people of Seville would have found it ironic; breaking with the more humane practices of the past, Fernando determined to make al-Andalus's capital a Christian city once and for all, and after starving the population into submission by siege he expelled every one of them, allowing them to take only the goods they could carry. **Alfonso X** (the Wise, 1252–84), noted for his poetry and the brilliance of his court, completed the conquest of western Andalucía in the 1270s and 1280s.

In the conquest of Seville, important assistance had been rendered by one of Fernando's new vassals, **Mohammed ibn-Yusuf ibn-Nasr**, an Arab adventurer who had conquered Granada in 1235. The **Nasrid Kingdom of Qarnatah** (Granada) survived partly from its cooperation with Castile, and partly from its mountainous, easily defensible terrain. For the next 250 years it would be the only remaining Muslim territory on the peninsula. Two other factors helped keep Granada afloat. One was a small but very competent army, which made good use of a chain of strong border fortresses in the mountains to make Castile think twice about any serious invasion. Granada was also able to count on help from the Marenid emirs of Morocco, who succeeded to power in North Africa after the collapse of the Almohad state. The Marenids half-heartedly invaded Spain twice, in 1264 in support of a Muslim revolt, and again in 1275; for a long time afterwards they were able to hold on to such coastal bases as Algeciras, Tarifa and Gibraltar.

As a refuge for Muslims from the rest of Spain, Granada became al-Andalus in miniature, a sophisticated and generally peaceful state, stretching from Gibraltar to Almería. It produced the last brilliant age of Moorish culture in the 14th century, expressed in its poetry and in the art of the Alhambra. It was not, however, always a happy land. When they were not raiding Granada's borders, the Castilians enforced heavy tributes on it, as they had with the Party Kings of the 11th century. It wasn't easy to prosper under such conditions, and things were made worse by the monopoly over trade and shipping forced on the Granadans by the predatory Genoese, who in those days were an affliction to Christian and Muslim Spaniards alike. Affected by a permanent siege mentality, and filled with refugees from the lands that had been lost, Granada seems to have acquired the air of melancholy that still clings to the city today.

In the rest of Andalucía, the Reconquista meant a profound cultural dislocation, as the majority of the Muslim population chose to flee the rough northerners and their priests. The Muslims who stayed behind (the **Mudéjars**, meaning those 'permitted to remain') did not fare badly at first. Their economy remained intact, and many Spaniards remained fascinated by the extravagant culture they had inherited. In the 1360s, King Pedro of Castile (1350–69) was signing his correspondence 'Pedro ben Xancho' in a flowing Arabic script, and spending most of his time in Seville's Alcázar, built by artists from Granada. There was even a considerable return of Muslim populations, to Seville and a few other towns from which they had been forced out; this took place with the approval of the Castilian kings, who needed their labour and skills to rebuild the devastated land. Throughout the period, though, the culture and the society that built al-Andalus were becoming increasingly diluted, as Muslims either left or converted, while the Castilians imported large numbers of Christian settlers from the north. Religious intolerance, fostered as always by the Church, was a growing problem.

1492–1516
A rotten Queen and a rotten King send the Andalucíans down a road of misery

The final disaster, for Andalucía and for Spain, came with the marriage in 1469 of **King Ferdinand II of Aragón** and **Queen Isabella I of Castile**, opening the way, ten years later, for the union of the two most powerful states on the peninsula. The glory of the occasion has tended to obscure the historical realities, and writers too often give a free ride to two of the most vicious and bigoted figures in Spanish history. If Ferdinand and Isabella did not invent genocide, they did their hypocritical best to sanctify it, forcing a maximalist solution to a cultural diversity they found intolerable. As state-sponsored harassment of the Mudéjars increased across Spain, the 'Catholic Kings' also found the time was right for the extinction of Granada. Ferdinand, a tireless campaigner, nibbled away at the Nasrid borders for a decade, until little more than the capital itself remained. It had not been easy, but Ferdinand was fortunate enough to have one of the greatest soldiers of his day running the show – Gonzalo de Cordoba, El Gran Capitán, who would later use the tactics developed on the Granada campaign to conquer southern Italy for Spain.

Granada fell in 1492, completing the Reconquista; Ferdinand and Isabella expelled all the Jews from Spain the same year; their **Inquisition** – founded by Ferdinand and Isabella, not by the Church, and entirely devoted to their purposes – was in full swing, terrorizing 'heretical' Christians and converted Jews and Muslims and effectively putting an end to all differences of opinion, religious or political. In the same year, **Columbus** (who had been present at the fall of Granada) sailed from Andalucía to the New World, initiating the Age of Discovery.

Under the conditions of Granada's surrender in 1492, the Mudéjars were to be allowed to continue their religion and customs unmolested. Under the influence of the Church, in the person of the famous Archbishop of Toledo, Cardinal Cisneros, Spain soon reneged on its promises and attempted forced conversion, a policy cleverly designed to justify itself by causing a revolt. The **First Revolt of the Alpujarras**, the string of villages near Granada in the Sierra Nevada, in 1500, resulted in the expulsion of all Muslims who failed to convert – the majority of the population had already fled – as well as decrees prohibiting Moorish dress and such un-Christian institutions such as public bathhouses.

Beyond that, the Spanish purposely impoverished the Granada territories, ruining their agriculture and bankrupting the important silk industry with punitive taxes and a ban on exports. The Inquisition enriched the Church's coffers, confiscating the entire property of any converted Muslims who could be found guilty of backsliding in the faith. A second revolt in the Alpujarras occurred in 1568, after which Philip II ordered the prohibition of the Arabic language and the dispersal of the remaining Muslim population throughout the towns and cities of Castile. By this time, paranoia had a partial justification. Spain was locked in a bitter struggle against the Ottoman Empire, and the Turks had established bases as close as the Maghreb coast; the threat of a Muslim revival was looking very real. But paranoia was not directed at Muslims alone. In the same year, the Inquisition began incinerating suspected Protestants in Seville, and the systematic persecution of the *conversos* – Jews who had converted to Christianity, in some cases generations before – was well under way. Intolerance had become a way of life.

1516–1700
The new Spain chokes on its riches and power, and Andalucía suffers the most

In the 16th century, the new nation's boundless wealth, energy and talent were squandered by two rulers even more vile than Los Reyes Católicos. Carlos I, a Habsburg who gained the throne by marriage when Ferdinand and Isabella's first two heirs died, emptied the treasury to purchase his election as Holy Roman Emperor. Outside Spain he is better known by his imperial title, **Charles V** (1516–56), a sanctimonious tyrant who had half of Europe in his pocket and dearly wanted the other half. His megalomaniac ambitions bled Spain dry, a policy continued by his son **Philip II** (1556–98), under whom Spain went bankrupt three times.

Throughout the century, Andalucía's ports were the base for the exploration and exploitation of the New World. Trade and settlement were planned from Seville, and gold and silver poured in each year from the Indies' treasure fleet; in the 16th century the city's population increased fivefold, to over 100,000. Unfortunately, what money did not immediately go to finance the wars of Charles and Philip was gobbled up by the nobility, the Genoese and German bankers, or by inflation – the 16th-century 'price revolution' caused by the riches from America. The colonies needed vast amounts of manufactured goods, and had solid bullion to pay for them, but despite Seville's monopoly on the colonial trade, Andalucía found itself too badly misgoverned and economically primitive to supply any of them.

The historical ironies are profound. Awash in money, and presented with the kind of opportunity that few regions ever see through their entire history, Andalucía instead declined rapidly from one of the richest and most cultured provinces of Europe to one of the poorest and most backward. Ferdinand and Isabella had begun the process, distributing the vast confiscated lands of the Moors to their friends, or to the Church and military orders; from its birth the new Andalucía was a land of huge estates, exploited by absentee landlords and worked by sharecroppers – the remnants of the original population as well as the hopeful colonists from the north, most of whom were reduced in a generation or two to virtual serfdom. It was the story of Roman Spain all over again, and in the end Andalucía found that it had become just as much a colony as Mexico or Peru.

By the 17th century, the destruction of Andalucía was complete. The Inquisition's terror had done its work, eliminating any possibility of intellectual freedom and reducing the population to the lowest depths of superstition and subservience. Their trade and manufactures ruined, the cities stagnated; agriculture suffered as well, as the complex irrigation systems of the Moors fell into disrepair and were gradually abandoned. The only opportunity for the average man lay with emigration, and Andalucía contributed more than its share to the American colonies. The shipments of American bullion peaked about 1610–20, and after that the decline was precipitous. As for the last surviving Muslims, the *moriscos*, they were expelled from Spain in 1609. The greatest concentration of them, surprisingly, was not in Andalucía, but in the fertile plains around Valencia. The king's minister, the Duke of Lerma, was a Valencian, and apparently he came up with the plan in hope of snatching some of their confiscated land. The leaders of the Inquisition opposed the expulsions, since they made most of their profits shaking down *moriscos*, but the land-grabbers won out, and by 1614 some 275,000 Spanish Muslims had been forced from their homes.

1700–1931
Bourbon reformers, Napoleonic hoodlums, and a long parade of despots cross the stage; the Andalucians start to fight back

For almost the next two centuries, Andalucía has no history at all. The perversity of Spain's rulers had exhausted the nation. Scorned for its backwardness, Spain was no longer even taken seriously as a military power. The **War of the Spanish Succession**, during which the English seized Gibraltar (1704), replaced the Habsburgs with the Bourbons, though their rule brought little improvement. Bourbon policies, beginning with **Philip V** (1700–46) followed the lead of their cousins in France, and a more centralized, rationalized state did attempt to bring improvements in roads and other public works, as well as state-sponsored industries in the French style, such as the great royal tobacco factory in Seville. The high point of reform in the 18th century was the reign of **Carlos III** (1759–88), who expelled the Jesuits, attempted to revive trade and resettled the most desolate parts of Andalucía. New towns were founded – the Nuevas Poblaciones – such as La Carolina and Olavide, though in such a depressed setting that the foreign settlers Carlos brought in could not adapt, and the new towns never really thrived. One bright spot was an ancient city, long in the shadows, that found a new prominence. Cadiz, which succeeded Seville as the major port for the colonial trade, became in these years one of the most prosperous and progressive cities in Spain.

Despite three centuries of decay, Andalucians responded with surprising energy to the French occupation during the **Napoleonic Wars**. The French gave them good reason to, stealing as much gold and art as they could carry, and blowing up castles and historical buildings just for sport. As elsewhere in Spain, irregulars and loyal army detachments assisted the British under Wellington. In 1808, a force made up mostly of Andalucíans defeated the French at the **Battle of Bailén**. In 1812, a group of Spanish liberals met in Cadiz to declare a constitution, and under this the Spanish fitfully conducted what they call their **War of Independence**.

With victory, however, came not reforms and a constitution, but reaction and the return of the Bourbons. For most Andalucíans, times may have been worse than ever, but Romantic-era Europe was about to discover the region in a big way. The trend had already started with Mozart's operas set in Seville, and now the habit resumed with Washington Irving's *Tales of the Alhambra* in 1832, and Richard Ford's equally popular *Handbook for Travellers in Spain* in 1845. Between the lost civilization of the Moors, which Europeans were coming to value for the first time, and the natural colour of its daily life, backward, exotic Andalucía proved to be just what a jaded continent was looking for. The region provided some of the world's favourite stereotypes, from gypsies and flamenco to *toreadors* and Don Juans. Bizet's *Carmen* had its debut in 1873.

The real Andalucíans, meanwhile, were staggering through a confusing century that would see the loss of Spain's American colonies, coups, counter-coups, civil wars on behalf of pretenders to the throne (the two Carlist Wars of the 1830s and 1870s), a short-lived First Republic in 1874 and several *de facto* dictatorships. Andalucía, disappointed and impoverished as ever, contributed many liberal leaders. It also knew a mining boom, especially at the famous Río Tinto mines in Huelva province, the same that had been worked in Phoenician times. Typically, in what had become a thoroughly colonial economy, all the mines were in the hands of foreign, mostly British owners, and none of the profits stayed in Andalucía. The desperate peasantry, living at rock bottom of an archaic feudal structure, became one of the most radicalized rural populations in Europe.

At first, this manifested itself as simple outlawry, especially in the Sierra Morena (and in northern Spain, Corsica, Sardinia, southern Italy, north Africa – the 19th century was a great age for bandits all over the Mediterranean). In 1870, an Italian agitator and associate of Bakunin named Giuseppe Fanelli brought **Anarchism** to Andalucía. In a land where government had never been anything more than institutionalized oppression, the idea was a hit; Anarchist ideas and institutions found a firmer foothold in Spain than anywhere else in Europe, oddly concentrated in two very different milieus: the backward Andalucían peasantry and the modern industrial workers of Barcelona. Anarchist-inspired guerrilla warfare and terrorism increased steadily in Andalucía, reaching its climax in the years 1882–6, directed by a secret society called the **Mano Negra**. Violence continued for decades, met with fierce repression by the hated but effective national police, the Guardia Civil. In 1910 the national Anarchist trade union, the CNT, was founded at a congress in Seville.

Despite their poverty and troubles, Andalucíans could occasionally make a game attempt to show they were at least trying to keep up with the modern world – most spectacurly at the 1929 *Exposición Iberoamericana*, Seville's first World Fair, which left the city a lovely park and some impressive monuments. The Fair project had been pushed along by Spain's dictator of the 1920s, General **Miguel Primo de Rivera**. Though a native Andalucian, from Jerez, Primo de Rivera did little else for the region. Rising discontent forced his resignation in 1929, and two years later municipal elections turned out huge majorities all over Spain for republican parties. King Alfonso XIII abdicated, and Spain was about to become a very interesting place.

1931–9
Civil War – the second Reconquista

The coming of the democratic **Second Republic** in 1931 brought little improvement to the lives of Andalucía, but it opened the gates to a flood of political agitation from extremists of every faction. Andalucía often found itself in the middle, as in 1932 when General Sanjurjo attempted unsuccessfully to mount a coup from Seville. Peasant rebellions intensified, especially under the radical right-wing government of 1934–6, when attempted land seizures led to such incidents as the massacre at Casas Viejas in 1934. Spain's alarmed Left formed a Popular Front to regain power in 1936, but street fighting and assassinations were becoming daily occurrences, and the new government seemed powerless to halt the country's slide into anarchy. In July 1936 the army uprising, orchestrated by Generals **Francisco Franco** and **Emilio Mola**, led to the **Civil War**. The Army of Africa, under Franco's command, quickly captured eastern Andalucía, and most of the key cities in the province soon fell under Nationalist control. The Army of Africa, battle-hardened from campaigns against the Rif in the mountains of Spanish Morocco in the 1920s, was the most effective force in the Spanish Army. Many of its battalions were made up of native Moroccans, who brought with them another bitter Spanish irony: generals fighting in the name of old Christian, Monarchist Spain, bringing mercenary Muslim troops into the country for the first time in 500 years.

In Seville, a flamboyant officer named Gonzalo Queipo de Llano (later famous as the Nationalists' radio propaganda voice) singlehandedly bluffed and bullied the city into submission, and then led an armoured column to destroy the working class district of Triana. In arch-reactionary Granada, the authorities and local fascists massacred thousands of workers and Republican loyalists, including the poet Federico García Lorca. Malaga, the last big town under Republican control, fell to Mussolini's Italian 'volunteers' in February 1937. Four thousand more loyalists were slaughtered there, and Franco's men bombed and strafed civilian refugees fleeing the city. Thereafter Andalucía saw little fighting, though its people shared fully in Nationalist reprisals and oppression; Franco, who had spent most of his career in the colonial service, had no problem using the same terror tactics on fellow Spaniards that the Army had habitually practised on Africans. A Nationalist officer estimated that some 150,000 people were murdered in Andalucía by 1938, and in Seville alone at that time the Nationalists were still shooting up to 80 people a day.

1939–Present
Forty years of Francisco Franco, and finally, a happy ending

After the war, in the dark days of the 1940s, Andalucía knew widespread destitution and, at times, conditions close to famine. Emigration, which had been significant ever since the discovery of America, now became a mass exodus, creating the huge Andalucían colonies in Madrid and Barcelona, and smaller ones in nearly every city of northern Europe.

Economic conditions improved marginally in the 1950s, with American loans to help get the economy back on its feet, and the birth of the Costa del Sol, on the empty coast west of Malaga. A third factor, often overlooked, was the quietly brilliant planning of Franco's economists, setting the stage for Spain's industrial take-off of the 1960s and '70s. In Andalucía, their major contributions were industrial programmes around Seville and Cadiz and a score of dams, providing cheap electricity and ending the endemic, terrible floods.

When **King Juan Carlos**, grandson of Alfonso III, ushered in the return of democracy in 1975 after Franco's death, Andalucíans were more than ready. **Felipe González**, the Socialist charmer from Seville, ran Spain from 1982 to 1996, and other Andalucíans are well represented in every sector of government and society. They took full advantage of the revolutionary regional autonomy laws of the late 1970s, building one of the most active regional governments, and giving Andalucía some control over its destiny for the first time since the Reconquista. And in other ways, history seems to be repeating itself over the last 20 years: the Arabs have returned in force, building a mosque in the Albaicín in Granada, making a home from home along the western Costa del Sol, and bringing economic if not exactly cultural wealth to the area; Jews once more are free to worship, and do so, in small communities in Malaga, Marbella and Seville. In 1978 the first synagogue to be built since the Inquisition was consecrated at El Real in Malaga province.

Five centuries of misery and misrule, however, cannot be redeemed in a day. The average income is less than half of that in Catalunya or the Basque country; the unemployment rate, despite the relief which tourism brings along the coast, often stands at a brutal 40 per cent. None of this will be readily apparent, unless you visit the more dismal suburbs of Seville or Malaga, or the mountain villages of Almería province, where the new prosperity is still a rumour. In the flashy, vibrant cities and the tidy whitewashed villages, Andalucíans hold fast to their ebullient, extrovert culture, living as if they were at the top of the world.

Art and Architecture

04

Until the coming of the Moors, southern Spain produced little of note, or at least little that has survived. To begin at the beginning, there are the 25,000-year-old cave drawings at the Cueva de la Pileta, near Ronda, and Neolithic dolmens near Antequera and Almería. No significant buildings have been found from the Tartessians or the Phoenicians, though remains of a 7th-century BC temple have been dug up at Cadiz. Not surprisingly, with their great treasury of metals, the Iberians were skilled at making jewellery and figurines in silver and bronze (also ivory, traded up from North Africa where elephants were still common). They built walled towns on defensible sites, and their most significant religious buildings (besides the eastern-style temples built by the Phoenicians and Carthaginians) were great store-houses where archaeologists have discovered caches containing thousands of simple ex-voto statuettes.

Real art begins with the arrival of the Greeks in the 7th century BC. The famous Lady of Elche in the Madrid museum, though found in the region of Murcia, may have been typical of the Greek-influenced art of all the southern Iberians; their pottery, originally decorated in geometrical patterns, began to imitate the figurative Greek work in the 5th century BC. The best collections of early work are in the Archaeological Museum at Seville and the museum at Malaga – though everything really exceptional ends up in Madrid.

During the long period of Roman rule, Spanish art continued to follow trends from the more civilized east (ruins and amphitheatres at Itálica, Carmona, Ronda; a recon-structed temple at Cordoba; museums in Seville, Cordoba and Cadiz). Justinian's invasion in the middle of the 6th century BC brought new influences from the Greek world, though the exhausted region by that time had little money or leisure for art. Neither was Visigothic rule ever conducive to new advances. The Visigoths were mostly interested in gaudy jewellery and gold trinkets (best seen not in Andalucía, but in the museums of Madrid and Toledo). Almost no building work survives; the Moors purchased and demolished all of the important churches, but made good use of one architectural innovation of the Visigothic era, the more-than-semicircular 'horseshoe' arch.

Moorish Art

The greatest age for art in Andalucía began not immediately with the Arab conquest, but a century and a half later, with the arrival of Abd ar-Rahman and the establishment of the Umayyad emirate. The new emir and his followers had come from Damascus, the old capital of Islam, and they brought with them the best tradi-tions of emerging Islamic art from Syria. 'Moorish' art, like 'Gothic', is a term of convenience that can be misleading. Along with the enlightened patronage of the Umayyads, this new art catalysed the dormant culture of Roman Spain, creating a brilliant synthesis; of this, the first and finest example is **La Mezquita**, the Great Mosque of Cordoba.

La Mezquita was recognized in its own time as one of the wonders of the world. We are fortunate it survived, and it is chilling to think of the (literally) thousands of mosques, palaces, public buildings, gates, cemeteries and towers destroyed by the Christians; the methodical effacement of a great culture. We can discuss Moorish architecture from its finest production, and from little else. As architecture, La Mezquita is full of subtleties and surprises (*see* pp.167–70). Some Westerners have tended to dismiss the Moorish approach as 'decorative art', without considering the philosophical background, or the expression of ideas inherent in the decoration. Figurative art was prohibited in Islam, and though lions, fantastical animals and human faces peek out frequently from painted ceramics and carvings, for more serious matters artists had to find other forms. One of them was Arabic calligraphy, which soon became an Andalucían speciality. In architecture and the decorative arts, the emphasis was on repetitive geometric patterns, mirroring a Pythagorean strain that had always been present in Islam; these made the pattern for an aesthetic based on a meticulously clever arrangement of forms, shapes and spaces, meant to elicit surprise and delight. The infinite elements of this decorative universe, and the mathematics that underlie them (*see* **Snapshots**, pp.54–6) come together in the most unexpected of conclusions – a reminder that unity is the basic principle of Islam.

The 'decorative' sources are wonderfully eclectic, and easy enough to discern. From Umayyad Syria came the general plan of the rectangular, many-columned mosques, along with the striped arches; from Visigothic Spain, the distinctive horseshoe arch. The floral arabesques and intricate, flowing detail, whether on a mosque window, a majolica dish or a delicately carved ivory, are the heritage of late-Roman art, as can be clearly seen on the recycled Roman capitals of La Mezquita itself. The Umayyads in Syria had been greatly impressed by Byzantine mosaics, and had copied them in their early mosques. This continued in Spain, often with artists borrowed from Constantinople. Besides architectural decoration, the same patterns and motifs appear in the minor arts of al-Andalus, in painted ceramics, textiles and in metalwork, a Spanish speciality since prehistoric times – an English baron of the time might have traded a village for a fine Andalucían dagger or brooch.

Such an art does not seek progress and development, in our sense; it shifts slowly, like a kaleidoscope, carefully and occasionally finding new and subtler patterns to captivate the eye and declare the unity of creation. It carried on, without decadence or revolutions, until the end of al-Andalus and beyond. The end of the caliphate and the rise of the Party Kings, ironically enough, was an impetus for art. Now, instead of one great patron there were thirty, with thirty courts to embellish. Under the Almoravids and Almohads, a reforming religious fundamentalism did not mean an end to art, though it did cut down some of its decorative excesses. The Almohads, who made their capital at Seville, created the **Torre del Oro** and the tower called **La Giralda**, model for the great minarets of Morocco.

The Christian conquest of Cordoba, Seville, and most of the rest of al-Andalus (1212–80), did not finish Moorish art. The tradition continued intact, with its Islamic foundations, for another two centuries in the kingdom of Granada. In the rest of Spain, Muslim artists and artisans found ready employment for nearly as long; their *mudéjar* art briefly contended with imported styles from northern Europe to become the national art of Spain. Most of its finest productions are not in Andalucía at all; you can see them in the churches and synagogues of Toledo, the towers of Teruel and many other towns of Aragón. The trademarks of *mudéjar* building are geometrical decoration in *azulejo* tiles and brickwork, and elaborately carved wooden *artesonado* ceilings. *Mudéjar* styles and techniques would also provide a strong influence in Spain, for centuries to come, in all the minor arts, from the *taracea* inlaid woodcraft of Granada to fabrics, ceramics and metalwork. And the Moorish love of intricate decoration would resurface again and again in architecture, most notably in the Isabelline Gothic and the Churrigueresque (*see* p.49).

Granada, isolated from the rest of the Muslim world and constantly on the defensive, produced no great advances, but this golden autumn of Moorish culture brought the decorative arts to a state of serene perfection. In the **Alhambra** (built in stages throughout the 14th century, during the height of the Nasrid kingdom), where the architecture incorporates gardens and flowing water, the emphasis is on panels of ornate plaster work, combining floral and geometric patterns with calligraphy – not only Koranic inscriptions, but the deeds of Granada's kings and contemporary lyrical poetry. Another feature is the stucco *muqarnas* ceilings (sometimes called 'stalactite ceilings'), translating the Moorish passion for geometry into three dimensions.

Granada's art and that of the *mudéjares* cross paths at Seville's **Alcázar**, expanded by Pedro the Cruel in the 1360s; artists from Granada did much of the work. Post-1492 *mudéjar* work can also be seen in some Seville palaces, such as the **Palacio de las Dueñas** or the **Casa de Pilatos**. The smaller delights of late Moorish decorative arts include painted majolica ware, inlaid wooden chests and tables (the *taracea* work, still a speciality of Granada), and exquisite silver and bronze work in everything from armour to astronomical instruments; the best collection is in the Alhambra's Museo Nacional de Arte Hispano-Musulmán.

Gothic and Renaissance

For art, the Reconquista and the emergence of a united Spain was a mixed blessing. The importation of foreign styles gave a new impetus to painting and architecture, but it also gradually swept away the nation's Moorish and *mudéjar* tradition, especially in the south, where it put an end to 800 years of artistic continuity. In the 13th and 14th centuries, churches in the reconquered areas were usually built in straightforward, unambitious Gothic, as with **Santa Ana** in Seville, built under Pedro the Cruel, and the simple and elegant parish churches of Cordoba. In the 1400s, Gothic lingered on without noticeable inspiration; Seville's squat and ponderous cathedral, the largest Gothic building anywhere, was probably the work of a German or Frenchman.

The Renaissance was a latecomer to Andalucía, as to the rest of Spain. In 1506, when the High Renaissance had already hit Rome, the Spaniards were building a Gothic chapel in Granada for the tombs of Ferdinand and Isabella. This time, though, they had an architect of distinction; **Enrique de Egas** (*c*. 1445–1534), who had already created important works in Toledo and Santiago de Compostela, made the Capilla Real Spain's finest late-Gothic building, in the lively style called 'Isabelline Gothic', roughly corresponding to the contemporary French Flamboyant or English Perpendicular. Isabelline Gothic is only one part of the general tendency of Spanish art in these times, which has come to be called the **Plateresque**. A *platero* is a silver-smith or a jeweller, and the style takes its name from the elaborate decoration applied to any building, whether Gothic or Renaissance.

The Plateresque in the decorative arts had already been established in Seville (the huge cathedral retablo, begun in 1482), and would continue into the next century (the cathedral's Capilla Real and sacristy, and the 1527 Ayuntamiento, by Diego de Riaño). Other noteworthy figures of this period are the Siloés: **Gil de Siloé**, a talented sculptor, and his son **Diego**, who came to Andalucía after creating the famous Golden Staircase in Burgos cathedral, and began the cathedrals at Granada (1526) and Úbeda. The Granada cathedral provided a precursor for High Renaissance architecture in Spain; Diego de Siloé was responsible for most of the interior, taking over the original Gothic plan and making it into a lofty, classical space in a distinctive, personal style. He is also responsible for the cathedral of Guadix, and contributed to the Capilla del Salvador at Úbeda.

Charles V took a personal interest in Granada, and de Siloé had a hard time convincing the King that his new architecture was really an advance over the more obvious charms of Isabelline Gothic. Charles eventually came around, while at the same time mainstream Renaissance architecture arrived with **Pedro Machuca** (1485–1550), who had studied in Italy. Strongly influenced by the monumental classi-cism of Bramante, his imposing Palacio de Carlos V (1527–8), built for the King in the Alhambra at Granada, was the most famous and influential work of the Spanish Renaissance; it actually predates the celebrated High Renaissance Roman palaces it so closely resembles. Andalucía's Renaissance city is Úbeda, with an ensemble of exceptional churches and palaces; its Sacra Capilla del Salvador contains some of the finest Renaissance reliefs and sculpture in Spain.

In the stern climate of the Counter-Reformation, architecture turned towards a disciplined austerity, the *estilo desornamentado* introduced by **Juan de Herrera** at Philip II's palace-monastery of El Escorial, near Madrid. Herrera gave Seville a textbook example in his Lonja, a business exchange for the city's merchants (1582). His most accomplished follower, **Andrés de Vandelvira**, brought the 'unornamented style' to a striking conclusion with his Hospital de Santiago in Úbeda, and other works in Úbeda and Baeza; he also began the ambitious cathedral at Jaén.

Baroque and Beyond

This style, like the Renaissance, was slow in reaching southern Spain. One of the most important projects of the 17th century, the façade for the unfinished Granada cathedral, wound up entrusted to a painter from Granada, **Alonso Cano** (1601–67), called in his time the 'Spanish Michelangelo' for his talents at painting, sculpture and architecture. The idiosyncratic and memorable result (1664), with its three gigantic arches, shows some appreciation for the new Roman style, though it is firmly planted in the Renaissance. Real Baroque arrived three years later, with Eufrasio López de Rojas's façade for Jaén Cathedral (1667).

The most accomplished southern architect in the decades that followed was **Leonardo de Figueroa** (1650–1730), who combined Italian styles with a native Spanish delight in colour and patterns in brickwork; he worked almost entirely in Seville (El Salvador and San Luis, both begun 1699, Palacio San Telmo, 1724, and the Convento de la Merced, now the Museo de Bellas Artes). His son Ambrosio Figueroa continued in the same style. Spanish sculpture was largely a matter of gory realism done in wood, as in the work of **Juan Martínez Montañés** (Seville cathedral). **Pedro de Mena** (1628–88), an artist from Granada known for wood sculpture, started out as Alonso Cano's assistant, and later did the relief panels in the choir of Malaga cathedral.

The 17th century has often been described as a golden age of painting in Andalucía. It begins with **Francisco Pacheco** of Sanlúcar de Barrameda (1564–1664). Not much of a painter himself, Pacheco is still a key figure in the beginning of this Andalucían school: founder of an academy, teacher and father-in-law of Velázquez, author of an influential treatise, the *Arte de la Pintura* – and official censor to the Seville Inquisition. Giving ample room for exaggeration, this 'golden age' does include **Velázquez** (1599–1660), a native *sevilleno* who left the region for ever in 1623 when he became painter to the king. Almost none of his work can be seen in the south. Of those who stayed behind, the most important was Alonso Cano. Cano studied sculpture under Montañés, and painting under Pacheco alongside Velázquez. His work often has a careful architectonic composition that betrays his side career as an architect, but seldom ranges above the pedestrian and devotional. Cano's sculpture, often in polychromed wood, can be seen in Granada cathedral, including the *Immaculate Conception* (1655) that many consider his masterpiece.

Francisco Herrera of Seville (1576–1656) shows more backbone, in keeping with the dark and stormy trends of contemporary Italian painting, under the influence of Caravaggio. His son, Francisco Herrera the younger (1627–85) was a follower of Murillo who spent little time in Seville. One of the most intriguing painters of the time is **Juan Sánchez Cotán** (1561–1627), the 'father of Baroque realism' in Spain, noted for his strange, intense still lifes. Sánchez Cotán, whose work had a great influence on Zurbarán, spent the last years of his life as a monk in Granada.

Best of all is an emigrant from Extremadura, **Francisco de Zurbarán** (1598–1664), who arrived in Seville in 1628. He is often called the 'Spanish Caravaggio', and though his contrasts of light and shadow are equally distinctive, this is as much a disservice as a compliment. Set in stark, bright colours, Zurbarán's world is an unearthly vision of monks and saints, with portraits of heavenly celebrities that seem painted from life, and uncanny, almost abstract scenes of monastic life like the *Miracle of Saint Hugo* in Seville's Museo de Bellas Artes. Later in life, Zurbarán went a bit soft, coming increasingly under the influence of his younger contemporary Murillo. Seeing the rest of his work would require a long trip across two continents; Napoleon's armies under Maréchal Soult stole hundreds of his paintings, and there are more than 80 in the Louvre alone.

In the next generation of southern artists, the worst qualities of a decaying Spain are often painfully evident. Sculpture declined precipitously, with artists adding glass eyes and real human hair in an attempt to heighten even more the gruesome realism of their religious subjects. Among the painters, **Bartolomé Esteban Murillo** (1617–82), another *sevilleno*, is the best of the lot; two centuries ago he was widely considered among the greatest painters of all time. Modern eyes are often distracted by the maudlin, missal-illustration religiosity of his saints and Madonnas, neglecting to notice the exceptional talent and total sincerity that created them. Spaniards call his manner the *estilo vaporoso*. Like Zurbarán's, Murillo's reputation suffered a lot in the 19th century from the large number of lesser works by other painters who copied their subjects and styles, and whose works were later attributed to the two masters. Murillo founded the Academy of Painting at Seville and was its first leader; he died after a fall from the scaffolding in 1682.

Somewhat harder to digest is **Juan de Valdés Leal** (1622–90), who helped Murillo organize the Seville Academy. His work is considerably more intense and dramatic than Murillo, and he is best known for the ghoulish, death-obsessed allegories he painted for the reformed Don Juan, Miguel de Mañara, at the Hospital de la Caridad in Seville (these two artists can be compared in Seville's museum and at the Caridad). After 1664, the head of sculpture at the Academy was **Pedro Roldán** (1624–99). Born in Antequera, Roldán was a fellow student of Pedro de Mena at Granada. Roldán was perhaps the most notable exponent of the Spanish desire to combine painting, sculpture and architecture in unified works of art. He is best known for his altarpiece at Seville's Caridad, which Valdés Leal polychromed, and he also contributed works for the facade of Jaén Cathedral. Roldán's daughter Luisa became a sculptor too – the only Spanish woman ever to become a king's court sculptor (for Charles II).

If any style could find a natural home in Spain, it would be the **rococo**. Eventually it did, though a lack of energy and funds often delayed it. Spain's most important architecture in this time, the elaborately decorated work of the Churriguera family and their followers, is mostly in the north, in Salamanca and Madrid. In Andalucía, **Vicente Acero** introduced the tendency early on, with a striking façade for the cathedral at Guadix. He had a chance to repeat it on a really important building project, the new Cadiz cathedral, but the money ran out, and the result was a stripped-down Baroque shell – ambition without the decoration. The great Fábrica de Tabacos in Seville (1725–65), the largest project of the century in Andalucía, met a similar end, leaving an austere work, an unintentional precursor of the Neoclassical. Whenever the resources were there, Andalucían architects responded with a tidal wave of eccentric embellishment worthy of the Moors – or the Aztecs. Pre-Columbian architecture may have been a bigger influence on Spain than is generally credited; judge for yourself at the chapel and sacristy of the Cartuja in Granada (1747–62), the most blatant interior in Spain.

Elsewhere, the decorative freedom of the rococo led to some unique and delightful buildings, essentially Spanish and often incorporating eclectic references to the styles of centuries past. José de Bada's church of San Juan de Dios (1737–59) in Granada is a fine example. In Cordoba, there is the elegant Convento de la Merced (1745), and the

Coro of the cathedral, inside La Mezquita, a 16th-century Gothic work redecorated (1748–57) with elaborate stucco decoration by **Juan de Oliva** and stalls and overall design by **Pedro Duque Cornejo**. Seville, in its decline, was still building palaces, blending the new style with the traditional requirements of a patio and grand staircase; the best of the century's palaces, however, is in Écija, the Palacio de Peñaflor (1728). Many smaller towns, responding to the improved economic conditions under Philip V and Charles III, built impressive churches, notably in Priego de Cordoba, Lucena, Utrera, Estepa and Écija.

In view of all Andalucía's troubles, it should not be surprising that little has been produced in the last two centuries. **Pablo Picasso**, born in Malaga, was the outstanding example of the artist who had to find his inspiration and his livelihood elsewhere. Despite the lack of significant recent architecture, Andalucíans hold on to the glories of their past with tenacity; splashes of *azulejo* tiles and Moorish decoration turn up in everything from bus stations and market houses to simple suburban cottages. For some 500 years now, Andalucíans have most often been constrained by their sorry history to follow styles and inspirations from outside. Few regions of Europe, however, can show such a remarkable heritage of locally nurtured arts and crafts, styles and motifs, the heritage of both Moor and Christian. Now that prosperity and confidence are slowly coming back, we might hope that Andalucía can find something in its old glories that fits a modern age, and amaze and delight the world once again.

Snapshots of Andalucía

05

City Slickers

You're on the train for Cordoba, passing the hours through some of the loneliest landscapes in Europe. For a long time, there's been nothing to see but olive trees – gnarled veterans, some of them planted in the time of Ferdinand and Isabella. You may see a donkey pulling a cart. At twilight, you pull in at the central station, and walk four blocks down to the Avenida del Gran Capitán, an utterly Parisian boulevard of chic boutiques and pompous banks, booming with traffic. The loudspeakers from the *Galerías Preciados* department store broadcast the latest chart singles. In a different way, southern Spanish cities have probably had much the same ambience for over 2,000 years; the atmosphere may be hard to recapture, but we can learn a lot by looking at decoration and design.

We know little about city life in Roman times – only that for relatively small populations, towns such as Itálica had amphitheatres and other amenities comparable to any in the empire. The cities of Moorish Spain were a revelation – libraries, public gardens and street lighting, at a time when feudal Europe was scratching its carrot rows with a short stick. Their design, similar to that of North African and Middle Eastern cities, can be discerned (with some difficulty) in parts of Granada, Cordoba and Seville today. It is difficult to say what aspects of the design of Andalucía's Moorish cities are legacies from Roman Baetica, and what was introduced by the Moors themselves. Enclosure was the key word in Moorish architecture: a great mosque and its walled courtyard occupied the centre, near the fortified palace (*alcázar or alcazaba*) and its walled gardens. Along with the markets and baths, these were located in the *medina*, and locked up behind its walls each night. The residential quarters that surrounded the *medina* were islands in themselves, a maze of narrow streets where the houses, rich or poor, looked inwards to open patios while turning blank walls to the street. Some of these survive, with their original decoration, as private homes in Granada's Albaicín.

In Roman times, the patio was called a *peristyle*. The gracious habit of building a house around a colonnaded central court was perfected by the Greeks, and became common across the Roman Mediterranean. Today, while most of us enjoy the charms of our cramped flats and dull, squarish houses, the Andalucíans have never given up their love of the old-fashioned way. In Cordoba especially, the patios of the old quarters spill over with roses, wisteria and jasmine; each year there is a competition for the prettiest. Besides the houses, some of the cellular quality of Moorish cities survived the Reconquista. In 16th-century Seville, thick with artful bandits, the silversmiths had their own walled quarter (and their own cops to guard it). The Moorish urban aesthetic evolved gracefully into the modern Andalucían: the simple, unforgettable panorama of almost any town – an oasis of brilliant white rectangularity, punctuated sharply by upright cypresses and by the warm sandstone of churches, palaces and towers.

One Spanish invention, combining Italian Renaissance planning with native tradition, was the arcaded, rectangular square usually called *Plaza Mayor*. The best are in Madrid and Salamanca, but many Andalucían towns have one, and there is a huge dilapidated specimen in Cordoba. Architecturally unified – the four walls often seem like a building turned inside-out – the *Plaza Mayor* translated the essence of the patio into public space. Such a square made a perfect stage for the colourful life of a Spanish city. Spanish theatres in the great age of Lope de Vega and Calderón took the same form, with three sides of balconies, the fourth for the stage, on the narrow end, and a Shakespearean 'pit' at ground level. In the last two centuries, while the rest of Spain continued to create innovations in urban design and everyday pageantry, impoverished Andalucía contributed little – some elegant bullrings, certain exquisite redesigns of the old Moorish gardens, a few grand boulevards like the Alameda of Malaga and the *paseos* of Granada, and some eccentric decorations, such as the gigantic, sinister stone birds of prey that loom over most city centres – symbols of an insurance company.

Modern Spain, even in the worst of times, never lost its talent for city building. The world's planners honour the memory of Arturo Soria, who in the 19th century proposed the Ciudad Lineal as a new form for the industrial age, a dense ribbon of city, three blocks wide but stretching for miles, where everyone would be a block or two from open countryside, and transportation to any point made easy and quick by a parallel railway line. A Ciudad Lineal was actually begun northeast of Madrid, though it has long since been swallowed up by the expanding suburbs.

During the last 30 years, the time of Spain's 'take-off' into a fully fledged industrial economy, *urbanización* has continued at a furious pace—in all senses of the word. As migrants streamed into the cities during the 1960s, endless blocks of high-rise suburban developments grew up, ugly but unavoidable. To the people who moved into them from poor villages or ancient tenements, they must have represented an exciting new way of life. The name for these is *urbanizaciones*, and the Spanish also use the word for their big seaside vacation developments, where they package north-erners into urbanized holidays on the beach.

Since the 1970s and the end of Francoism, one can sense a slickness gathering momentum: a touch of anonymous good design in a shop sign, new pavements and lighting, ambitious new architecture with a splash of colour and surprise. The El Corte Inglés department store in Malaga has been known to be entirely covered in computer-controlled electric lights at Christmas, nearly a vertical acre of permanent fireworks, flashing peacock tails and other patterns in constantly changing, brilliant colours – as spectacular and futuristic a decoration as any city has ever had. Watch out for these sharp Andalucíans – and for Spaniards in general. While we fog-bound northerners are nodding off with Auntie at twelve o'clock, they may well be plotting the delights of the future.

Castrum

In laying out their military camps, as in anything else, the Romans liked to go by the book. From Britain to Babylonia, they established hundreds of permanent forts (*castrum* in Latin) all seemingly stamped out of the same press, with a neatly rectangular circuit of walls and two straight streets, the *cardo* and *decumanus*, crossing in the middle. Many of these grew into towns – any place in Britain, for example, that ends in -*chester* or -*caster*.

In Spain, where the Roman wars of conquest went on for 200 years, there are perhaps more of these than anywhere else, and it's interesting to try and trace out the outlines of the Roman *castrum* while you're exploring a Spanish city. In Barcelona's Barri Gòtic, the plan is obvious, and in Ávila and Cáceres the streets and walls have hardly changed since Roman times. But with a little practice and a good map, you can find the *castra* hiding inside Cordoba and a score of other towns.

Roses of the Secret Garden

Western art and Islamic art are two worlds that will never agree. Even today, the sort of folk who believe in the divinity of Michelangelo or the essential greatness of the Baroque can be found in print, sniffing at the art of the Alhambra as merely 'decorative'. On the other side, you will discover a state of mind that can dismiss our familiar painting and sculpture as frivolous, an impious obsession with the appearances of the moment that ignores the transcendent realities beneath the surface. A powerful idea was in the air in the 7th–8th centuries, perhaps a reaction against the worldliness and incoherence that drowned classical civilization. It was not limited to Islam alone; the 'iconoclastic' controversy in Byzantium, following the attempt of Emperor Leo III to end the idolatrous veneration of icons, was about the same issue.

However this argument started, Islam grew up with an aversion to figurative art. At the same time, Islam was gaining access to the scientific and mathematical heritage of Greece and Rome, and finding it entirely to its liking. A new approach to art gradually took form, based on the sacred geometry of Byzantine architecture, and on a trend of mathematical mysticism that goes back to Pythagoras. Number, proportion and symmetry were the tools God used to create the world. The same rule could be found in every aspect of creation, and could be reproduced in art by the simple methods of Euclidean geometry. This geometry now found its place not only in the structure of a building, but also in its decoration.

Once the habit of thinking this way was established, it profoundly affected life and art in all the Islamic world, including Spain. The land itself became a careful mosaic, with neat rows of olive trees draped over the hills and the very beans and carrots in the gardens laid out in intricate patterns (Andalucían farmers still do it: you can see a remarkable example of such a landscape from the *mirador* in Úbeda). While nature was being made to imitate art, Muslim artists, consciously or not, often imitated the hidden processes of nature – the Cordoba mosque grew like a crystal with the columns and aisles of each new addition. Often, they created novelties by changing scales, reducing and replicating old forms to make new, more complex ones. One example of this is the Visigothic horseshoe arch. You can see it in its simplest form at Cordoba or Medinat az-Zahra; later, as in Seville's Alcázar, the same arch is made of smaller versions of itself. And in the Alhambra, you'll see arches made of arches made

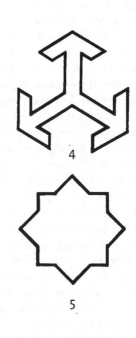

1

2

3

4

5

of arches, seeming to grow organically down from the patterns on the walls. A tree or a snowflake finds its form in much the same way. Fans of chaos theory, take note – the Moors had anticipated fractals and Koch curves 600 years ago.

Three dimensions is the domain of the mundane shell, the worldly illusion. The archetypes, the underlying reality, can be more fittingly expressed in two. With their straight-edge and compass, Islamic artists developed a tradition of elaborate geometrical decoration, in painted tiles, stucco, or wooden grilles and ceilings. The highest levels of subtlety reached by this art were in Isfahan, Persia, in Egypt, and in Granada. The foundation, as in all constructive geometry, is the circle – *man's heart is the centre, heaven the circumference*, as a medieval Christian mystic put it. From this, they wove the exquisite patterns that embellish the Alhambra, exotic blooms interlaced in rhythms of 3, 5, 6, 8 or 12. This is not the shabby, second-hand symbolism of our times. A 12-pointed flower does not *symbolize* the firmament and the 12 signs of the zodiac, for example; it *recalls* this, and many other things as well. For philosophers, these patterns could provide a meditation on the numerical harmony of creation; for the rest of us, they stand by themselves, lovely, measured creations, whispering a sweet invitation to look a bit more closely at the wonders around us. The patterns of the Alhambra haunt Andalucía to this day. In Granada especially, these geometric flowers are endlessly reproduced on *azulejo* tiles in bars and restaurants, and in the *taracea* (marquetry) work boxes and tables sold in the Alcaicería.

One of the favourite games of the Islamic artists was filling up space elegantly, in the sense that a mathematician understands that word. In geometry, only three regular polygons, when repeated, can entirely fill a flat plane: the hexagon (as in a honeycomb); the square (as on a chessboard); and the equilateral triangle. Some not-so-regular polygons (any triangle or parallelogram, for example) can do it too. Try and find some more complex forms; it isn't easy. One modern artist fascinated by these problems was M. C. Escher, whose tricks of two-dimensional space are beloved of computer programmers and other Pythagoreans of our own age. The first four figures on the previous page can fill a plane. The first, with a little imagination and geometrical know-how, could be made into one of Escher's space-filling birds or fish. The third doesn't quite do the job, but properly arranged it creates a secondary pattern of eight-pointed stars (fig.5) in between. For a puzzle, try and multiply each of the four on paper to fill a plane. Answers can be found on the walls of the Alhambra.

By now, you may suspect that these shapes were not employed without reason. In fact, according to the leading authority on such matters, Keith Critchlow (in his book *Islamic Patterns*), the patterns formed by figs.1 and 3 mirror the symmetrical arrangement of numbers in a magic square. Triangular figs.2 and 4 are based on the *tetractys*, a favourite study of the Pythagoreans. But a Spanish Muslim did not need to be a mathematician to appreciate the lesson of this kind of geometry. Everyone understood the basic tenet of Islam – that creation is One: harmonious and complete. Imagine some cultured minister of a Granadan king, musing under the arcades of the Court of the Lions, reflecting perhaps on the nature that shaped the roses in the court, and how the same laws are proclaimed by the ceramic blossoms within.

Flamenco

For many people, flamenco is the soul of Spain – like bullfighting – an essential part of the culture that sets it apart from the rest of the world. Good flamenco, with that ineffable quality of *duende*, has a primitive, ecstatic allure that draws in its listeners until they feel as if their very hearts were pounding in time with its relentless rhythms, their guts seared by its ululating Moorish wails and the sheer drama of the dance. Few modern experiences are more cathartic.

As folklore goes, however, flamenco is newborn. It began in the 18th century in Andalucía, where its originators, the gypsies, called one another '*flamencos*' – a derogatory term dating back to the days when Charles V's Flemish (*flamenco*) courtiers bled Spain dry. These gypsies, especially in the Guadalquivir delta cities of Seville, Cadiz and Jerez, sang songs of oppression, lament and bitter romance, a kind of blues that by the 19th century began to catch on among all the other downtrodden inhabitants of Andalucía.

Yet despite flamenco's recent origins, the Andalucían intelligentsia, especially Lorca and Manuel de Falla, found (or invented) much to root it deeply in the south's soil and soul. Its rhythms and Doric mode are as old as Andalucía's ancient Greek settlers; its spirit of improvisation and spontaneity date from the famous Cordoba school of music and poetry, founded in 822 by Abu al-Hassan Ali ibn Nafi, better known as

Ziryab, the 'Blackbird' (see **History**, w33); the half-tonal notes and lyrics of futility of the *cante jondo*, or deep song, the purest flamenco, seem to go straight back to the Arab troubadours of al-Andalus.

But just how faithfully the music of al-Andalus was preserved among the gypsies and others to be reincarnated as flamenco will never be known; the Arabs knew of musical notation, but disdained it in their preference for improvisation.

By the late 19th century, flamenco had gone semi-public, performed in the back rooms of cafés in Seville and Malaga. Its very popularity in Spain, and the enthusiasm set off by Bizet's *Carmen* abroad, began seriously to undermine its harsh, true quality. At the same time, flamenco's influence spread into the popular and folk repertories to create a happier, less intense genre called the *sevillena* (often songs in praise of you know where). When schoolchildren at a bus stop in Cadiz burst into an impromptu dance and hand-clapping session, or when some old cronies in Malaga's train-station bar start singing and reeling, you can bet they're doing a *sevillena*.

In the 1920s attempts were made to establish some kind of standards for the real thing, especially *cante jondo*, though without lasting results; the 'real, original flamenco' was never meant to be performed as such, and will only be as good as its 'audience'. This should ideally be made up of other musicians and flamenco *aficionados*, whose participation is essential in the spontaneous, invariably late-night combustion of raw emotion, alcohol, drugs and music, to create *duende*.

Flamenco not only remains popular in Spain, but is undergoing something of a renaissance. It all started in the 1970s and 1980s when Paco de Lucia, a native of Algeciras, took his art to the international stage, fusing it with jazz. Paco's music is a must for any lover of flamenco guitar and he continues to produce traditional records as well as recording crossover with other musicians like John McLaughlin and Al Di Meola. Within Spain, Ketama, a popular gypsy band from Granada, have fused flamenco with rock, and singers like Niña Pastori are following in their wake. On a pop level, flamenco has achieved an international audience thanks to the Gypsy Kings (who are French) and the Michael Flatley-style dance spectaculars of Joaquin Cortés.

The Founding Father

Andalucía for itself, for Spain and for Humanity.

So reads the proud device on the regional escutcheon, hurriedly cooked up by the Andalucians after the regional autonomy laws of the 1970s made them masters in their own house once again. Above the motto we see a strong fellow, mythologi-cally underdressed and accompanied by two lions. Though perhaps more familiar to us for his career among the Hellenes, he is also the first Andalucían – HERCULES DOMINATOR FUNDATOR.

The Greeks themselves admit that Hercules found time for two extended journeys to the distant and little-known West. In the eleventh of his Twelve Labours, the Apples of the Hesperides caper, he made it as far as the environs of Tangier, where he dispatched the giant Antaeus. The tenth Labour brought Hercules into Spain, sailing in the golden goblet of Helios and using his lion skin for a sail. In the fabled land of Tartessos, on the 'red island' of Erytheia, he slew the three-headed titan Geryon and stole his cattle. Before heading back to Greece, he founded the city of Gades, or Cadiz, on the island (Cadiz, surrounded by marshes, is almost an island). He also erected his well-known Pillars, Gibraltar and Mount Abyle, across the way in Africa. His return was one of the all-time bad trips; whenever you're crazed and dying on some five-hour 'semi-direct' Andalucían bus ride (say, Granada to Cordoba via Rute), think of Hercules, marching Geryon's cows through Spain and over the Pyrenees, then making a wrong turn that took him halfway down the Italian peninsula before he noticed the mistake. After mortal combats with several other giants and monsters, he finally made it to Greece – but then his nemesis, Hera, sent a stinging blue-tail fly to stampede the cattle. They didn't stop until they reached the Scythian Desert. To most people, Hercules is little more than mythology's most redoubtable Dog Warden, rounding up not only Cerberus, the Hound of Hell, but most of the other stray monsters that dug up the roses and soiled the footpaths of the Heroic Age. But there is infinitely more than this to the character of the most-travelled, hardest-working hero of them all. In antiquity, wherever Hercules had set foot the people credited him with founding nations and cities, building roads and canals, excavating lakes and draining swamps. And there is the intellectual Hercules, the master of astronomy and lord of the zodiac, the god of prophecy and eloquence who taught both the Latins and the Spaniards their letters. One version has it that the original Pillars of Hercules were not moun-tains at all, but columns, like those of the Temple of Jerusalem, and connected with some alphabetical mysticism.

Ancient mythographers had their hands full, sorting out the endless number of deities and heroes known to the peoples of Europe, Africa and the Middle East, trying to decide whether the same figure was hiding behind different names and rites. Varro recorded no fewer than 44 Hercules, and modern scholars have found the essential Herculean form in myths from Celtic Ireland to Mesopotamia. Melkarth, the Phoenician Hercules, would have had his temples in southern Spain long before the first Greek ever saw Gibraltar. Not a bad fellow to have for a founding father – and a reminder that in Andalucía the roots of culture are as strong and as deep as in any corner of Europe.

Bullfights

In Spanish newspapers, you will not find accounts of the bullfights (*corridas*) on the sports pages; look in the 'arts and culture' section, for that is how Spain has always thought of this singular spectacle. Bullfighting combines elements of ballet with the primal finality of Greek tragedy. To Spaniards it is a ritual sacrifice without a religion, and it divides the nation irreconcilably between those who find it brutal and demeaning, an echo of the old Spain best forgotten, and those who couldn't live without it. Its origins are obscure. Some claim it derives from Roman circus games, others that it started with the Moors, or in the Middle Ages, when the bull faced a mounted knight with a lance.

There are bullrings all over Spain, and as far afield as Arles in France and Guadalajara, Mexico, but modern bullfighting is quintessentially Andalucían. The present form had its beginnings around the year 1800 in Ronda, when Francisco Romero developed the basic pattern of the modern *corrida*; some of his moves and passes, and those of his celebrated successor, Pedro Romero, are still in use today.

The first royal *aficionado* was Fernando VII, the reactionary post-Napoleonic monarch who also brought back the Inquisition. He founded the Royal School of Bullfighting in Seville, and promoted the spectacle across the land as a circus for the discontented populace. Since the Civil War, bullfighting has gone through a period of troubles similar to those of boxing in the USA. Scandals of weak bulls, doped-up bulls, and bulls with the points of their horns shaved have been frequent. Attempts at reform have been made, and all the problems seem to have decreased bullfighting's popularity only slightly.

In keeping with its ritualistic aura, the *corrida* is one of the few things in Andalucía that begins strictly on time. The show commences with the colourful entry of the *cuadrillas* (teams of bullfighters or *toreros*) and the *alguaciles*, officials dressed in 17th-century costume, who salute the 'president' of the fight. Usually three teams fight two bulls each, the whole taking only about two hours. Each of the six fights, however, is a self-contained drama performed in four acts. First, upon the entry of the bull, the members of the *cuadrilla* tease him a bit, and the *matador*, the team leader, plays him with the cape to test his qualities. Next comes the turn of the *picadores*, on padded horses, whose task is to slightly wound the bull in the neck with a short lance or pica, and the *banderilleros*, who agilely plant sharp darts in the bull's back while avoiding the sweep of its horns. The effect of these wounds is to weaken the bull physically without diminishing any of its fighting spirit, and to force it to keep its head lower for the third and most artistic stage of the fight, when the lone *matador* conducts his *pas de deux* with the deadly, if doomed, animal. Ideally, this is the transcendent moment, the matador leading the bull in deft passes and finally crushing its spirit with a tiny cape called a *muleta*. Now the defeated bull is ready for 'the moment of truth'. The kill must be clean and quick, a sword thrust to the heart. The corpse is dragged out to the waiting butchers.

More often than not the job is botched. Most bullfights, in fact, are a disappointment, especially if the *matadores* are beginners, or *novios*, but to the *aficionado* the chance to see one or all of the stages performed to perfection makes it all worthwhile. When a *matador* is good, the band plays and the hats and handkerchiefs fly; a truly excellent performance earns as a reward from the president one, or both, of the bull's ears; or rarely, for an exceptionally brilliant performance, both ears and the tail.

You'll be lucky to see a bullfight at all; there are only about 500 each year in Spain, mostly coinciding with holidays or a town's fiesta. During Seville's *feria* there is a bullfight every afternoon at the famous Maestranza ring, while the rings in Malaga and Puerto de Santa María near Cadiz are other major venues. Tickets can be astronomically expensive and hard to come by, especially for a well-known *matador*; sometimes touts buy out the lot. Get them in advance, if you can, and directly from the office in the *plaza de toros* to avoid the hefty commission charges. Prices vary according to the sun – the most expensive seats are entirely in the shade.

Dust in the Wind

The poets of al-Andalus devoted most of their attention to sensuous songs of love, nature, wine, women and boys, but amidst all the lavish beauty there would linger, like a *basso continuo*, a note of refined detachment, of melancholy and futility. Instead of forgetting death in their man-made paradises, the poets made a point of reminding their listeners of how useless it was to become attached to these worldly delights. After all, only God is forever, and why express love to something that would one day turn to dust? Why even attempt to build something perfect and eternal – the main ingredients of the lovely, delicate Alhambra are plaster and wood. The Nasrid kings, were they to return, might be appalled to find it still standing.

The Christians who led the Reconquista had no time for futility. In their architecture and art they built for eternity, plonking a soaring church right in the middle of the Great Mosque and an imperial palace on the Alhambra – literal, lapidarian, emanating the power and total control of the temporal Church and State. Their oppression reduced the sophisticated songs of the Moorish courts to a baser fatalism. The harsh realities of everyday life encouraged people to live for the moment, to grab what happiness they could in an uncertain world. This uncertainty was expressed by the 17th-century Spanish playwright Pedro Calderón de la Barca, especially in his great *La Vida es Sueño* (Life is a Dream), known as the Catholic answer to *Hamlet*.

There wasn't much poetry in Granada between 1492 and the advent of Federico García Lorca, born in 1898 in the Vega just outside of town. Lorca, a fine musician as well as a poet and playwright, found much of his inspiration in what would be called nowadays Granada's 'alternative' traditions, especially those of the gypsies. In 1922, Lorca was a chief organizer of Granada's first *cante jondo* festival, designed to bring flamenco singing to international attention and prevent it from sliding into a hackneyed Andalucían joke. In 1927, he published the book of poems that made him the most popular poet in Spain, the *Romancero Gitano* (Gypsy Ballads); his plays, like *Bodas de Sangre* (Blood Wedding) and *Yerma* (The Barren One), have the lyrical, disturbing force of the deepest *cante jondo*.

But of post-Reconquista Granada he was sharply critical, accusing Ferdinand and Isabella of destroying a much more sophisticated civilization than their own – and as for the modern inhabitants of Granada, they were an imported reactionary bourgeois contingent from the north, not 'real' Andalucíans. Lorca criticized, but he kept coming back, and had dreams of bringing the city's once great culture back to life.

In Granada, a commemorative park at Víznar marks the spot where, on 18 August 1936, local police or rebel soldiers took Lorca and shot him dead. No one knows who gave the orders, or the reason why; the poet had supported the Republic but was not

actively political. When news of his secret execution leaked out, it was an embarrass-
ment to Franco, who managed to hush up the affair until his own death. But most
historians agree that the killing was a local vendetta for Lorca's outspoken views
of his home town, a blood sacrifice to the stone god of Ferdinand and Isabella and
Charles V who fears all change, closing (one can only hope) once and for all the circle
of bittersweet futility, frustration, and death.

Hot-blooded Andalucian Women

Andalucía holds roughly a fifth of Spain's people, which means more than one tenth
of the population consists of the most sultry, sensuous women in Europe. Ah, *señores*,
how they arch their supple torsos in an improvised *sevillena*, clicking their magic
castanets! *Dios*, how provocative they are behind the iron grilles of their windows
with their come-hither burning black eyes over flickering fans, serenaded by their
handsome guitar-strumming *caballero*, tossing him a red rose of promise and desire!

Ever since the first boatload of dancing girls from Cadiz docked at the slave-markets
of ancient Rome, the women of Andalucía have had to put up with this – an extraordinary reputation for grace, beauty, and amorous dispositions. Travellers' accounts and
novels elaborate on their exotic charms, spiced by the languor of the Moorish harem
odalisque and the supposed promiscuity of the passionate gypsy. After all, when
Leporello counts off his master's conquests in Mozart's *Don Giovanni*, which country
comes out on top? Spain, of course, with 1003 victims to the arch-libertine's art of
persuasion.

Nothing kept this fond male fancy afloat as much as the fact that nubile
Andalucían women were tantalizingly inaccessible, thanks to a rigid Latin code of
honour second to none. It took the Industrial Revolution, the Seville tobacco factory,
and a French visitor, Prosper Mérimée, to bring this creature of the imagination out
into the open, in the form of the beautiful gypsy tomato *Carmen* (1845), rendered
immortally saucy in Bizet's opera of 1873. Step aside, Don Juan, or be stepped on! This
new stereotype was as quick to light up a cheroot as to kick aside her sweetheart for
a strutting matador in tight trousers. Not surprisingly, it wasn't long before the
tobacco factory and its steamy, scantily-clad examples of feminine pulchritude
(labouring for a handful of pesetas each day) attracted as many tourists as the
Giralda tower.

Alas, where is the kitsch of yesteryear? Modern young Andalucian women are, like
modern Andalucían men, among the most normal, mentally well-balanced people in
the world. Ask them about the cloistered *señoritas* of the past and they'll laugh. Ask
them about the unbridled Carmen, and they'll laugh. Ask them about the bizarre
wind called the *solano* that troubles Cadiz in the springtime, a wind that in the old
days drove the entire female population en masse to the beach, where they would
fling off their clothes and dive into the sea to seek relief while the local cavalry regi-
ment stood guard. Ask them about it, and they'll just laugh.

Spain and Britain

Where would the English be without Spain? Where would they get their brussels sprouts in January, or canaries, or Seville oranges for marmalade? Long ago the ancient Iberians colonized Cornwall (of course historians can be found who say they arrived in Spain from Britain), and ever since, these two lands have been bound by the oldest of crossed destinies, either as the closest of allies, as in the Hundred Years' War, or the most implacable of enemies.

Strange little connections would fill a book. Morris dancing, or Moorish dancing if you like, is said to have come up with John of Gaunt after his unsuccessful campaign to snatch the throne of Castile. One of Elizabeth II's biggest crown jewels was a gift from Pedro the Cruel to the Black Prince; Pedro had murdered an ambassador from Muslim Granada to get it off his turban. In politics, we can thank Spain for words like propaganda, Fifth Column (both from the Civil War), and liberal (from the 1820s), and among the Jews expelled by Ferdinand and Isabella in 1492 were the ancestors of Disraeli.

In Spain, the Welsh may feel right at home in the green mining country of Asturias, and the Irish can honour the memory of the 19th-century prime minister O'Donnell, the famous governor of Cadiz, Conde O'Reilly, or the thousands of their countrymen who escaped persecution to settle in Galicia in the 16th century. The true Scotsman will make a pilgrimage to the Vega of Granada to look for the heart of Robert the Bruce, hero of the battle of Bannockburn. In 1329 Sir James Douglas was taking the Bruce's heart to be buried in the Holy Land, when crusading zeal side-tracked him to Spain. In battle against the Moors of Granada, Douglas and his knights became surrounded beyond hope of rescue. Spurring his horse for a last attack, Douglas flung the Bruce's heart into the enemy ranks, crying, 'Go ye first, as always!'

Bats

A fine country for bats, is Spain. Almost everywhere in the country (but especially around Granada) you'll see clouds of them cavorting in the twilight, zooming noise-lessly past your ears and doing their best to ensure you get a good night's sleep by gobbling up all the mosquitoes they can. Spaniards don't mind them a bit, and the medieval kings of Aragón even went so far as to make them a dynastic emblem, derived from a Muslim Sufi symbol. Lots of bats, of course, presumes lots of caves, and Spain has more than its share. The famous grottoes of Nerja and Aracena are only a couple of the places where you can see colossal displays of tinted, aesthetically draped stalactites. Hundreds were decorated in one way or another by Palaeolithic man; even though the most famous, at Altamira, are closed to the public, you can still see some cave art by asking around for a guide in Vélez Rubio west of Murcia. This last area, from Vélez as far west as Granada, actually has a huge population still living in caves – quite cosily fitted out these days – and in Granada itself you can visit the 'gypsy caves' for a little histrionic flamenco and diluted sherry.

Food and Drink

Read an old guidebook to Spain and, when the author gets around to the local cooking, expressions like 'eggs in a sea of rancid oil' and 'mysterious pork parts' or 'suffered palpitations through garlic excess' pop up with alarming frequency. One traveller in the 18th century fell ill from a local concoction and was given a purge 'known on the comic stage as angelic water. On top of that followed four hundred catholic pills, and a few days later...they gave me *escordero* water, whose efficacy or devilry is of such double effect that the doctors call it ambidexter. From this I suffered agony'.

You'll fare better; in fact, the chances are you'll eat some of the tastiest food you've ever had at half the price you would have paid for it at home. The massive influx of tourists has had its effect on Spanish kitchens, but so has the Spaniards' own increased prosperity and, perhaps most significantly, the new federalism. Each region, each town even, has come to feel a new interest and pride in the things that set it apart, and food is definitely one of those; the best restaurants are almost always those that specialize in regional cooking.

The greatest attraction of *andaluz* cuisine is the use of simple, fresh ingredients. Seafood plays a big role, and marinated or fried fish (*pescatos fritos*, known in Sevilla as *pescaíto frito*) is a speciality. (The traditional marinade, or *adobo*, is a mixture of water, vinegar, salt, garlic, paprika, cumin and marjoram.) Other specialities include the wholesome broth made with fish, tomato, pepper and paprika, and the famous cured hams of **Jabugo** and **Trevélez**. Almost everybody has heard of *gazpacho*; there are literally dozens of varieties, ranging from the *pimentón* of **Antequera** made with red peppers, to the thick, tasty Córdoban version, *salmorejo*, sometimes topped with finely chopped ham and boiled egg. Olives, preserved in cumin, wild marjoram, rosemary, thyme, bay leaves, garlic, savoury fennel and vinegar, are a particular treat, especially the plump, green manzanilla olives from **Seville**.

In **Granada**, an unappetizing mixture of brains, bulls' testicles, potatoes, peas and red peppers results in a very palatable tortilla Sacromonte, and many restaurants in the city work wonders with slices of beef *filete* or loin larded with pork fat and roasted with the juice from the meat and sherry. However, watch out for odd little dishes like *revoltillos*, whose name gives you a fair warning of what flavours to expect in this subtle dish of tripe, rolled and secured with the animal's intestines, mercifully lined with ham and mint.

The province of **Cadiz** takes the place of honour in *andaluz* cuisine; its specialities to look out for are *cañailles* (sea snails), *pastel de pichones* (pigeon pâté), *calamares con habas* (squid with beans), *archoba* (a highly seasoned fish dish) or *bocas* (small crab). **Cordoba**, too, has a fine culinary tradition, including dishes with a strong Arab and Jewish influence, like *calderetas*, lamb stew with almonds. But Cordoba is also the home of one of the most famous *andaluz* dishes, *rabo de toro*, a spicy concoction of oxtail, onions and tomatoes. Also try the *buchón* (rolled fish filled with ham, dipped in breadcrumbs, then fried). As one might expect, the **Sierras** offer dishes based on the game and wild herbs found in the mountains. Here freshwater lakes teem with trout, and wild asparagus grows on the slopes. The town of **Jaén** is particularly well known for its high-quality oil and vinegar, and delectable salads are a feature of most menus (try the *pipirrana*).

Fish and seafood, fresh from the coast, dominates cuisine in **Malaga** but there are plenty of *gazpachos*, particularly *ajo blanco con uvas* – a creamy white garlic soup with grapes. Prawns and mussels are plump and, served simply with lemon, are divine. The **Costa del Sol**'s traditional beachside delicacy is sardines, speared on a stick and cooked over a wood fire – best when eaten with a good salad and washed down with chilled white wine. *Boquerones* (often mistaken for the peculiarly English whitebait but in fact a variety of anchovy) feature widely in restaurants and tapas bars, along with *pijotas*, small hake that suffer the indignity of being sizzled with tail in mouth. Forget British fried fish; in Malaga *fritura mixta* is one of Spain's culinary art forms.

Nearly every village in the province has its own dessert, usually influenced by the Moors. Try the almond tarts in **Ardales**, the honey-coated pancakes in **Archidona** and the mixture of syrup of white roses, oil and eggs called *tocino de cielo* in **Vélez**. There again you can always substitute a sweet Malaga dessert wine for pudding – delicious sipped with dry biscuits.

All over Andalucía you will find *pinchitos*, a spicier version of its Greek cousin the *souvlaki*, a mini-kebab of lamb or pork marinated in spices. To finish off your meal there are any number of desserts (*postres*) based on almonds and custards, and the Arab influence once again shows through in, for example, the excellent sweetmeats from Granada and the *alfajores* (puff pastry) from **Huércal**, Almería.

The presence of 1.5 million foreign residents, mainly clustered along the southern coast, has had an effect on the Costa del Sol culinary scene, although Spanish restaurants still manage to hold their own. A bewildering choice of Indonesian, Belgian, Swedish, Chinese, French, Italian and numerous other nationalities' cuisines confront the tourist. The standard is in fact quite high in most 'ethnic' restaurants, and prices are reasonable because of the fierce competition. A host of British establishments (mostly pubs) offer the whole shebang: roast beef, Yorkshire pudding and three veg, apple pie and custard, and all for bargain prices.

Practicalities

Eating Out

Sticklers for absurd bureaucracy, the Spanish government rates **restaurants** by forks (this has become a bit of a joke – a car repair shop in Granada has rated itself two wrenches). The forks have nothing to do with the quality of the food, though they hint somewhat at the prices. Unless it's explicitly written on the bill (*la cuenta*), service is not included in the total, so tip accordingly. Be careful, though: eating out in southern Spain – especially away from the Costa and big towns – is still a hit-and-miss affair. You will need luck as well as judgement. Spain has plenty of bad restaurants; the worst offenders are often those with the little flags and 10-language menus in the most touristy areas. But common sense will warn you off these. On the

Menu Reader

Hors d'œuvres (*Entremeses*)
aceitunas olives
alcachofas con mahonesa artichokes with mayonnaise
ancas de rana frogs' legs
caldo broth
entremeses variados assorted hors d'œuvres
huevos de flamenco baked eggs in tomato sauce
gambas pil pil shrimp in hot garlic sauce
gazpacho cold soup
huevos al plato fried eggs
huevos revueltos scrambled eggs
sopa de ajo garlic soup
sopa de arroz rice soup
sopa de espárragos asparagus soup
sopa de fideos noodle soup
sopa de garbanzos chickpea soup
sopa de lentejas lentil soup
sopa de verduras vegetable soup
tortilla Spanish omelette, with potatoes
tortilla a la francesa French omelette

Fish (*Pescados*)
acedías small plaice

adobo fish marinated in white wine
almejas clams
anchoas anchovies
anguilas eels
angulas baby eels
ástaco crayfish
atún tuna fish
bacalao codfish (usually dried)
besugo sea bream
bogavante lobster
bonito tunny
boquerones anchovies
caballa mackerel
calamares squid
cangrejo crab
centollo spider crab
chanquetes whitebait
chipirones cuttlefish
... en su tinta ...in its own ink
chirlas baby clams
lubina sea bass
escabeche pickled or marinated fish
gambas prawns
langosta lobster
langostinos giant prawns
lenguado sole
mariscos shellfish

other hand, kitsch 'Little Chef' type cut-outs are rampant along country roads, beckoning you inside – and, unlike in the UK, they're not necessarily indicative of a second-class establishment.

If you dine where the locals do, you'll be assured of a good deal, if not necessarily a good meal. Almost every restaurant offers a *menú del día*, or a *menú turístico*, featuring an appetizer, a main course, dessert, bread and drink at a set price, always cheaper than if you had ordered the items *à la carte*. These are always posted outside the restaurant, in the window or on the plywood chef at the door; decide what you want before going in if it's a set-price menu, because these bargains are hardly ever listed on the menu the waiter gives you at the table.

One step down from a restaurant are **comedores** (literally, dining-rooms), often tacked on to the backs of bars, where the food and décor are usually drab but cheap, and **cafeterías**, usually those places that feature photographs of their offerings of *platos combinados* (combination plates) to eliminate any language problem. **Asadores** specialize in roast meat or fish; **marisqueras** serve only fish and shellfish – you'll usually see the sign for '*pescados y mariscos*' on the awning. Keep an eye out for **ventas**, usually modest family-run establishments offering excellent *menús del día* for working people. They specialize in typical *andaluz* dishes of roast kid or lamb, rabbit, paella, game (partridge crops up often) and many pork dishes, chorizo sausage and varieties of ham. Try and visit one on a Sunday lunchtime when all Spanish families go

mejillones mussels		*cerdo* pork	
merluza hake		*chorizo* spiced sausage	
mero grouper		*chuletas* chops	
navajas razor-shell clams		*cochinillo* sucking pig	
ostras oysters		*conejo* rabbit	
pejesapo monkfish		*corazón* heart	
percebes barnacles		*cordero* lamb	
pescadilla whiting		*faisán* pheasant	
pez espada swordfish		*fiambres* cold meats	
platija plaice		*filete* fillet	
pulpo octopus		*hígado* liver	
rape anglerfish		*jabalí* wild boar	
raya skate		*jamón de York* raw cured ham	
rodaballo turbot		*jamón serrano* baked ham	
salmón salmon		*lengua* tongue	
salmonete red mullet		*lomo* pork loin	
sardinas sardines		*morcilla* blood sausage	
trucha trout		*paloma* pigeon	
veneras scallops		*pato* duck	
zarzuela fish stew		*pavo* turkey	
		perdiz partridge	

Meat and Fowl (*Carnes y Aves*)

albóndigas meatballs		*pinchitos* spicy mini kebabs	
asado roast		*pollo* chicken	
bistec beefsteak		*rabo/cola de toro* bull's tail with onions and tomatoes	
buey ox		*riñones* kidneys	
callos tripe		*salchicha* sausage	

out – with a bit of luck things may get out of hand, and guitars and castanets could appear from nowhere, in which case abandon all plans for the rest of the day.

If you're travelling on a budget, you may want to eat one of your meals a day at a **tapas bar** or *tasca*. Tapas means 'lids', since they started out as little saucers of goodies served on top of a drink. They have evolved over the years to become the basis of the world's greatest snack culture. Bars that specialize in them have platter after platter of delectable tidbits – shellfish, mushrooms baked in garlic, chicken croquettes, *albóndigas*, the ubiquitous Spanish meatball, quails' eggs and stews. (*Tortilla* is seldom as good as it looks, unless you like eating re-heated shoe-leather). All you have to do is pick out what looks best and point to it. At about 150 pts (€1)a go, it doesn't really matter if you pick a couple of duds. Order a *tapa* (hors-d'œuvre), or a *ración* (big helping) if it looks really good. It's hard to generalize about prices, but on average 750 pts (€5) of tapas and wine or beer really fill you up. Sitting down at a table rather than eating at the bar may attract a token surcharge. Another advantage of tapas is that they're available at what most Americans or Britons would consider normal dining hours. Spaniards are notoriously late diners; 2pm is the earliest they would consider sitting down to their huge 'midday' meal – at Jerez's premier restaurant, no self-respecting local would be seen dead in the place before 4pm. Then after work at 8pm a few tapas at the bar hold them over until supper at 10 or 11pm. After living in Spain for a few months this makes perfect sense, but it's exasperating to the

salchichón salami
sesos brains
solomillo sirloin steak
ternera veal
    Note: *potajes, cocidos, guisados, estofados, fabadas* and *cazuelas* are all different kinds of stew.

Vegetables (*Verduras y Legumbres*)
ajo garlic
alcachofas artichokes
apio celery
arroz rice
arroz marinera rice with saffron and seafood
berenjena aubergine (eggplant)
cebolla onion
champiñones mushrooms
col, repollo cabbage
coliflor cauliflower
endibias endives
ensalada salad
espárragos asparagus
espinacas spinach
garbanzos chickpeas
judías (verdes) French beans
lechuga lettuce
lentejas lentils

patatas potatoes
...fritas/salteadas ...fried/sautéed
...al horno ...baked
pepino cucumber
pimiento pepper
puerros leeks
remolachas beetroots (beets)
setas Spanish mushrooms
zanahorias carrots

Fruits (*Frutas*)
albaricoque apricot
almendras almonds
cerezas cherries
ciruelas plums
ciruela pasa prune
frambuesas raspberries
fresas strawberries
...con nata ...with cream
higos figs
limón lemon
manzana apple
melocotón peach
melón melon
naranja orange
pera pear
piña pineapple

average visitor. On the coasts, restaurants tend to open earlier to accommodate foreigners (some as early as 5pm) but you may as well do as the Spaniards do.

See 'Food and Drink', pp.81–2, in **Practical A–Z** for restaurant price categories.

Drinking

No matter how much other costs have risen in Spain, **wine** (*vino*) has remained awesomely inexpensive by northern European or American standards; what's more, it's mostly very good and there's enough variety from the regions for you to try something different every day. If you take an empty bottle into a *bodega*, you can usually bring it out filled with the wine that suits your palate that day. A *bodega* can be a bar, wine cellar or warehouse, and is worth a visit whatever its guise.

If you want to learn how to discern a *fino* from an *amontillado*, go to one of the warehouse *bodegas* of Jerez where you can taste the sherry as you tour the site. While dining out, a restaurant's *vino del lugar* or *vino de la casa* is always your least expensive option; it usually comes out of a barrel or glass jug and may be a surprise either way. Some 20 Spanish wine regions bottle their products under strict controls imposed by the Instituto Nacional de Denominaciones de Origen (these almost always have the little maps of their various regions pasted on the back of the bottle). In many parts of Andalucía you may have difficulty ordering a simple bottle of white wine, as, on requesting *una botella de vino blanco de la casa*, you will often be served

plátano banana
pomelo grapefruit
sandía watermelon
uvas grapes

Desserts (*Postres*)
arroz con leche rice pudding
bizcocho/pastel/torta cake
blanco y negro ice cream and coffee float
flan crème caramel
galletas biscuits (cookies)
helados ice creams
pajama flan with ice cream
pasteles pastries
queso cheese
requesón cottage cheese
tarta de frutas fruit pie
turrón nougat

Drinks (*Bebidas*)
agua con hielo water with ice
agua mineral mineral water
...sin/con gas ...without/with fizz
batido de leche milkshake
café (con leche) coffee (with milk)
cava Spanish champagne
cerveza beer

chocolate hot chocolate
jerez sherry
granizado slush, iced squash
leche milk
té (con limón) tea (with lemon)
vino (tinto, rosado, blanco) wine (red, rosé, white)
zumo de manzana apple juice
zumo de naranja orange juice

Restaurant Vocabulary
menu *carta/menú*
bill/check *cuenta*
change *cambio*
set meal *menú del día*
waiter/waitress *camarero/a*
Do you have a table? *¿Tiene una mesa?*
  for one/two? *¿... para uno/dos?*
What is there to eat? *¿Qué hay para comer?*
Can I see the menu, please? *Déme el menú, por favor*
Do you have a wine list *¿Hay una lista de vinos?*
Can I have the bill (check), please? *La cuenta, por favor*
Can I pay by credit card *¿Puedo pagar con tarjeta de crédito?*

something resembling diluted sherry. To make things clear, specify a wine by name or by region – for example *una botella de Rioja blanco* – or ask for *un vino seco*, and the problem should be solved. Spain also produces its own champagne, known as *cava*, which seldom has the depth of the French, nor the lightness of an Italian *prosecco*, but is refined enough to drink alone. The principal house, Cordoniú, is always a safe bet. Some *andaluz* wines have achieved an international reputation for high quality. Best known is the *jerez*, or what we in English call **sherry**. When a Spaniard invites you to have a *copita* (glass) it will nearly always be filled with this Andalucían sunshine. It comes in a wide range of varieties: *munzanillas* are very dry; *fino* is dry, light and young (the famous Tío Pepe); *amontillados* are a bit sweeter and rich and originate from the slopes around Montilla in Córdoba province; *olorosos* are very sweet dessert sherries, and can be either brown, cream, or *amoroso*.

The white wines of Cordoba grown in the Villaviciosa region are again making a name for themselves, after being all but wiped out by phylloxera in the last century. In Sevilla, wine is produced in three regions: Lebrija; Los Palacios (white table wines); and Aljarafe, where full-bodied wines are particular favourites. Jaén also has three wine-producing regions. Torreperogíl, east of Úbeda, produces wine little known outside the area, but extremely classy. In Bailén, the white, rosé and red table wines resemble those of the more famous La Mancha vineyards. In the west of the province, Lopera white wines are also sold from the barrel. Malaga and Almería do not produce much wine, although the sweet, aromatic wines of Malaga are famous (and famously undrinkable to most English palates, but persevere). Two grapes, muscatel and Pedro Ximénez, define Malaga province wines and sherries. All are sweet, enjoyed with gusto in bars and the best known are the Malaga Virgen.

Many Spaniards prefer **beer** (*cerveza*), which is also good, though not quite the bargain wine is. The most popular brands are Cruzcampo and San Miguel – most bars sell it cold in bottles or on tap; try Mahón Five Star if you see it. Imported whisky and other spirits are pretty inexpensive, though even cheaper are the versions Spain bottles itself, which may come close to your home favourites. Gin, believe it or not, is often drunk with Coke. Bacardi and Coke is a popular thirst-quencher but beware, a Cuba Libre is not necessarily a rum and Coke, but Coke with anything, such as gin or vodka – you have to specify; then, with a flourish worthy of a matador, the barman will zap an ice-filled tumbler in front of you, and heave in a quadruple measure. No wonder the Costa del Sol has a staggering six chapters of Alcoholics Anonymous.

Coffee, tea, all the international soft-drink brands and *Kas*, the locally made orange drink, round out the average café fare. If you want tea with milk, say so when you order, otherwise it may arrive with a piece of lemon. Coffee comes with milk (*café con leche*) or without (*café solo*). Spanish coffee is good and strong, and if you want a lot of it order a *doble* or a *solo grande*; one of those will keep you awake through the guided tour of any museum.

Travel

07

Getting There

By Air from the UK

From the UK, **British Airways** flies up to six times a day to Andalucía with 22 flights a week from London (Gatwick and Heathrow) to Malaga, and five flights a week from Gatwick to Seville; flights are operated by GB Airways. The Spanish airline, **Iberia**, operates on many of the same routes, and also offers direct services from the UK to Seville, and flies to Granada via Madrid or Barcelona. **Monarch Airlines** flies from Luton to Malaga, with increased frequency in summer. Malaga is also served by **British Midland Airways** with a weekly service from East Midlands Airport. The low-cost carrier **easyJet** also operates a daily service from Luton to Malaga, and **Go** flies to Malaga from London Stansted.

Lufthansa have twice weekly services to Granada via Barcelona.

APEX and other discounted fares carry various restrictions, such as minimum and maximum stays and no change of reservation is allowed. They do, however, represent substantial savings on standard published fares. Most companies offer promotional fares from time to time outside the peak seasons of mid-summer, Christmas and Easter, although a degree of flexibility over travel dates may be necessary to secure them.

Charter Flights

These can be incredibly cheap, and offer the added advantage of departing from local airports. Companies such as **Thomson**, **Airtours** and **Unijet** offer return flights from as little as £80. This theoretically includes basic accommodation, but nobody expects you to make use of this facility. Some of the best

Airline Carriers

UK
Air France, t (020) 8759 2311, Paris **t** 01 43 17 22 00, www.airfrance.com.
Alitalia, t (020) 8745 8200, Rome **t** (06) 65 621, www.alitalia.it.
British Airways, t (0845) 773 3377, www.britishairways.com.
British Midland Airways, t 0870 607 0555, www.flybmi.com.
easyJet, t (0870) 600 000, www.easyjet.com.
Go, t (0845) 605 4321, www.go-fly.com.
Iberia, Venture House, 27–29 Glasshouse Street, London W1R 6JU, **t** (0845) 601 2854.
KLM, t (01279) 660400, Amsterdam **t** (20) 474 7747, www.klm.com.
Lufthansa, t (0845) 773 7747, Frankfurt **t** (69) 255 255; Düsseldorf, **t** (211) 868 686.
Monarch Airlines, t (01582) 398 333, www.fly-crown.com.

USA
Air Canada, toll free **t** (800) 268 2262.
American Airlines, toll free **t** (800) 433 7300.
Continental Airlines, toll free **t** (800) 231 0856.
Iberia, toll-free **t** (800) 772 4642, www.iberia.com.
TWA, toll free **t** (800) 892 4141.
United Airlines, toll free **t** (800) 538 2929.

Other Airlines with Routes via Europe
British Airways, toll free **t** (800) 403 0882.
KLM, toll free **t** (800) 447 4747.
Lufthansa, toll free **t** (800) 645 3880.
TAP, toll free **t** (800) 221 7370.
Virgin Atlantic, toll free **t** (800) 862 8621.

Charters, Discounts and Special Deals

UK
Flightline.com, Flightline House, Turners Hill, West Sussex, RH10 4QH, **t** (0870) 040 1757, www.flightlineinternational.com.
STA Travel, 117 Euston Road NW1 and 86 Old Brompton Road SW7 are the main London centres, **t** (020) 7361 6161.
USIT Campus, 52 Grosvenor Gardens, London SW1, **t** (0870) 240 1010, www.usitcampus.com.

USA
DER, toll free **t** (800) 782 2424.
Spanish Heritage, 116–47 Queens Blvd, Forest Hills, NY 11375, **t** 718 520 1300.
TFI, 34 West 32nd Street, New York, NY 10001, **t** (212) 736 1140, toll free **t** (800) 745 8000.

deals have return dates limited strictly to one week or two, sometimes four, the maximum allowed under the regulations. In many cases a return charter ticket is a big saving over a one-way regular fare, even if your itinerary means you have to let the return half lapse. Check it out at your local economy travel agent, bucket shop, in your local paper, or in the Sunday papers. In London, look in the *Evening Standard* and in *Time Out*.

TV Teletext and the Internet are also good sources of information on cheap charter flights to Spain, with some remarkable last-minute deals.

Get your ticket as early as possible, but try to be sure of your plans, as there are no refunds for missed flights – most travel agencies sell insurance, and indeed, most charter companies now insist upon it so that you don't lose all your money if you become ill. Students and anyone under 26 have the additional option of special discount charters, departing from the UK, but make sure you have proof of student status. An STA Youth card costs about £6; there is also a Go-25 card.

By Air from the USA

There are numerous carriers that serve Spain, but most regular flights from the USA or Canada are to Madrid or Barcelona. **Iberia**, the national airline, offers fly-drive deals and discounts: inquire about the 'Visit Spain' offer. Also try **American Airlines** and **Continental Airlines**.

Charter Flights

These require a bit more perseverance to find, though you can save considerably on the cost of a regular or even APEX flight – currently a charter from New York to Madrid varies between $400–700 depending on the season, with winter charters from New York to Malaga at around $350. You may want to weigh this against the current transatlantic fares to London, where in most cases you will be able to get a low-cost flight to Spain departing within a day or two of your arrival. This is an especially cheap way to go in the off season. The Sunday *New York Times* has the most listings.

By Sea

Sea links between the UK and Spain are operated by Brittany Ferries and P&O European Ferries. This is a good way to go if you mean to bring your car or motorbike or caravan or bicycle, but you will then have a long journey down to the south of Spain from the north coast.

Brittany Ferries operates between Plymouth and Santander twice weekly, three times during high season.

P&O European Ferries operates the Portsmouth–Bilbao route with crossings twice weekly throughout the year except for a three-week break in January.

Brittany Ferries: Millbay Docks, Plymouth PL1 3EW, t (08705) 360 360, *www.brittanyferries.com*. In Santander the address is the Estación Marítima, t (94) 221 4500.

P&O European Ferries Ltd: Peninsular House, Wharf Road, Portsmouth, PO2 8TA, t (0870) 2424 999. In Bilbao, Cosmé Echevarría 1, 48009 Bilbao, t (94) 423 4477.

By Rail

From London to Andalucía takes at least a day and a half and requires a change of trains in Paris and Madrid or Barcelona. A two-month return, London–Madrid costs from £320; for London–Seville you will need to change in Madrid anyway. Students, those under 26 and holders of a Senior Citizen's Railcard can get reductions. Time can be saved by taking the Eurostar rail service, t (08705) 186 186, which runs very frequently and takes three hours from London (Waterloo) to Paris (Gare du Nord). Fares are lower if booked at least 14 days in advance.

Rail Passes

If you've been a resident in Europe for the past six months you can take advantage of the two-zone **InterRail Pass**, available at British Rail or any travel agent, giving you a month's rail travel for £239 (under-26 £169), as well as half-price discounts on Channel crossings and ferries to Morocco, where the pass is also valid. The full InterRail Pass, covering all of Europe, costs £229 for one month. **Bookings**: rail tickets to Spain from England, or vice versa, and couchette and sleeper reservations in France, can be obtained from Rail Europe, 179 Piccadilly, London, W1 (take your passport), or booked and paid for over the telephone, t (08705) 848 848, or online, *www.raileurope.co.uk*. Tickets for local Spanish services can be obtained from certain UK travel agents, but bookings must be made weeks in advance.

The American **EurRail Pass**, which must be purchased before you leave the States, is a good deal only if you plan to use the trains every day in Spain and elsewhere – and it's not valid in the UK, Morocco or countries outside the EU. A month is $623 for those under 26, 21 days is $499, and two weeks is $388; those over 26 can get a 15-day pass for $554, a 21-day pass for $718 or one for a month for $890. In Spain you'll have to pay supplements for any kind of express. **Contact**: CIT Tours, 15 West 44th Street, New York 10173 t (800) 248 7245.

By Bus or Coach

One major company, **Eurolines**, offers departures several times a week in the summer (once a week out of season) from London to Spain, along the east coast as far as Alicante, or to Algeciras via San Sebastián, Burgos, Madrid, Cordoba, Granada and Malaga. Journey time is 33 hours from London to Granada, and 37 hours to Algeciras. Fares from London to Granada start from £126 return for under-26s, £139 for over-26s. Peak season fares between 1 July and 31 August are slightly higher. There are discounts for anyone under 26, senior citizens and children under 12. The national coach companies operate services that connect with the continental bus system. In the summer, the coach is the best bargain for anyone over 26; off-season you'll probably find a cheaper charter flight.

Information and booking: Eurolines, 52 Grosvenor Gardens, London SW1, t (020) 7730 8235, *www.eurolines.co.uk*; National Express, t (08705) 808 080, *www.gobycoach.com*.

By Car

From the UK via France you have a choice of routes. Ferries from Portsmouth cross to Cherbourg, Caen, Le Havre and St-Malo. From any of these ports the most direct route takes you to Bordeaux, down the western coast of France to the border at Irún, and on to San Sebastián, Burgos and Madrid, from where you can head south and choose your entry point into Andalucía.

An alternative route is from Paris to Perpignan, crossing the border at the Mediterranean side of the Pyrenees, then along the coast to Barcelona, where the E15 will take you south. Both routes take an average of two days' steady driving.

You may find it more convenient and less tiring to try the ferry from Portsmouth to Bilbao or Plymouth to Santander, which cuts out driving through France and saves expensive autoroute tolls. For the scenery, opt for one of the routes over the Pyrenees, through Puigcerdá, Somport-Canfranc or Andorra, but expect heavy traffic; if you're not in a hurry, take the classic route through Roncesvalles, Vall d'Arán, or through Tarbes and Aragnouet through the tunnel to Parzán.

Entry Formalities

Passports and Visas

There are no formal entry requirements for EU passport holders travelling to Spain, regardless of the purpose or duration of the

> ### Spanish Consulates
> **Canada**: 1 West Mount Square, Montreal H3Z 2P9, t (514) 935 5235; 200 Cross Street West, Toronto, Ontario t (416) 977 1661.
> **Ireland**: 17a Merlyn Park, Ballsbridge, Dublin 4, t (1) 269 1640, 269 1854.
> **UK**: 20 Draycott Place, London SW3 2RZ, t (020) 7589 8989; 1a Brook House, 70 Spring Gardens, Manchester M2 2BQ, t (0161) 236 1233, f (0161) 228 7467; 63 North Castle Street, Edinburgh EH2 2LJ, t (0131) 220 1843.
> **USA**: 545 Boylston Street, Boston, MA 02116, t (617) 536 2506; 180 North Michigan Avenue, Chicago, IL 60601, t (312) 782 4588; 2655 Lejeune Road, 203 Coral Gable, Florida, t (305) 446 5511; 5055 Wilshire Blvd, Suite 960 Los Angeles, CA 90036, t (323) 938 0158; 150 East 58th Street, New York, NY 10155, t (212) 355 4090; 2375 Pennyslvania Avenue NW, Washington, DC 20009, t (202) 728 2330.

Specialist Tour Operators

Abercrombie & Kent International, 1520 Kensington Road, Oak Brook, Illinois, IL 60521, toll free **t** (800) 323 7308, and in the UK, Sloane Square House, Holbein Place, London SW1W 8NS, **t** (020) 7730 9600, *www.abercrombiekent.co.uk*. Tailor-made breaks in Granada, Seville and Cordoba.

ACE Study Tours, Sawston Road, Babraham, Cambridge CB2 4AP, **t** (01223) 835 055, **f** 837394, *www.study-tours.org*. Organizes tours focusing on Moorish art, architecture, archaeology and history in Granada, Seville and Ronda.

Al-Andalus Expreso, booked through Cox & King's (*see* below). Offers luxury train tours across Andalucía.

Andante Travel, The Old Barn, Old Road, Alderbury, Salisbury, SP5 3AR, Wilts, **t** (01722) 713 800, *www.andantetravels.co.uk*. Arranges archaeological and historical study tours of Roman and Moorish Seville and Cordoba.

BA Holidays, 156 Regent St, London W1R 6LB, **t** (020) 7434 4700. City breaks in Granada and Seville.

Cadogan Travel, 9–10 Portland Street, Southampton SO14 7EB, **t** (01703) 828 300, *www.cadoganholidays.com*. 3- and 4-star hotel city breaks in Granada.

Club Nautique, Puerto Deportivo Marina del Este, Punta de la Mona, 18690 Almuñécar, (Granada), **t** 95 863 9197. An excellent scuba-diving centre.

Cox & King's Travel Ltd, Gordon House, 10 Green Coat Place, London SW1P 1PH, **t** (020) 7873 5000. Agents for the al-Andalus luxury train tour of Andalucía, plus tours of Islamic Spain; gardens in Seville, Roman ruins in Cordoba and Granada's Alhambra.

CV Travel, 43 Cadogan Street, London SW3 2PR, **t** (020) 7581 0851. Has a 24-hour brochure service: **t** (020) 7589 0132, **f** (020) 7584 5229. Includes small luxury hotels in Seville.

Kirker Holidays, 3 New Concordia Wharf, Mill Street, London SE1 2BB, **t** (020) 7231 3333. Specializes in tailor-made travel in Seville, Granada, Cordoba, rural Andalucía and the *paradores*.

Learning for Pleasure, Apartado 25, Las Limas, 11330 Jimena de la Frontera (Cádiz), **t** 95 664 01 02, **f** 95 664 12 89. Offers courses in painting, creative writing, cooking, herbal medicine and gardening, and organizes riding and walking tours.

Mundicolor Holidays, 276 Vauxhall Bridge Road, London SW1V 1BE, **t** (020) 7828 6021, *www.mundicolor.co.uk*. Specializes in tailor-made holidays throughout Spain; it also offers a luxury train tour of Andalucía and gastronomy and wine tours.

Page & Moy Ltd, 136–140 London Road, Leicester LE2 1EN, **t** (0116) 250 7000, *www.page-moy.com*. Cultural guided tours.

Plantagenet Tours, 85 The Grove, Moordown, Bournemouth BH9 2TY, **t** (01202) 521 895, *www.plantagenet-tours.freeserve.co.uk*. Organizes a 12-day Isabelline tour of medieval Andalucía every March.

Prospect Music & Art Tours, 36 Manchester Street, London W1 U7LH, **t** (020) 7486 5704, **f** (020) 7486 5868, *sales@prospecttours.com*. Arranges tours led by art historians.

Ramblers Holidays, Box 43, Welwyn Garden City, Herts AL8 6PQ, **t** (01707) 331 133, *www.ramblersholidays.co.uk*. Offers easygoing 1-week walking tours in Granada and Seville; 2-star hotels and hostels.

Rancho Los Lobos, 11339 Estación de Jimena (Cádiz), **t** 95 664 04 29, **f** 95 664 11 80. Offers riding holidays.

Safari Andalucía, Apartado 20, 29480 Gaucín, (Málaga), **t** 95 215 11 48, **f** 95 215 13 76. Walking holidays in the Serranía de Ronda with tented camp and hunting lodge accommodation and mules to carry baggage.

The Spirit of Andalucía, c/o Sally von Meister, Apartado 20, El Nobo, 29480 Gaucín, (Málaga), **t** 95 215 13 03. Offers courses in cooking and painting.

Thomson Breakaways, Centenary House, 3 Water Lane, Richmond, Surrey, **t** (0181) 210 4500, city breaks in 2, 3 and 4 star hotels in Granada, Seville and Cordoba.

Thomas Cook, Units 1–3, Coningsby Road, Peterborough TE3 8BX, **t** (0990) 666222, city breaks in Seville, minimum stay 2 nights.

Time Off, 1 Elmfield Park, Bromley, Kent BR1 1OU, **t** (0990) 846363. City breaks in 2, 4 and 5 star hotels in Seville.

Unicorn Holidays, 2–10 Crossroad, Tadworth, KT20 5UJ, **t** (01737) 812 255. Specializes in tailor-made holidays, with high-quality character hotels.

visit. In fact, nationals of the EU countries that are signatories to the *Schengen* agreement no longer require even a passport. However, the UK is *not* a signatory and passengers arriving at Spanish airports from Britain must still present a valid passport.

Holders of US or Canadian passports can enter Spain for up to 90 days without a visa; holders of Australian or New Zealand passports need a visa, available from any Spanish consulate.

Customs

Customs are usually polite and easy to get through – unless you come in via Morocco, when they'll search everything you own. EU limits for goods bought in a tax-free shop are: 1 litre of spirits or 2 litres of liquors (port, sherry or champagne) plus 2 litres of wine and 200 cigarettes. Larger quantities (10 litres of spirits, 90 litres of wine, 110 litres of beer, 800 cigarettes) can be taken through Customs if they have been bought locally in a non-tax-free shop, you are travelling between EU countries, and you can prove that they are for private consumption only.

If you are travelling from the UK or the USA, don't bother to pick up any alcohol in transit – aside from the fact that duty-free shopping is no longer possible when travelling between EU countries, it's cheaper to buy drink off the supermarket shelves in Spain.

Getting Around

By Air

Internal flights in Spain are primarily on Iberia, Aviaco, Binter and Air Europa. However, there are several other carriers on national routes, such as the Alitalia service between Malaga and Barcelona. Cordoba, Granada,

---

Iberia Offices

Granada: Pza Isabel la Católica 2, **t** 95 822 7592.
Malaga: Molina Larios 13, **t** 95 213 6147.
Seville: Avda de la Buhaira, 8, **t** 95 422 8901.

You can also call Iberia throughout Spain on their 24hr number in Madrid, **t** 902 400 500. Otherwise log on to *www.iberia.com*.

Malaga and Seville have airports. Prices are less of a bargain than they used to be, although if you shop around and are willing to travel at night you can pick up some cheap deals, especially if you're going on a round trip. Also, check out the national charters in Spanish travel agencies.

By Rail

Mister Traveler, take the Spanish Train!
RENFE brochure

Democracy in Spain has made the trains run on time, but Western Europe's most eccentric railway company, **RENFE**, still has a way to go. The problem isn't the trains themselves; they're almost always clean and comfortable, and do their best to keep to the schedules, but the new efficient RENFE remains so complex it will foul up your plans at least once if you spend much time in Spain. To start with, there are no fewer than 13 varieties of train, from the luxury **TEE** (Trans-Europe Express) to the excruciating *semidirecto* and *ferrobús*. Watch out for these; they stop at every conceivable hamlet to deliver mail.

The best are the **Talgo** trains, speedy and stylish beasts in gleaming stainless steel, designed and built entirely in Spain; the Spaniards are very proud of them. **TER** trains are almost as good. Note that a majority of lines are still, incredibly, single-track, so whatever train you take, you'll still have to endure delays for trains coming the other way. This said, there has been one great leap forward in Spanish rail transport in the last few years, and that is the introduction of **AVE** services – high-speed rail links.

Every variety of train has different services and a different price. RENFE ticket people and conductors can't always get them straight, and confusion is rampant, except again on Talgo and AVE routes where the published prices are straightforward and easy to read. There are discounts for children (under-4s free; 4–12 half-price), large families, senior citizens (half-price) and regular travellers, and 25 per cent discounts on *Días Azules* ('blue days') for round-trip tickets only. 'Blue days' are posted in the RENFE calendars in every station – really almost every day is a 'blue day'.

Interpretations of the rules for these discounts differ from one ticket-window to the next, and you may care to undertake protracted negotiations over them like the Spaniards do. There is a discount pass for people under 26, the *tarjeta joven*, and BIGE or BIJ youth fares are available from TIVE offices in the large cities.

Every city has a **RENFE travel office** in the centre (*see* list below), and you can make good use of these for information and tickets. Always buy tickets in advance if you can; one of RENFE's little tricks is to close station ticket-windows 10 minutes before your train arrives. Other stations don't open the ticket-windows until the train is a couple of minutes away, causing panic and confusion. Don't rely on the list of trains posted; always ask at the station or travel office. **Fares** average 500 pts for every 100km (63 miles) – 750 pts first class – but there are supplements on the faster trains that can put another 80 per cent on top of the basic price. If you plan to do a lot of riding on the rails, buy the *Guía RENFE*, an indispensable government publication with all the schedules and tariffs, available from any station newsagent.

Rail Excursions

Andalucía's answer to the famous *Transcantábrica*, which operates in northwest Spain, is the *Al-Andalus Expreso*, a luxury tour taking passengers from Seville to Cordoba, Granada, Malaga and Jerez. Although expensive, the trip is a memorable experience – the carriages are done out in fancy period décor and the cuisine is superb. The trip takes 4–5 days, depending on which 'cruise' you take, but a common complaint we have heard is that the train spends an excessive amount of time in a railway siding!

UK: Cox & King's Travel Ltd, Gordon House, 10 Green Coat Place, London SW1P 1PH, **t** (020) 7873 5000.

USA: Marketing Ahead Inc., 433 Fifth Avenue, New York, NY 10016, **t** (212) 686 9213.

RENFE Offices

Cordoba: Ronda de los Tejares 10, **t** 95 749 02 02.

Granada: Reyes Católicos 63, **t** 95 827 12 72.

Seville: Zaragoza 29, **t** 95 441 41 11.

By Car

If you are not part of a tour which includes inter-city travel, this is certainly the most convenient way of getting about, and often the most pleasurable. However, there are no petrol concessions or coupons for tourists. Another problem is that only a few hotels – the more expensive ones – have garages or any sort of parking. And in cities parking is always difficult, although a useful tip to remember is that space which appears to be private – e.g. underground car parks of apartment blocks and offices – is often public, and rates are usually modest. Spain's highway network is adequate, usually in good repair, and sometimes impressive. The system of *autovías* (motorways) is constantly expanding. Spanish road building is remarkable for its speed if not always its durability.

To drive in Spain you'll need registration and insurance documents, and a driving licence. If you're coming from Ireland or the UK, adjust the dip of your headlights to the right. Drivers with a valid licence from an EU country, the USA, Canada or Australia no longer need an international licence.

Americans should not be intimidated by driving in Europe. Learn the international road-sign system (charts available to members from most auto clubs), brush up on your gear-changing technique, and get used to the idea of few signals, and traffic constantly converging from all directions. Seat belts are mandatory. The speed limit is 100km (62 miles) per hour on national highways, unless otherwise marked, and 120km (75 miles) per hour on motorways. Drive with the utmost care at all times – having an accident will bring you untold headaches, and to make matters worse, many Spaniards drive without insurance.

Hitchhiking is likely to involve a long, hot wait. Drivers in Andalucía are rarely inclined to give lifts and temperatures in midsummer can soar; few Spaniards ever hitchhike.

Car Hire

This is moderately cheaper than elsewhere in Europe. The big international companies are the most expensive, and seldom the most service-orientated. Smaller companies will, for example, deliver a car to your hotel when you want it, and collect it again when you no longer require it. Prices for the smallest cars begin at about £100 ($155) per week, which includes unlimited mileage and full insurance (CDW), according to season. An all-in weekly rate for a two-door Opel Corsa in mid-season picked up from and returned to Malaga Airport should run to about 21,000 pts. If your car rental begins at Malaga Airport, try booking it locally in advance. You will do no better than with **Mustang Rent-a-Car**, Aeropuérto de Málaga, **t** 95 223 51 59, **f** 95 288 33 13. Apart from offering good rates and friendly service, Mustang is also a car-repair garage. Two other firms with a good reputation are **Marinsa**, **t** 95 223 23 04, **f** 95 223 99 25, and **Helle Hollis**, **t** 95 224 55 44, **f** 95 224 51 86. Local firms, such as **Turarche**, C/Roger de Flor 1 (by the bus station), **t** 95 231 80 69, **f** 95 231 63 42, *www.turarche.es*, also rent mopeds and bicycles, especially in tourist areas. From the UK, try **Holiday Autos**, **t** (08705) 300 400, or **Hertz**, **t** (08705) 996 699. However, pre-booked car rentals offer no refunds should your plans change.

Taxis

Taxis are still cheap enough for the Spaniards to use them regularly on their shopping trips. The average fare for a ride within a city will be 500–750 pts. Taxis are not always metered, but the drivers are usually quite honest; they are entitled to certain surcharges (for luggage, night or holiday trips, to the train or airport, et cetera), and if you cross the city limits they can usually charge double the fare shown. It's rarely hard to hail a cab from the street, and there will always be a few around the stations. If you get stuck where there are no taxis to hail, call information for the number of a radio taxi.

By Bus

With literally dozens of companies providing services over Andalucía, expect choice at the price of confusion. Not all cities have bus stations; in some, including Seville and Cordoba, there may be a dozen little offices spread around town for each firm. Buses, like the trains, are cheap by northern European standards, but still no bargain; if you're travelling on the cheap, you'll find that transportation is your biggest expense. Usually, whether you go by train or bus will depend on simple convenience; in some places the train station is far from the centre, in others the bus station is. As is the custom at RENFE stations, tickets on the inter-city bus routes are sometimes sold at the last minute.

If you want to escape the city heat and venture out on day trips, small towns and villages can normally be reached by bus only through their provincial capitals. Buses are usually clean, dependable and comfortable, and there's plenty of room for baggage in the compartment underneath. On the more luxurious buses which link the main cities of Andalucía, as well as the services along the coast, you get air-conditioning and even a movie (*Rambo, Kung Fu*, sappy Spanish flicks from the Franco era or locally produced rock videos). **Tourist information offices** are the best sources for information.

City Buses

Every Spanish city has a perfectly adequate system of public transportation. You won't need to make much use of it, though, for in almost every city all attractions are within walking distance of each other. City buses usually cost 120 pts, and if you intend to use them often there are books of tickets called *abonamientos* or *bono-Bus* or *tarjeta* cards to punch on entry, available at reduced rates from tobacco shops.

Bus drivers will give change but don't give them a 1,000 pts note. In many cities, the bus's entire route will be displayed on the signs at each stop (*parada*). And don't take it for granted that the bus will stop just because you are waiting – nearly every stop apart from the terminus seems to be a *request* stop. Flamboyant signals and throwing yourself across its path are the only ways of ensuring the bus will stop for you.

Practical A–Z

Children

Spaniards adore children, and they'll welcome yours almost everywhere. Baby foods, and other supplies are widely available, but don't expect to find babysitters except at the really smart hotels; Spaniards always take their children with them, even if they're up until 4am. Nor are there many special amusements for children. Ask at a local tourist office for a list of attractions in its area geared towards children.

Climate and When to Go

Andalucía is hot and sunny in the summer, generally mild and sunny by day in the winter – in fact, with an average 320 days of sunshine in the region, you can count on more sun here than anywhere else in Europe. Autumn weather is normally warm and comfortable, but can pack a few surprises, from torrential rains to droughts. The mild winters in coastal regions give way to warm springs with minimal rainfall. Temperatures inland can be considerably lower, especially in the mountainous regions, and the *Levante* wind can make life uncomfortable, even in summer, when it will not only blow your beach umbrella away, but might even make you a bit kooky. For comfort, spring and autumn are the best times to visit.

Disabled Travellers

Facilities for disabled travellers are limited within Spain and public transport is not particularly wheelchair-friendly, though RENFE usually provides wheelchairs at main city stations. You are advised to contact the Spanish Tourist Office, which has compiled a fact sheet and can give general information on accessible accommodation, or any of the organizations that specifically provide services for people with disabilities.

Organizations in Spain
ECOM, in Barcelona, **t** 93 451 55 50. The federation of private Spanish organizations offering services for the disabled. Ask for Emilio Grande, who speaks good English.
ONCE (Organización Nacional de Ciegos de España), Pso de la Castellana 95, Planta 28, Madrid, **t** 91 597 47 27. The Spanish association for blind people.

Organizations in the UK
Holiday Care Service, 2 Old Bank Chambers, Station Rd, Horley, Surrey RH6 9HW, **t** (01293) 774 535. Travel information and details of accessible accommodation and care holidays.
RADAR (The Royal Association for Disability and Rehabilitation), 12 City Forum, 250 City Road, London EC1V 8AF, **t** (020) 7259 3222. Has a wide range of travel information.
Royal National Institute for the Blind, 224 Great Portland Street, London W15 5TB, **t** (020) 7388 1266. Its mobility unit offers a 'Plane Easy' audio-cassette which advises blind people on travelling by plane. It will also advise on accommodation.
Tripscope, The Courtyard, Evelyn Road, London W4 5JL, **t** (020) 8994 9294, or **t** (08457) 585 641 (calls from within the UK charged at cheap rate). Offers advice on the practicalities of travel for elderly and disabled travellers.

In the USA
American Foundation for the Blind, 15 West 16th Street, New York, NY 10011, **t** (212) 620 2000; toll free **t** 800 232 5463. The best source of information in the USA for visually impaired travellers.

Average Temperatures in °C (°F)

	Jan		April		July		Oct	
	max	min	max	min	max	min	max	min
Seville	15 (59)	6 (43)	23 (74)	11 (52)	35 (95)	21 (70)	26 (79)	14 (58)

Average monthly rainfall in mm (inches)

	Jan	April	July	Oct
Seville	99 (4)	80 (3)	0 (0)	37 (1.5)

Federation of the Handicapped, 211 West 14th Street, New York, NY 10011, t (212) 747 4262. Organizes summer tours for members; there is a nominal annual fee.

Mobility International USA, PO Box 3551, Eugene, OR 97403, t (503) 343 1248. Offers a service similar to that of its sister organization in the UK.

SATD (Society for the Advancement of Travel for the Disabled), Suite 610, 347 5th Avenue, New York, NY 10016, t (212) 447 7284. Advice on travel for the disabled for a $5 charge, or free to members ($45, concessions $30).

Electricity

The current is 225 AC or 220 V, the same as most of Europe. Americans will need converters, and the British will need two-pin adapters for the different plugs. If you plan to stay in the less expensive *hostales*, it may be better to leave your gadgets at home. Some corners of Spain, even some big cities, have pockets of exotic voltage – 150V for example – guaranteeing a brief display of fireworks. Big hotels always have the standard current.

Embassies and Consulates

Australia: Pso de la Castellana, 143 Edificio Cuzco, Madrid, t 91 279 85 04.

Canada: C/Núñez de Balboa 35, Madrid t 91 431 43 00; Malaga, t 95 222 33 46.

France: C/Salustiano Olózaga 9, Madrid, t 91 435 55 60; Malaga, t 95 221 48 88.

Ireland: C/Claudio Coello 73, Madrid, t 91 576 35 00; Malaga, t 95 247 51 08.

Italy: C/Joaquín Costa 29, Madrid, t 91 262 55 46; Malaga, t 95 230 61 50.

New Zealand: Plaza de la Lealtad 2, Madrid, t 91 523 02 26.

UK: C/de Fernando el Santo 16, Madrid, t 91 319 0208; Pza Nueva 8, Seville, t 95 422 88 75; Edificio Duquesa, C/Duquesa de Parcent 8, Malaga, t 95 221 7571.

USA: C/Serrano 75, Madrid, t 91 587 22 00; consular office for passports, around the corner at Pso de la Castellana, 52 Pso de las Delicias 7, Seville, t 95 423 18 85; C/Martínez Catena, Portal 6, Apartado 5B, Complejo Sol Playa, Fuengirola (Malaga), t 95 247 98 91.

Festivals

One of the most spiritually deadening aspects of Francoism was the banning of many local and regional fiestas. These are now celebrated with gusto, and if you can arrange your itinerary to include one or two you'll be guaranteeing an unforgettable holiday.

Besides those listed overleaf, there are literally thousands of others, and new ones spring up all the time. Many village patronal fiestas feature *romerías* (pilgrimages) up to a venerated shrine. Getting there is half the fun, with everyone in local costume, riding on horseback or driving covered wagons full of picnic supplies. Music, dancing, food, wine and fireworks are all necessary ingredients of a proper fiesta, while the bigger ones often include bullfights, funfairs, circuses and competitions. *Semana Santa* (Holy Week) is a major tourist event, especially in Sevilla. The processions of *pasos* (ornate floats depicting scenes from the Passion) carried in a slow march to lugubrious tuba music, and accompanied by children and men decked out in costumes later copied by the Ku Klux Klan, are worth fighting the crowds to see. And while a certain amount of merry-making goes on after dark, the real revelry takes place after Easter, in the unmissable April *feria*. Fiestas or *ferias* are incredibly important to Andalucíans, no matter what the cost in money and lost sleep; they are a celebration of being alive in a society constantly aware of the inevitability of death.

Dates for most festivals tend to be fluid, flowing towards the nearest weekend; if the actual date falls on a Thursday or a Tuesday, Spaniards 'bridge' the fiesta with the weekend to create a four-day whoopee. Check dates at the tourist office in advance.

Food and Drink

See also **Food and Drink** chapter, pp.63–70.

Spaniards are notoriously late diners; 2pm is the earliest they would consider sitting down to their huge 'midday' meal. Then after work at 8pm a few tapas at the bar hold them over until supper at 10 or 11pm. After living in Spain for a few months this makes perfect sense, but it's exasperating to the average visitor. On the coasts, restaurants tend to open earlier to

Calendar of Events

January
First week Granada: commemoration of the city's capture by the Catholic Kings.
Malaga: Epiphany parade of Los Reyes Magos (Three Wise Men).

March
Easter week Seville: sees the most important *Semana Santa*: celebrations, with over 100 processions, broken by the singing of *saetas* (weird laments).
Cordoba: the city's 26 processions are perhaps the most emotionally charged of all, making their way around the streets of the great Mosque.
Malaga, Granada, Úbeda: also put on major celebrations.

April
Last week Seville: the capital's *Feria*, originally a horse-fair, has now grown into the greatest festival of Andalucía. Costumed parades of the gentry in fine carriages, lots of flamenco, bullfights, and drinking.

May
First week Granada: everyone dresses up and decorates the streets with carpets and flowers for the *Fiesta de la Santa Cruz*.
Second week Cordoba: every third year the *Concurso Nacional de Arte Flamenco* takes place, with over 100 singers, guitar players and dancers.

June
Mid-month Granada: start of the month-long *Festival Internacional de Música y Danza*, which attracts big names from around the world; classical music, jazz and ballet; flamenco competitions are also held in odd-numbered years.

July
First Sunday Cordoba: International Guitar Festival – classical, flamenco and Latino.
Last two weeks Lebrija, near Seville: flamenco festival.

August
5 Trevélez (near Granada): has a midnight pilgrimage up Mulhacén, Spain's highest mountain, so that pilgrims arrive exhausted but in time for prayers at midday.

---

accommodate foreigners (some as early as 5pm) but you may as well do as the Spaniards do. A few rounds of tapas – available at what most Americans or Britons would consider normal dining hours – will fill in the gaps.

Unless it's explicitly written on the bill (*la cuenta*), service in most restaurants is not included in the total, so tip accordingly. Almost every restaurant offers a *menú del día*, or a *menú turístico*, featuring an appetizer, a main course, dessert, bread and drink at a set price, always cheaper than if you had ordered the items *à la carte*.

Price categories quoted in the 'Eating Out' sections throughout this book are prices for the set menus or for a three-course meal with drinks, per person.

Restaurant Price Categories
Expensive over 5,000 pts / €30
Moderate 3,000–5,000 pts / €18–30
Inexpensive under 3,000 pts / €18

Health and Insurance

There is now a standard agreement for citizens of EU countries, entitling them to a certain amount of free medical care, but it's not straightforward. You must complete all the necessary paperwork before you go to Spain, and allow a couple of months to make sure it comes through in time. Ask for a leaflet entitled *Before You Go* from the Department of Health and fill out form E111, which on arrival in Spain you must take to the local office of the *Instituto Nacional de Seguridad Social* (INSS), where you'll be issued with a Spanish medical card and some vouchers enabling you to claim free treatment from an INSS doctor. At time of writing, the government is trying to implement a much easier system.

If you have a particular diet or need special treatment then obtain a letter from your doctor and get it translated into Spanish before you go. In an emergency, ask to be taken to the nearest *hospital de la seguridad social*.

Before resorting to a *médico* (doctor) and his £20 ($30) fee (ask at the tourist office for a list of English-speaking doctors), go to a **pharmacy** and tell them your woes. Spanish *farmacéuticos* are highly skilled, and if there's a prescription medicine that you know will cure you, they'll often supply it without a doctor's note. (The newspaper *Sur* lists *farmacías* in large cities that stay open all night and every pharmacy displays a duty roster outside so you can locate one nearby which is open.)

No **inoculations** are required to enter Spain, though it never hurts to check that your tetanus jab is up to date, as well as some of the more exotic inoculations (typhoid, cholera and gamma globulin) if you want to venture on into Morocco.

The **tap water** is safe to drink in Spain, but of horrendously poor quality after periods of drought. At the slightest twinge of queasiness, switch to the bottled stuff.

Insurance

You may want to consider travel insurance, available through most travel agents. For a small monthly charge, not only is your health insured, but your bags and money as well. Some will even refund a missed charter flight if you're too ill to catch it.

Many English and English-speaking doctors now have arrangements with European insurance companies and send their account directly to the company without you, the patient, having to fork out. But whether you pay on the spot or not, be sure to save all doctors' bills, pharmacy receipts and police documents (if you're reporting a theft).

Left Luggage

Since terrorists stopped leaving bombs in rail stations, RENFE has started to reintroduce *consignas*, or left-luggage facilities; you'll have about an even chance of finding one in a bus station or small bus company office, and sometimes bars near train or bus stations are willing to let you leave your bags. But don't rely on it.

Media

The Socialist *El País* is Spain's biggest and best national **newspaper**, though circulation is painfully low at under 400,000; Spaniards just don't read newspapers (the little magazine *Teleprograma*, with television listings, is far and away the best-selling periodical).

El País has the best regional **film** listings, indicating where you can see some great films subtitled instead of dubbed (look out for *versión original* or its abbreviation 'vo'). English films are occasionally shown on the Costa del Sol and dozens of shops rent English-language video releases. Films are cheap and Spaniards are great cinema-goers; there are lots of inexpensive outdoor movie theatres in the summer. Hollywood hearthrob Antonio Banderas is a native *malagueño*; his occasional visits to the Costa del Sol are greeted with a media frenzy.

The other big papers are *Diario 16* (centrist), *ABC* (conservative, in a bizarre 1960s magazine format), and the *Alcázar* (neo-fascist). Major British papers are available in all tourist areas and big cities by around 4pm the same day; the American *New York Herald Tribune*, the *Wall Street Journal*, and *USA Today* are readily available wherever Americans go. Most hit the newsstands a day late; issues of *Time* and *Newsweek* often hang about for a while.

Money

1 January 1999 saw the beginning of the transition to the **Euro**. It became the official currency in Spain (and 10 other nations within the European Union). **The official exchange rate was set at 166.386 pts.** Euro notes and coins will be issued from 1 January 2002 and will circulate in parallel with *pesetas* for just two months. From March 2002 until 30 June, you will be able to exchange *pesetas* for euros in any bank for no charge. From 1 July you will only be able exchange *pesetas* at the Bank of Spain (offices situated only in major cities).

Pesetas (pts) come in notes of 1,000, 2,000, 5,000, 10,000, all in different colours, and coins of 1, 5, 10, 25, 100, 200 and 500 pts. At street markets, and in out-of-the-way places, you may hear prices given in *duros* or *notas*. A *duro* is a 5 pts piece, and a *nota* is a 100 pts note.

There will be 7 **euro** notes: 500, 200, 100, 50, 20, 10 and 5; and 8 coins: 2 euros, 1 euro, 50 cents, 20 cents, 10 cents, 5 cents, 2 cents and 1 cent.

Exchange rates vary, but until any drastic changes occur £1 is roughly 270 pts, and $1 equivalent to about 190 pts. Spain's city centres seem to have a bank on every street corner, and most of them will exchange money; look for the *cambio* or *exchange* signs and the little flags. There is a slight difference in the rates, though usually not enough to make shopping around worthwhile. Beware exchange offices, as they can charge a hefty commission on all transactions. You can often change money at travel agencies, hotels, restaurants or the big department stores. Even big supermarkets tend to have *telebancos* or automatic tellers. There are 24-hour *cambios* at the big train stations in Barcelona and Madrid.

Traveller's cheques, if they are from one of the major companies, will pass at most bank exchanges. Wiring money from overseas entails no special difficulties; just give yourself two weeks to be on the safe side, and work through one of the larger institutions (Banco Central, Banco de Bilbao, Banco Español de Crédito, Banco Hispano Americano, Banco de Santander, Banco de Vizcaya). All transactions have to go through Madrid.

Credit cards will always be helpful in towns, rarely in the country. Direct debit cards are also useful ways of obtaining money, though you should check with your bank before leaving to ensure your card can be used in Spain. But do not rely on a hole-in-the-wall machine as your only source of cash; if the machine swallows your card, it usually takes 10 days to retrieve it.

Opening Hours

Banks

Most banks are open Mon–Thurs 8.30–2.30, Fri 8.30–2 and Sat in winter 8.30–1.

Churches

The less important churches are often closed. Some cities probably have more churches than faithful communicants, and many are unused. If you're determined to see one, it will never be hard to find the *sacristán* or caretaker. Usually they live close by, and would be glad to show you around for a tip. Don't be surprised when cathedrals and famous churches charge for admission – just consider the costs of upkeep.

Shops

Shops usually open from 9.30am. Spaniards take their main meal at 2pm and, except in the larger cities most shops shut down for 2–3 hours in the afternoon, usually from 1pm or 2pm. In the south, where it's hotter, the siesta can last from 1pm to 5pm. In the evening most establishments stay open until 7pm or 8pm, or later still in tourist resorts.

Museums

Although their opening times have become more chaotic lately, major **museums** and historical sites tend to follow shop hours, but abbreviated in the winter months; nearly all close on Mondays. We have tried to list the hours for the important sights. Seldom-visited ones have a raffish disregard for their official hours, or open only when the mood strikes them. Don't be discouraged; bang on doors and ask around.

We haven't bothered to list **admission prices** for all museums and sites. Usually the sum is trivial and often fluctuating – hardly anything will cost more than 250 pts, usually much less; EU nationals are admitted free to many monuments. The Alhambra in Granada, La Mezquita in Cordoba and La Giralda in Seville are the most notable exceptions.

Photography

Film is quite expensive everywhere; so is developing it, but in any city there will be plenty of places – many in opticians' shops (*ópticas*) or big department stores – where you can get processing done in a hurry.

Serious photographers must give some consideration to the strong sunlight and high reflectivity of surfaces (pavements and build-ings) in towns. If you're there during the summer use ASA100 film.

Police Business

Crime is not really a big problem in Spain and Spaniards talk about it perhaps more than is warranted. Pickpocketing and robbing parked cars are the specialities; in Seville they like to take the whole car. The big cities are the places where you should be careful, especially Seville. You're still probably safer in Spain than you would be at home; the crime rate is roughly a quarter of that in Britain. Note that in Spain less than 8 grams of cannabis is legal; buying and selling it, however, is not. And anything else may easily earn you the traditional 'six years and a day'.

There are several species of **police**, and their authority varies with the area. Franco's old goon squads, the *Policía Armada*, have been reformed and relatively demilitarized into the *Policía Nacional*, whom the Spaniards call 'chocolate drops' for their brown uniforms; their duties largely consist of driving around in cars and drinking coffee. They are, however, more highly thought of than the *Policía Armada*, and their popularity increased when their commander, Lt General José Antonio Sáenz de Santa María, ordered his men to surround the Cortes to foil Tejero's attempted coup in 1981, thereby proving that he and his *Policía Nacional* were strongly on the side of the newly born democracy. The *Policía Municipal* in some towns do crime control, while in others they simply direct traffic.

Post Offices

Every city, regardless of size, seems to have one post office (*correos*) and no more. It will always be crowded, but unless you have packages to mail, you may not ever need to visit one. Most tobacconists sell stamps (*sellos*) and they'll usually know the correct postage for whatever you're sending. The standard charge for sending a letter is 60 pts (European Union) and 87 pts (North America). Send everything air mail (*por avión*) and don't send postcards unless you don't care when they arrive. Mailboxes are bright yellow and scarce. The post offices also handle telegrams, which normally take 4hrs to arrive within Europe but are very expensive – a one-word message plus address costs around 2,000 pts. There is also,

> ## Public Holidays in Spain
> **1 Jan** Año Nuevo (New Year's Day)
> **6 Jan** Epifanía (Epiphany)
> **March/April** Viernes Santo (Good Friday)
> **1 May** Día del Trabajo (Labour Day)
> **May/June** Corpus Christi
> **25 July** Día de Santiago (St James's Day)
> **15 Aug** Asunción (Assumption)
> **12 Oct** Día de la Hispanidad (Columbus's Day)
> **1 Nov** Todos los Santos (All Saints' Day)
> **6 Dec** Día de la Constitución (Constitution Day)
> **8 Dec** Inmaculada Concepción (Immaculate Conception)
> **25 Dec** Navidad (Christmas Day)

of course, the *poste restante* (general delivery). In Spain this is called *lista de correos*, and it is as chancy as anywhere else. Don't confuse post offices with the *Caja Postal*, the postal savings banks, which look just like them.

Public Holidays

The Spaniards, like the Italians, try to have as many public holidays as possible. And everything closes. The big holidays, celebrated throughout Spain, are *Corpus Christi* in late May, *Semana Santa* during the week before Easter, *Asunción* on 15 August and *Día de Santiago* on 25 July, celebrating Spain's patron, Saint James.

No matter where you are, there are bound to be fireworks or processions on these dates, especially for *Semana Santa* and *Corpus Christi*. But be aware that every region, town, and village has at least one of its own holidays as well (*see* 'Festivals').

Shopping

There are some delightful tacky tourist wares – Toledo 'daggers', plastic bulls and flamenco dolls *ad nauseam*. There are also some good buys to be had, for instance the high-quality **leather goods** from Cordoba and the town of Ubrique, which has been producing leatherwork since Roman times. Moorish craftsmen later had a major influence on the method of treating the cured skin for export. But, though the quality is good, the design seldom compares with its Italian counterpart. While Cordoba is better known for its ornate embossed leather for furniture decoration and **filigree jewellery**, Ubrique specializes in handmade items such as diaries, suitcases, bags and wallets.

Ceramic plates, pottery and colourful *azulejo* tiles are made all over Andalucía; the quality varies enormously, from the shoddy factory-made products adorning tourist shop shelves, to the sophisticated **ceramic ware** you will find in the Triana district of Seville. Granada is well known for its **inlaid wood** *taracea* work (chests, chessboards and music boxes), although these can be rather crudely produced. Spanish **woven goods** are reasonably priced; Seville produces exquisite *mantillas* and embroidered shawls, and is the centre for the extraordinary designs that adorn the bullfighter's costume. In the Alpujarras a concentrated effort is being made to revive old skills, using the wooden loom particularly, to produce the typical **woollen blankets** and **rugs** for which this area has long been known – a fascinating mixture of ancient Christian and Arab designs. To encourage the nation's craftsmen, the government has organized a kind of co-operative, *Artespaña*, with various outlets selling their work. In Andalucía these can be found at: Rodríguez Jurado 4, Seville; Corral del Carbón, Granada.

The major **department store** chains in Spain, El Corte Inglés and Galerías Preciados, often have good selections of crafts. All of the above will ship items home for you. You can also get bargains at the roving **weekly markets**, where Spaniards do a good deal of their shopping. Good-quality **antiques** can occasionally be picked up at a *rastro* (flea market), but they aren't the great finds they once were – Spaniards have learned what they're worth and charge accordingly. Guitars, mandolins and bagpipes, fine wooden furniture and Goya tapestries are some of the bulky, more expensive items you may want to ship home.

EU citizens are not entitled to tax refunds.

Sports and Activities

Bars and **cafés** collect much of the Spaniards' leisure time. They are wonderful institutions, where you can eat breakfast or linger over a glass of beer until four in the morning; in any of them you could see an old sailor delicately sipping his camomile tea next to a young mother, baby under her arm, stopping by for a beer break during her shopping. Some have music – jazz, rock or flamenco; some have great snacks, or tapas, some have games or pinball machines. Every Spaniard is a gambler; there seem to be an infinite number of lotteries run by the State (the *Lotería Deportiva*), for the blind (ONCE), the Red Cross or the Church; there's at least one bingo-hall in every town and there are **casinos** in all major resorts. Every bar has a slot machine, doling out electronic versions of **La Cucaracha** whenever it gets lonely.

Discos and **night clubs** are easily found in the big cities and tourist spots; most are expensive. Ask around for the favourites. Watch out for posters for **concerts, ballets**, and especially for **circuses**. The little travelling Spanish troupes with their family acts, tents, tinsel and names like 'The National Circus of Japan' will charm you; they often gravitate to the major fiestas throughout the summer.

Football has pride of place in the Spanish heart, while **bullfighting** (*see* **Snapshots**, pp.58–60) and cycling vie for second place; all are shown regularly on television, which, despite a heavy fare of dubbed American shows, everyone is inordinately fond of watching. Both channels are state-run.

Cycling

Cycling is taken extremely seriously in Spain and you don't often see people using a bike as a form of transport. Instead, Lycra-clad enthusiasts pedal furiously up the steepest of hills, no doubt trying to reach the standards set by Miguel Indurain, who was the Spanish winner of the *Tour de France* for three years running.

If you do want to bring your own **bicycle** to Spain, you can make arrangements by ferry or train; by air, you'll almost always have to dismantle it to some extent and pack it in some kind of crate. Each airline seems to have its own policy. The south of Spain would be suicide to bike through in summer, though all right in winter.

Information: call the Cycling Federation of Andalucía, Ferraz 16, 28028 Madrid, t 91 542 04 21, f 91 542 03 41.

Football

Soccer is Spain's most popular sport, and the Spanish Primera is possibly the best football league in the world. Barcelona, Real Madrid and Valencia are the best teams to watch; fans of Malaga, Sevilla and Real Betis will argue over whose team is the best in Andalucía. The season lasts from September to June, and matches are usually trouble-free.

Information: Spanish Football Federation, Alberto Bosch 13, 28014 Madrid, **t** 91 420 33 21, **f** 91 420 20 94.

Golf

English settlers built Spain's first golf course at the Río Tinto mines in the 19th century, and since the advent of Severiano Ballesteros Spaniards too have gone nuts for the game. The sunny warm winters, combined with greens of international tournament standard, attract golfing enthusiasts from all over the world throughout the year. Any real-estate agent on the coast hoping to sell villas to foreigners, especially Scandinavians and the latest newcomers, the Russians, stands little chance of closing a deal unless his property is within 5mins of a golf course – or preferably *on* a golf course. It's a rage in the Costa del Sol; the Marbella area alone boasts over two dozen fine courses, some so 'exclusive' that if you manage to get in you could find yourself teeing off next to Sean Connery. On the other hand, there is an abundance of humbler clubs where a mere 3,000 pts will get you a round. Most places hire out clubs. Inland you'll find courses around the big cities and, at the last count, there were 60 courses along the Costa del Sol, over a third of all golf courses in Spain. Many hotels cater specifically for the golfer and there are numerous specialist tour operators (*see* **Travel**, pp.77–78). **Information:** the Spanish tourist office, or the Royal Spanish Golf Federation, Capitán Haya 9–5, 28020 Madrid, **t** 91 555 27 57, **f** 91 556 32 90.

Hiking and Mountaineering

Thousands of hikers and mountaineers are attracted to the paths in the Sierra Nevada above Granada and the Serranía de Ronda. The tourist office or the Spanish Mountaineering Federation provide a list of *refugios*, which offer mountain shelter in many places. Some are well equipped and can supply food. Most,

however, do not, so take your own sleeping bags, cooking equipment and food with you. Hiking boots are essential, as is a detailed map of the area, issued by the Instituto Geográfico Nacional, or the Servicio Geográfico Ejército. **Information:** Spanish Mountaineering Federation, Alberto Aguilera 3, 28015 Madrid, **t** 91 445 13 82.

Horse Racing

Horse racing in Spain is centred in Madrid, but there is a winter season at the Pineda racecourse in Seville. **Information:** Spanish Horse Racing Federation, Calle Montesquinza 8, 28006 Madrid, **t** 912 577 78 92, **f** 912 575 07 70.

Pelota

Pelota, although a Basque game by origin, has a following in Andalucía. This is a fast, thrilling game, where contestants wearing long basket-like gloves propel a hard ball with great force at high walls; rather like squash. The fast action on the *jai-alai* court is matched by the wagering frenzy of the spectators. **Information:** Spanish Pelota Foundation, Los Madrazo 11, 28014 Madrid, **t** 91 521 42 99, **f** 91 532 38 79.

Skiing

Many of the mountains popular with hikers at other times of the year attract ski crowds in the winter. An hour from Granada you can be among the Iberian Peninsula's highest peaks and Europe's southernmost ski resorts, whose après-ski life is steadily improving. In Spain, it's easy to arrange all-inclusive ski packages through a travel agent. A typical deal would include six nights' accommodation in a three- or four-star hotel with half board and unlimited use of ski lift for the week, at a cost of around 100,000 pts. With instruction fees, count on 10–15,000 pts extra per week. **Information:** write to the tourist office or the Spanish Winter Sports Federation, Infanta Maria Teresa 14, 28016 Madrid, **t** 91 344 09 44.

Tennis

There is just as much fervour for tennis as for golf, inspired by international champion Arantxa Sánchez Vicario, and more recently by Conchita Martínez, both of whom are revered in their native Spain. Again, the best clubs are to be found on the coast, and every resort hotel has its own courts; municipal ones are rare or hard to get to. The most famous tennis school in Andalucía lies just behind Fuengirola on the Mijas road, and is owned by Australian Lew Hoad, the Wimbledon favourite of the 1950s and 1960s. If you're looking for a game in Marbella, call Los Monteros Tennis Club, **t** 95 277 1700. **Information**: Royal Spanish Tennis Federation, Avda Diagonal 618, 08021 Barcelona, **t** 93 201 08 44.

Telephones

Emergency numbers: (in Spain) **Proteccíon civil t** 006; **police t** 091.

Save for a few annoying quirks, Spain has one of the best and cheapest telephone systems in Europe (25 pts for a short local call), although it can be rather confusing to use. All local telephone numbers in Spain contain seven digits plus a code, which now must be dialled even from within a province. In Andalucía, this code is 95. Spain is one of the few countries where you can make an international call conveniently from a phone booth. In newer phone booths there are complete instructions (in English) and the phone itself has a little slide on top that holds coins; keep it full of 100 pts, and you can gab all day as the Spaniards do. This can be done to the USA too, but take at least 3,000 pts in change with you in 100s.

Overseas calls from Spain are among the most expensive in Europe; calls to the UK cost about 250 pts a minute, to the USA substantially more. There are central telephone offices (*telefónicas*) in every big city, where you call from metered booths (and pay a fair percentage more for the comfort); they are indispensable, however, for reversed charge or collect calls (*cobro revertido*). *Telefónicas* are generally open 9–1 and 5–10 and closed on Sundays. Expect to pay a big surcharge if you telephone from your hotel or any public place that does not have a coin slot. Cheap rate is from 10pm–8am Monday–Saturday and all day Sunday and public holidays.

For calls to Spain from the UK, dial 00 followed by the country code, the area code (remember that if you are calling from outside Spain you drop the '9' in the area code) and the number. For international calls from Spain, dial 07, wait for the higher tone and then dial the country code, etc.

Toilets

Outside bus and train stations, public facilities are rare in Spain. On the other hand, every bar on every corner has a toilet; don't feel uncomfortable using it without purchasing something – the Spaniards do it all the time. Just ask for *los servicios* (on signs they are sometimes referred to as *aseos*). It has to be said that public lavatories and ones in private commercial establishments have improved tremendously over the last decade. Going to the loo in a marble cubicle at an airport or petrol station can be a delightful experience!

Tourist Information

After receiving millions of tourists each year for the last two decades, no country has more information offices, or more helpful ones, or more intelligent brochures and detailed maps. Every city will have an office, and about two-thirds of the time you'll find someone who speaks English. Sometimes they'll be less helpful in the big cities in the summer. More often, though, you'll be surprised at how well they know the details of accommodation and transportation. Many large cities also maintain **municipal tourist offices**, though they're not as well equipped as those run by the Ministry of Tourism, better known as **Turismo**. Hours for most offices are Monday to Friday, 9.30–1.30 and 4–7, open on Saturday mornings, closed on Sundays.

International Country Codes

Australia 61
Netherlands 31
Canada 1
New Zealand 64
France 33
Spain 34
Germany 49
UK 44
Italy 39
USA 1

Spanish National Tourist Offices

Australia: 203 Castlereagh Street, PO Box A-685, Sydney, t (2) 264 7966, f (2) 267 5111.
Canada: 102 Bloor Street West, Toronto, Ontario, M5S 1M8, t (416) 961 3131, f (416) 961 1992.
France: 43 Avenue Pierre 1 de Serbie, Paris, t 01 47 20 90 54, f 01 47 23 56 38.
Germany: Kurfürstendamm 180, 10707 Berlin, t (30) 882 6036, f (30) 882 6661.
Myliusstraße 14, 60323 Frankfurt, t (69) 72 50 33, f (69) 72 53 13.
Post Fach No. 151940, Schuberterstraße 10, München, t (89) 538 90 75.
Italy: Via del Mortaro 19, Interno 5, Roma 00187, t 06 678 3106, f 679 82 72.
Piazza del Carmine 4, Milano 20221, t 02 72 00 46 17, f 02 72 00 43 18.
Netherlands: Laan Van Meerdervoort 8, 2517 's-Gravenhage, t (70) 346 5900, f (70) 364 9859.
UK: 57–58 St James's Street, London SW1A 1LD, t (020) 7499 1169/0901, f (020) 7629 4257.
USA: Water Tower Place, Suite 915, East 845 North Michigan Avenue, Chicago, Illinois, IL 60611, t (312) 642 1992, f (312) 642 9817.
8383 Wilshire Boulevard, Suite 960, Beverly Hills, CA 90211, t (213) 658 7188, f (213) 658 1061.
665 Fifth Avenue, New York, NY 10022, t (212) 759 8822, f (212) 980 1053.

Where to Stay

Hotels in Spain are still bargains – though, as with prices for other facilities, Spain is gradually catching up with the rest of western Europe. One thing you can still count on is a consistent level of quality and service; the Spanish government regulates hotels intelligently and closely. Room prices must be posted in the hotel lobbies and in the rooms, and if there's any problem you can ask for the complaints book, or *Libro de Reclamaciones*. No one ever writes anything in these; any written complaint must be passed on to the authorities immediately. Hotel keepers would usually rather correct the problem for you.

The prices given in this guide are for double rooms with bath (unless stated otherwise) but do not include VAT (IVA) charged at 7% on all hotel rooms. Prices for single rooms will average about 60 per cent of a double, while triples or an extra bed are around 35 per cent more. Within the price ranges shown (*see* box), the most expensive are likely to be in the big cities, while the cheapest places are always in provincial towns. On the whole, prices throughout Andalucía are surprisingly consistent. No government, however, could resist the chance to insert a little bureaucratic confusion, and the wide range of accommodation in Spain is classified in a complex system. Look out for the little **blue plaques** next to the doors of all *hoteles, hostales*, etc., which identify the classification and number of stars.

Paradores

The government, in its plan to develop tourism in the 1950s, started this nationwide chain of classy hotels to draw some attention to little-visited areas. They restored old palaces, castles and monasteries for the purpose, furnished them with antiques and installed fine restaurants featuring local specialities. *Paradores* for many people are one of the best reasons for visiting Spain. Not all *paradores* are historical landmarks; in resort areas, they are as likely to be cleanly designed modern buildings, usually in a great location with a pool and some sports facilities. As their popularity has increased, so have their prices; in most cases both the rooms and the restaurant will be the most expensive in town. *Paradores* are classed as three- or four-star hotels, and their prices range from 10,000 pts in remote provincial towns to 23,000 pts and upwards for the most luxurious. Many offer out-of-season or weekend promotional rates. If you can afford a *parador*, there is no better place to stay. We've mentioned most of them throughout this book.

Advance Booking

Spain: Head office, Requena 3, 28013, Madrid t 91 516 66 66.
UK: Keytel International, 402 Edgware Road, London W2 1ED, t (020) 7402 81 82.
USA: Marketing Ahead, 433 Fifth Avenue, New York, NY 10016, t (212) 686 92 13.

Hoteles

Hoteles (H) are rated with from one to five stars, according to the services they offer. These are the most expensive places, and even

Accommodation Price Ranges

Note: Prices listed here and elsewhere in the book are for a double room with bathroom.

Luxury over 22,000 pts/ €132
Expensive 13,000–22,000 / €78–132
Moderate 8,000–13,000 / €48–78
Inexpensive 5,000–8,000 / €30–48
Cheap under 5,000 pts / €30

a one-star hotel will be a comfortable, middle-range establishment. *Hotel Residencias* (HR) are the same, only without a restaurant. Many of the more expensive hotels have some rooms available at prices lower than those listed. They won't tell you, though; you'll have to ask. You can often get discounts in the off season but will be charged higher rates during important festivals. These are supposedly regulated, but in practice hotel-keepers charge whatever they can get. If you want to attend any of these big events, book your hotel as far in advance as possible.

Hostales and Pensiónes

Hostales (Hs) and *Pensiónes* (P) are rated with from one to three stars. These are more modest places, often a floor in an apartment block; a three-star *hostal* is roughly equivalent to a one-star hotel. *Pensiónes* may require full- or half-board; there aren't many of these establishments, only a few in resort areas. *Hostal Residencias* (HsR), like hotel *residencias*, do not offer meals except breakfast, and not always that. Of course, *hostales* and *pensiónes* with one or two stars will often have rooms without private baths at considerable savings.

Fondas, Casas de Huéspedes and Camas

The bottom of the scale is occupied by the *fonda* (F) and *casa de huéspedes* (CH), little different from a one-star *hostal*, though generally cheaper. Off the scale completely are hundreds of unclassified cheap places, usually rooms in an apartment or over a bar and identified only by a little sign reading *camas* (beds) or *habitaciones* (rooms). You can also ask in bars or at the tourist office for unidentified *casas particulares*, private houses with a room or two; in many villages these will be the best

you can do, but they're usually clean – Spanish women are manic housekeepers. The best will be in small towns and villages, and around universities.

Occasionally you'll find a room over a bar, run by somebody's grandmother, that is nicer than a four-star hotel – complete with frilly pillows, lovely old furnishings, and a shrine to the Virgin Mary. The worst are inevitably found in industrial cities or dull modern ones. It always helps to see the room first. In cities, the best places to look are right in the centre, not around the bus and train stations. Most inexpensive establishments will ask you to pay a day in advance.

Alternative Accommodation

Youth hostels exist in Spain, but they're usually not worth the trouble. Most are open only in the summer; there are the usual inconveniences and silly rules, and often hostels are in out-of-the-way locations. You'll be better off with the inexpensive *hostales* and *fondas* – sometimes these are even cheaper than youth hostels – or ask at the local tourist office for rooms that might be available in **university dormitories**. If you fancy some peace and tranquillity, the national tourist office has a list of 64 **monasteries** and **convents** that welcome guests. Accommodation starts at about £10 a night, meals are simple and guests may usually take part in the religious ceremonies.

Women Travellers

On the whole, the horror stories of sexual harassment in Spain are a thing of the past – unless you dress provocatively and hang out by the bus station after dark. All Spaniards seem to melt when they see blondes, so if you're fair you're in for a tougher go. Even Spanish women sunbathe topless these days at the international *costa* resorts, but do be discreet elsewhere, especially near small villages. Apart from the coast, it often tends to be the older men who comment on your appearance as a matter of course. Whether you can understand what is being said or not, best to ignore them.

Granada

09

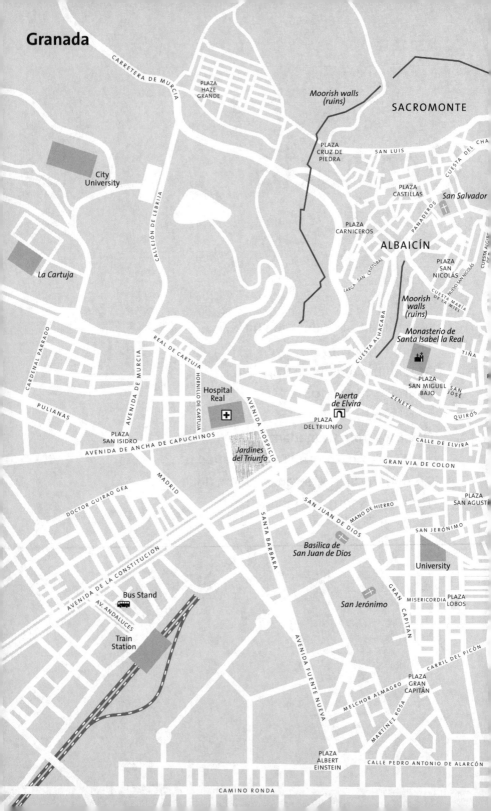

Granada

CARRETERA DE MURCIA

PLAZA HAZE GRANDE

Moorish walls (ruins)

SACROMONTE

PLAZA CRUZ DE PIEDRA

SAN LUIS

CUESTA DEL CHA

City University

PLAZA CASTILLAS

PANADEROS

San Salvador

PLAZA CARNICEROS

ALBAICÍN

CALLEJÓN DE LEBRIJA

PLAZA SAN NICOLÁS

CUESTA ALGIBE

La Cartuja

LARGA SAN CRISTÓBAL

NUEVO SAN NICOLÁS

CUESTA MARIA DE LA MIEL

Moorish walls (ruins)

REAL DE CARTUJA

Monasterio de Santa Isabel la Real

CARDENAL PARRADO

AVENIDA DE MURCIA

HORNILLO DE CARTUJA

Hospital Real

CUESTA ALHACABA

TIÑA

PLAZA SAN MIGUEL BAJO

SAN JOSÉ

PULIANAS

AVENIDA HOSPICIO

Puerta de Elvira

ZENETE

QUIRÓS

PLAZA SAN ISIDRO

AVENIDA DE ANCHA DE CAPUCHINOS

PLAZA DEL TRIUNFO

CALLE DE ELVIRA

Jardines del Triunfo

GRAN VIA DE COLON

MADRID

DOCTOR GUIRAO GEA

SAN JUAN DE DIOS

MANO DE HIERRO

PLAZA SAN AGUSTÍ

SANTA BARBARA

SAN JERÓNIMO

AVENIDA DE LA CONSTITUCION

Basílica de San Juan de Dios

University

Bus Stand

MISERICORDIA

PLAZA LOBOS

AV. ANDALUCES

San Jerónimo

GRAN CAPITÁN

Train Station

AVENIDA FUENTE NUEVA

CARRIL DEL PICÓN

PLAZA GRAN CAPITÁN

MELCHOR ALMAGRO

MARTÍNEZ ROSA

PLAZA ALBERT EINSTEIN

CALLE PEDRO ANTONIO DE ALARCÓN

CAMINO RONDA

Río Darro

cromonte
Caves

Casa
del Chapiz

GENERALIFE

El Generalife

CAMINO DE LA SILLA

500 metres
500 yards

CUESTA DEL REY CHICO

CAMINO VIEJO

La Alhambra

ALHAMBRA

Casa Museo
Manuel de Falla

ANTEQUERUELA ALTA

CAMINO NUEVO DEL CEMENTERIO

CUESTA DEL CAIDERO

VISTILLA DE LOS ÁNGELES

onvento
e Santa
atalina
e Zafra

Archaeological
Museum

rish
hs

Santa Ana

Torres
Bermejas

Audiencia

PLAZA
NUEVA

Bus Stand

Palacio
de la
Madraza

atedral

Corral del
Carbón

PLAZA Alcaicería
BIB-RAMBLA
ería

ALHÓNDIGA

PAVANERAS

SANTA ESCOLÁSTICA

PLAZA
PADRE SUAREZ

PLAZA
SAN JUAN
DE LA CRUZ

SAN MATIAS

PLAZA
CAMPOS

PLAZA
MARIANA
PINEDA

ANGEL GAVINET

ACERA DEL CASINO

REALEJO

Santo
Domingo

PACO SECO DE LUCENA

CALLE DE MOLINOS

CALLE DE SANTIAGO

SAN MATIAS

Cuarto Real
de Santo
Domingo

CONCEPCIÓN

CARRERA DEL GENIL

ALERA DE DARRO

SAN ANTON

CALLE DE SAN ANTON

SAN JOSÉ BAJA

CALLE DE GRACIA

CALLE DE RECOGIDAS

PLAZA
DE GRACIA

CALLE DE ALHAMAR

CALLE PEDRO ANTONIO DE ALARCÓN

CAMINO RONDA

PASEO DEL SALÓN

Río Genil

PASEO DE LA BOMBA

POETA MANUEL DE GÓNGORA

PABLO PICASSO

Bus Stand
(Sierra Nevada)

Palacio de
Congresos

DEL VIOLON

Ermita de
San Sebastián

CAMINO RONDA

Getting Around

By Air

There are two flights daily to Madrid (*Mon–Sat*), two daily to Barcelona (*Mon–Fri*) and three flights a week to the Balearics and Canaries. The airport is 16km west of Granada, near Santa Fé. **Information: t** 95 824 52 23.

By Train

Granada has connections to Guadix and Almería (three daily), to Algeciras, Seville, and Cordoba by way of Bobadilla Junction, and two daily to Madrid and Barcelona; three daily to Alicante, one a day to Valencia. The station is at the northern end of town, about a mile from the centre, on Avenida de los Andaluces. **Information: t** 90 224 02 02.

By Bus

All buses leave from the the new main bus station, on the outskirts of town on the Carretera de Jaén. **Information: t** 95 818 54 80; sales **t** 90 233 04 00. Bus No.3 runs between the bus station and the city centre.

The 'Alhambra' bus No.30 from the Plaza Nueva will save you the trouble of climbing up to the Alhambra.

By Car

Parking is a problem, so if you plan staying overnight make sure that your hotel has parking facilities and check whether there is a charge or not – it can cost as much as the accommodation in some places. Traffic police are vigilant. Fines of up to 20,000 pts are payable on the spot if you are a tourist. Ignore people at the bottom of the Alhambra trying to persuade you to park before you reach the top; there's plenty of parking space by the entrance and it's a steep walk to get there.

Tourist Information

Provincial tourist office, Pza Mariana Pineda 10, **t** 95 822 66 88. *Open Mon–Fri 9.30–7 and Sat 10–2.* There's a smaller office inside the Corral del Carbón, C/Liberos 2, **t** 95 822 59 90. *Open Mon–Sat 9–7 and Sun 10–2.* There is also an office in the Alhambra itself: Avda del Generalife s/n, **t** 95 822 95 75. *Open Mon–Fri 9–4 and Sat 9–1; closed Sun.*

Where to Stay

Granada ✉ 18000

The city centre, around the Acera del Darro, is full of hotels, and there are lots of inexpensive *hostales* around the Gran Vía – but the less you see of these areas the better. Fortunately, you can choose from a wide range around the Alhambra and in the older parts of town if you take the time to look.

Luxury

★★★★★**Parador Nacional San Francisco**, **t** 95 822 14 40, **f** 95 822 22 64, *granada@parador.es*. Right in the Alhambra itself, this is perhaps the most famous of all Paradores, housed in a convent where Queen Isabella was originally interred. It is beautiful, very expensive (though worth it), and small; you'll always need to book well in advance – a year would not be unreasonable.

Expensive

★★★★**Alhambra Palace**, C/Peña Partida 2-4, **t** 95 822 14 68, **f** 95 822 64 04. An alternative choice very near the Alhambra; outrageously florid, neo-Moorish, and most rooms have terrific views over the city.

★★★**Washington Irving**, Pso del Generalife 2, 95 822 75 50, **f** 95 22 88 40. This old place on the slopes below the Alhambra is a little faded but still classy.

★**Hotel América**, Real de la Alhambra 53, **t** 95 822 74 71, **f** 95 822 74 70. Right beside the *parador* but a third of the price, with simple, pretty rooms and a delightful garden and patio but, as for the *parador*, you'll need to book well in advance.

★★★**Palacio de Santa Inés**, Cuesta de Santa Inés 9, **t** 95 822 23 62, **f** 95 822 24 65, *www.lugaresdivino.com*. A 16th-century palace in the Albaicin with murals in the patio attributed to Alejandro Mayner, Rafael's disciple. Just nine rooms – some with priceless views of the Alhambra – and an art gallery.

Carmen de Santa Inés, Placeta de Porras 7, **t** 95 822 63 80, **f** 95 822 44 04. Another converted mansion nearby and under the same management as the Palacio de Santa Inés.

****Hotel Triunfo–Granada**, Pza del Triunfo 19, t 95 820 74 44, f 95 827 90 17, *h_triunfo_granada@granada.net*. Stands by the Moorish Puerta de Elvira at the foot of the Albaicín. It's a quiet place with a restaurant that is popular with locals.

***Hotel Plaza Nueva**, Plaza Nueva 2, t 95 850 18 97, f 95 850 18 13, *hotelplazanueva@ wanadoo.es*. Brand new and right on the square, with rooms offering views of the Alhambra, but you pay for the location.

****Melía Granada**, C/Angel Gavinet 7, t 95 822 74 00, f 95 822 74 03. In a good spot within striking distance of the old and new parts of the city and with most amenities.

****Carmen**, Acera del Darro 62, t 95 825 83 00, f 95 825 64 62. If you are after luxury, but are not overly concerned about position, then this recently refurbished hotel offers sumptuous bedrooms and bathrooms, a rooftop suite and a pool – all at a fairly reasonable price.

Moderate

Casa del Aljarife, Placeta de la Cruz Verde 2, t/f 95 822 24 25, *most@mx3.redestb.es*. This 17th-century Moorish house with tastefully refurbished rooms is one of a handful of hotels in the Albaicín, and one of the most delightful places to stay in the city, with a view of the Alhambra that you won't better elsewhere. There are only three rooms so be sure to book in advance. The friendly owners can arrange parking and will even collect you from the train station or airport.

***Hotel Navas**, C/Navas 24, t 95 822 59 59, f 95 822 75 23. In an excellent spot offering quiet, air-conditioned rooms with a good value restaurant attached.

***Los Ángeles**, Cuesta Escoriaza 17, t 95 822 14 24, f 95 822 21 25. On the slopes below the Alhambra you can get a pool and air conditioning at this hotel.

Hotel Macia Plaza, Plaza Nueva 4, t 95 822 75 36, f 95 822 75 33, *maciaplaza@macia-hoteles.com*. A good bet if you want a few more mod cons than the hostales and pensiones in this area.

La Ninfa, C/Cocheras de San Cecilio, t 95 822 26 61. In a good spot just off Campo de Principe,

offering simple rooms with air-conditioning and TV. Café attached.

Inexpensive

The residential area around the Campo Principe hides some possibilities.

Hostal Suecia, Huerta Los Angeles, t 95 822 50 44. A delightful budget option: clean, quiet, in its own grounds, with parking and views of the palace.

Failing this, try around Plaza del Carmen:

Lisboa, Pza del Carmen 27, t 95 822 14 13, f 95 822 14 87. Adequate if uninspiring.

Hotel Niza, C/Navas 16, t 95 822 54 30, f 95 822 54 27. Good value but in a noisy location sandwiched between a number of bars.

Cheap

For cheap *hostales*, the first place to look is the Cuesta de Gomérez, the street leading up to the Alhambra from Plaza Nueva.

Viena, t 95 822 18 59. One of three good Austrian-run places on and just off Cuesta de Gomérez; all are clean, friendly and functional.

Landázuri, Cuesta de Gomérez 24, t 95 822 14 06. A bit further up with a restaurant and a small roof terrace.

Britz, Cuesta de Gomérez 1, t 95 822 36 52. No bath.

Gomérez-Gallegos, Cuesta de Gomérez 2. Even more basic.

Off Calle San Juan de Dios, in the university area, there are dozens of small *hostales* used to accommodating students:

San Joaquín, C/Mano de Hierro 17, t 95 828 28 79. Has a pretty patio.

Hostal Angélica, C/Cristo de la Yedra 36, t 95 827 14 30. A couple of streets away from the Hospital Real.

Eating Out

Granada isn't known for its cuisine. There are too many touristy places around the Plaza Nueva, with very little to distinguish between them. Below are some better finds.

Expensive

Seville, C/Oficios 12, t 95 822 12 23. The best-known and best-loved restaurant in

Granada, where Lorca often met fellow poets and intellectuals. The character of the restaurant has been preserved and the specialities are still the local dishes of Granada and Andalucía. *Closed Sun evening*.

Ruta del Veleta, Ctra de la Sierra, km 50, t 95 848 61 34. Some of the finest cooking in Granada can be found here, with dishes including partridge with onion ragôut and salad of angler fish with vegetable stuffing; situated 5km away from the city towards the Sierra Nevada.

Moderate

Cunini, Pza de Pescadería 14, t 95 825 07 77. The *granadinos* trust dining out at this place, where the menu depends on availability. *Closed Mon*.

Mesón Antonio, Ecce Homo 6, t 95 822 95 99. There is no better in Granada for agreeable dining in an intimate family-run restaurant; international meat and fish dishes are served. *Closed Sun, July and Aug*.

Mirador de Morayma, Pianista García Carrillo 2, Albaicín, t 95 822 82 90. In a charming 16th-century house with views over the Alhambra from the top-floor dining room; *la sopa de espárragos verdes de Huétor* (asparagus soup) is particularly good, and be sure to leave room for an *andaluz* pudding. *Closed Sun eve*.

Chikito, Pza de Campillo 9, t 95 822 33 64. Popular with *granadinos*, serving classic Granada dishes in an intimate atmosphere.

Pilar de Toro, C/hospital de Santa Ana 12, Plaza Nueva, t 95 822 38 47. In a converted 17th-century house with a trendy bar sct round a delightful patio and more intimate dining upstairs.

Tendido 1, Avda. Doctor Oloriz 25, t 95 827 23 02. Makes for a memorable dining experience: right in the bullring itself.

Inexpensive

Cepillo, Calle Pescadería. Everyone's favourite rock-bottom, filling 750 pts menu is served up at this tiny restaurant. It's several doors away from the Cunini and is one of the few places where you can get paella for one – order fish or squid.

Bar Aliatar, C/San Sebastian (a small street between Plaza de Bib-Rambla and Calle Reyes Católicos). Try here for *bocadillos* (hot and cold sandwiches).

Tapas Bars

Granada rivals Seville for its tapas and has a fine tradition of serving up mini-meals for the price of a drink. Areas worth exploring are the roads off the top end of Gran Via, particularly calles Almireceros, Joaquin Costa, Elvira and Cetti Meriem; also try the streets off Plaza del Carmen, particularly Navas; around the cathedral, Plaza Bib-Rambla and C/Pescaderia are particularly good. On the streets leading up into the Albaicin are an increasing number of Moroccan-style tea bars, or *teterías*, where you can sip mint tea in Alhambra-style decor and nibble at Moorish-inspired dishes. Try in particular calles Calderias Vieja and Nueva and Carcel Alta.

Casteñada, Gran Via. A great Andaluz bar which serves up very generous and reasonably priced tapas, including the delicious Trevelez jamon.

Hannigans, C/Cetti Meriem 1. Serves up very good tapas and attracts an ex-pat crowd; Guinness on tap.

Las Copas, C/Navas. A big, open place.

Los Damantes, C/Navas. A spit- and sawdust-type place.

El Tabernaculo, C/Navas. Noisy and crowded.

El Fogon de Galicia, C/Navas. Specializes in shellfish.

Entertainment and Nightlife

Granada is one of the best places in Andalucia to catch flamenco. Though there are touristy shows in the caves of Sacromonte, there are also some more spontaneous venues, and it's well worth heading up to Sacromonte to wander around.

El Niño de los Almendras, Calle Muladar de Dona Sancha (near Plaza San Miguel Bajo). A popular venue in the Albaicín.

El Camborio, Sacromonte. One of several discos popular with the locals in Sacromonte; packed on Friday and Saturday nights.

Dale limosna mujer, que no hay en la vida nada
Como la pena de ser ciego y en Granada.

Francisco de Icaza

(Give him alms, woman, for there is nothing in life
so cruel as being blind in Granada.)

Everyone who comes to Andalucía stops in to see the Alhambra in Granada, but there is infinitely more to this magical (though somewhat complex and introverted) city. Not content with having the biggest collection of wonders from Moorish al-Andalus, Granada also possesses the greatest monuments of the Christian Reconquista. The city where Ferdinand and Isabella chose to be buried is still a capital of romance, a city where 'Nights in the Gardens of Spain' is not merely a fantasy, but something encouraged by the tourist office.

Granada's setting is a land of excess, where Spain's tallest mountain, Mulhacén in the Sierra Nevada, stands only 40km from the sea – it has become something of a tourist ritual to ski and swim on the same day. Mulhacén and its sister peaks provide the matchless backdrop for the Alhambra, while their southern face overlooks the hidden villages of the Alpujarras, the last redoubt of the Moors in Spain.

Beyond the Sierra Nevada the landscapes merge into the arid expanses typical of southeastern Spain. Out in the dry and lonely eastern reaches of Granada's province, the main attraction is the bizarre cave-city of Guadix. The province of Almería is another world – perfect for the filming of Sergio Leone's spaghetti westerns and complete with its own 'Mini-Hollywood' at Tabernas. The highlights are Almería itself, and the exotic, whitewashed (and increasingly trendy) coastal resort of Mojácar.

The first thing to do upon arrival is to pick up a copy of Washington Irving's *Tales of the Alhambra*. Every bookshop in town can sell you one in just about any language. It was Irving who put Granada on the map, and established the Alhambra as the necessary romantic pilgrimage of Spain. Granada, in fact, might seem a disappointment without Irving. The modern city underneath the Alhambra is a stolid, remarkably unmagical place, with little to show for the 500 years since the Catholic kings put an end to its ancient glory.

As the Moors were expelled, the Spanish Crown replaced them with Castilians and Gallcians from up north, and even today *granadinos* are thought of as a bit foreign by other Andalucíans. Their Granada has never been a happy place. Particularly in the last hundred years it has been full of political troubles. Around the turn of the century even the Holy Week processions had to be called off for a few years because of disruptions from the leftists, and at the start of the civil war the reactionaries who always controlled Granada made one of the first big massacres of Republicans. One of their victims was Federico García Lorca, the *granadino* who, in the decades since his death, has come to be recognized as one of the greatest Spanish dramatists and poets since the 'Golden Age'. If Irving's fairytales aren't to your taste, consider the works of Lorca, in which Granada and its sweet melancholy are recurring themes. Lorca once wrote that he remembered Granada 'as one should remember a sweetheart who has died'.

History: the Nasrid Kingdom of Qarnatah

First Iberian *Elibyrge*, then Roman *Illiberis*, the town did not make a name for itself until the era of the *taifas* in the early 11th century, when it emerged as the centre of a very minor state. In the 1230s, while the Castilians were seizing Cordoba and preparing to polish off the rest of the Almoravid states of al-Andalus, an Arab chieftain named Mohammed ibn-Yusuf ibn-Nasr established himself around Jaén. When that town fell to the Castilians in 1235, he moved his capital to the town the Moors called *Qarnatah*. Ibn Nasr (or Mohammed I, as he is generally known) and his descendants in the Nasrid dynasty enjoyed great success at first in extending their domains. By 1300 this last Moorish state of Spain extended from Gibraltar to Almería, but this accomplishment came entirely at the expense of other Moors. Mohammed and his successors were in fact vassals of the kings of Castile, and aided them in campaigns more often than they fought them.

Qarnatah at this time is said to have had a population of some 200,000 – almost as many as it has now – and both its arts and industries were strengthened by refugees from the fallen towns of al-Andalus. Thousands came from Cordoba, especially, and the Albaicín quarter was largely settled by the former inhabitants of Baeza. Although a significant Jewish population remained, there were very few Christians. In the comparatively peaceful 14th century, Granada's conservative, introspective civilization reached its height, with the last flowering of Arabic-Andaluz lyric poetry and the architecture and decorative arts of the Alhambra.

This state of affairs lasted until the coming of the Catholic kings. Isabella's religious fanaticism made the completion of the Reconquista the supreme goal of her reign; she sent Ferdinand out in 1484 to do the job, which he accomplished in eight years by a breathtakingly brilliant combination of force and diplomacy. Qarnatah at the time was suffering the usual curse of al-Andalus states – disunity founded on the egotism of princes. In this fatal feud, the main actors were Abu al-Hasan Ali (Mulay Hassan in Irving's tales), king of Qarnatah, his brother El Zagal ('the valiant') and the king's rebellious son, Abu abd-Allah, better known to posterity as Boabdil el Chico. His seizure of the throne in 1482 started a period of civil war at the worst possible time. Ferdinand was clever enough to take advantage of the divisions; he captured Boabdil twice, and turned him into a tool of Castilian designs. Playing one side against the other, Ferdinand snatched away one Nasrid province after another with few losses.

When the unfortunate Boabdil, after renouncing his kingship in favour of the Castilians, finally changed his mind and decided to fight for the remnants of Qarnatah (by then little more than the city itself and the Sierra Nevada), Ferdinand had the excuse he needed to mount his final attack. Qarnatah was besieged and, after two years, Boabdil agreed to surrender under terms that guaranteed his people the use of their religion and customs. When the keys of the city were handed over on 2 January 1492, the Reconquista was complete.

Under a gentlemanly military governor, the Conde de Tendilla, the agreement was kept until the arrival in 1499 of Cardinal Ximénez de Cisneros, the most influential cleric in Spain and a man who made it his personal business to destroy the last vestiges of Islam and Moorish culture. The new Spanish policy – cultural genocide (*see*

History, pp.36–7) – was as successful in the former lands of Granada as it was among those other troublesome heathens of the same period, the Indians of Central and South America. The famous revolt in Las Alpujarras (1568) was followed by a rising in the city itself, in the Albaicín. Between 1609 and 1614, the last of the Muslims were expelled, including most of those who had converted to Christianity, and their property confiscated. It is said that, even today, there are old families in Morocco who sentimentally keep the keys to their long-lost homes in Granada.

Such a history does not easily wear away, even after so many centuries. The Castilians corrupted Qarnatah to *Granada*; just by coincidence that means 'pomegranate' in Spanish, and the pomegranate has come to be the symbol of the city. With its associations with the myth of Persephone, with the mysteries of death and loss, no symbol could be more suitable for this capital of melancholy.

A Sentimental Orientation

In spite of everything, more of the lost world of al-Andalus can be seen in Granada than even in Cordoba. Granada stands where the foothills of the Sierra Nevada meet the fertile Vega de Granada, the greenest and best stretch of farmland in Andalucía. Two of those hills extend into the city itself. One bears the **Alhambra**, the fortified palace of the Nasrid kings, and the other the **Albaicín**, the most evocative of the 'Moorish' neighbourhoods of Andalucían cities. Parts of old Qarnatah extended down into the plain, but they have been largely submerged into the new city. How much you enjoy Granada will depend largely on how successful you are in ignoring the new districts, in particular three barbarically ugly streets that form the main automobile route through Granada: the **Gran Vía Colón** chopped through the centre of town in the 19th century, the **Calle Reyes Católicos**, and the **Acera del Darro**. The last two are paved over the course of the Río Darro, the stream that ran picturesquely through the city until the 1880s. Before these streets were built, the centre of Granada was the **Plaza Nueva**, a square that is also partly built over the Darro. The handsome building that defines its character is the **Audiencia** (1584), built by Philip II for the royal officials and judges. **Santa Ana** church, across the plaza, was built in 1537 by Diego de Siloé, one of the architects of Granada's cathedral. From this plaza the ascent to the Alhambra begins, winding up a narrow street called the **Cuesta de Gomérez**, past guitar-makers' shops and gypsies with vast displays of tourist trinkets, and ending abruptly at the **Puerta de las Granadas**, a monumental gateway erected by Charles V.

The Alhambra

Open daily March–Oct 8.30–7.45, Tues–Sat evenings 10pm–11.30pm (you can only see the Palacio Nazari at night); in winter open daily 8.30–5.45, Fri and Sat evenings from 8pm–9.30pm; adm.

The grounds of the Alhambra begin here with a bit of the unexpected. Instead of the walls and towers, not yet even in view, there is a lovely grove of great elms, the **Alameda**, planted at the time the Duke of Wellington passed through during the

Peninsular War. Take the path to the left – it's a stiff climb – and in a few minutes you'll arrive at the **Puerta de Justicia**, entrance of the Alhambra. The orange tint of the fortress walls explains the name *al-hamra* (the red), and the unusual style of the carving on the gate is the first clue that here is something very different. The two devices, a hand and a key, carved on the inner and outer arches, are famous. According to one of Irving's tales, the hand will one day reach down and grasp the key; then the Alhambra will fall into ruins, the earth will open, and the hidden treasures of the Moors will be revealed.

From the gate, a path leads up to a broad square. Here are the ticket booth, and the **Puerta del Vino**, so called from a long-ago Spanish custom of doling out free wine from this spot to the inhabitants of the Alhambra. To the left you'll see the walls of the **Alcazaba**, the fort at the tip of the Alhambra's narrow promontory, and to the right the huge **Palacio de Carlos V**; signs point your way to the entrance of the **Casa Real** (Royal Palace), with its splendidly decorated rooms that are the Alhambra's main attraction. Visit again after dark; seeing it under the stars is the treat of a lifetime.

The Alcazaba

Not much remains of the oldest part of the Alhambra. This citadel probably dates back to the first of the Nasrid kings. Its walls and towers are still intact, but only the foundations of the buildings that once stood within it have survived. The **Torre de la Vela** at the tip of the promontory has the best views over Granada and the *vega*. Its big bell was rung in the old days to signal the daily opening and closing of the water gates of the *vega*'s irrigation system; the Moors also used the tower as a signal post for sending messages. The Albaicín (*see* p.106), visible on the opposite hill, is a revelation; its rows of white, flat-roofed houses on the hillside, punctuated by palm trees and cypresses, provide one of Europe's most exotic urban landscapes.

Casa Real (Royal Palace)

Palace visits are limited to 30mins and the time must be specified at time of ticket purchase, otherwise it will be arranged for at least 1hr later.

Words will not do, nor will exhaustive descriptions help, to communicate the experience of this greatest treasure of al-Andalus. This is what people come to Granada to see, and it is the surest, most accessible window into the refinement and subtlety of the culture of Moorish Spain – a building that can achieve in its handful of rooms what a work like Madrid's Royal Palace cannot even approach with its 2,800.

It probably never occurs to most visitors, but one of the most unusual features of this palace is its modesty. What you see is what the Nasrid kings saw; your imagination need add only a few carpets and tapestries, some well-crafted furniture of wood inlaid with ivory, wooden screens, and big round braziers of brass for heat or incense, to make the picture complete. Most of the actual building is wood and plaster, cheap and perishable, like a World's Fair pavilion; no good Muslim monarch would offend Allah's sense of propriety by pretending that these worldly splendours were anything more than the pleasures of a moment (much of the plaster, wood, and all of the tiles,

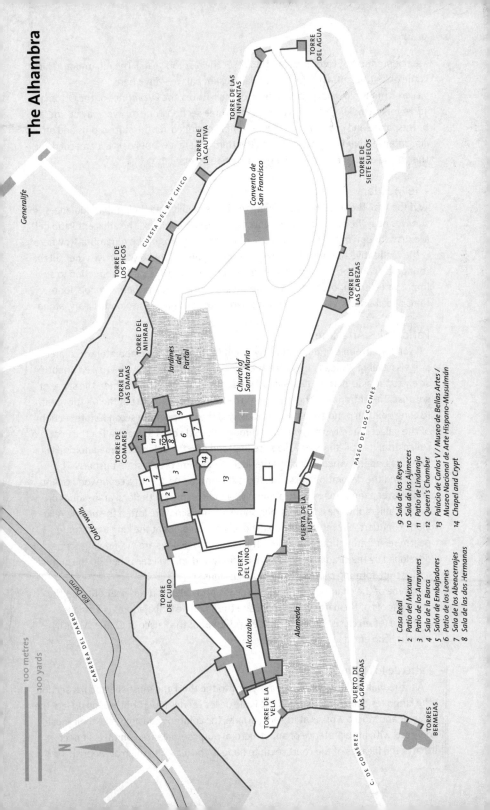

The Alhambra

Generalife

TORRE DEL AGUA

TORRE DE LAS INFANTAS

TORRE DE LA CAUTIVA

CUESTA DEL REY CHICO

TORRE DE LOS PICOS

TORRE DE SIETE SUELOS

Convento de San Francisco

TORRE DEL MIHRAB

TORRE DE LAS DAMAS

Jardines del Partal

TORRE DE LAS CABEZAS

TORRE DE COMARES

Church of Santa María

PASEO DE LOS COCHES

PUERTA DE LA JUSTICIA

TORRE DEL CUBO

PUERTA DEL VINO

Outer walls

RÍO DARRO

CARRERA DEL DARRO

Alcazaba

Alameda

TORRE DE LA VELA

PUERTO DE LAS GRANADAS

C. DE GOMEREZ

TORRES BERMEJAS

N

100 metres
100 yards

1   Casa Real
2   Patio del Mexuar
3   Patio de los Arrayanes
4   Sala de la Barca
5   Salón de Embajadores
6   Patio de los Leones
7   Sala de los Abencerrajes
8   Sala de las dos Hermanas
9   Sala de los Reyes
10 Sala de los Ajimeces
11 Patio de Lindaraja
12 Queen's Chamber
13 Palacio de Carlos V / Museo de Bellas Artes /
    Museo Nacional de Arte Hispano-Musulmán
14 Chapel and Crypt

are the products of careful restorations over the last 100 years). The Alhambra, in fact, is the only substantially intact medieval Muslim palace – anywhere.

Like so many old royal palaces (those of the Hittites, the Byzantines or the Ottoman Turks, for example), this one is divided into three sections: one for everyday business of the palace and government; the next, more secluded, for the state rooms and official entertainments of the kings; and the third, where few outsiders ever reached, for the private apartments of the king and his household.

The Mexuar

Of the first, the small Mexuar, where the kings would hold their public audiences, survives near the present-day entrance to the palace complex. The adjacent **Patio del Mexuar**, though much restored, is one of the finest rooms of the Alhambra. Nowhere is the meditative serenity of the palace more apparent (unless you arrive when all the tour groups do) and the small fountain in the centre provides an introduction to an important element of the architecture – water. Present everywhere, in pools, fountains and channels, water is as much a part of the design as the wood, tile and stone.

Patio de los Arrayanes

If you have trouble finding your way around, remember the elaborately decorated portals never really lead anywhere; the door you want will always be tucked unobtrusively to the side; here, as in Seville's Alcázar, the principle is to heighten the sense of surprise. The entrance to the grand Patio de los Arrayanes (Court of the Myrtles), with its long goldfish pond and lovely arcades, was the centre of the second, state section of the palace; directly off it, you pass through the **Sala de la Barca** (Hall of the Boat), so called after its hull-shaped wooden ceiling, and into the **Salón de Embajadores** (Hall of Ambassadors), where the kings presided over all important state business. The views and the decoration are some of the Alhambra's best, with a cedarwood ceiling and plaster panels (many were originally painted) carved with floral arabesques or Arabic calligraphy. These inscriptions, some Koranic scripture (often the phrase 'Allah alone conquers', the motto of the Nasrids), some eulogies of the kings, and some poetry, recur throughout the palace. The more conspicuous are in a flowing script developed by the Granadan artists; look closely and you will see others, in the angular Kufic script, forming frames for the floral designs.

In some of the chambers off the Patio de los Arrayanes, you can peek out over the domed roofs of the baths below; opposite the Salón de Embajadores is a small entrance (often closed) into the dark, empty **crypt** of the Palace of Charles V, with curious echo effects.

Patio de los Leones

Another half-hidden doorway leads you into the third and most spectacular section, the king's residence, built around the Patio de los Leones (Court of the Lions). Here the plaster and stucco work is at its most ornate, the columns and arches at their most delicate, with little pretence of any structural purpose; balanced on their slender shafts, the façades of the court seem to hang in the air. As in much of Moorish architecture, the overripe arabesques of this patio conceal a subtle symbolism. The 'enclosed garden' that can stand for the attainment of truth, or paradise, or for the cosmos, is a recurring theme in Islamic mystical poetry. Here you may take the 12 endearingly preposterous lions who support the fountain in the centre as the months, or signs of the zodiac, and the four channels that flow out from the fountains as the four corners of the cosmos, the cardinal points, or, on a different level, the four rivers of paradise.

The rooms around the patio have exquisite decorations: to the right, from the entrance, the **Sala de los Abencerrajes**, named after the legend of the noble family that Boabdil supposedly had massacred at a banquet here during the civil wars just before the fall of Granada; to the left, the **Sala de las dos Hermanas** (Hall of the Two Sisters). Both of these have extravagant domed *muqarnas* ceilings. The latter chamber is also ornamented with a wooden window grille, another speciality of the Granadan artists; this is the only one surviving in the Alhambra. Adjacent to the Sala de las dos Hermanas is the **Sala de los Ajimeces**, so called for its doubled windows. The **Sala de los Reyes** (Hall of the Kings), opposite the court's entrance, is unique for the paintings on its ceiling, works that would not be out of place in any Christian palace of medieval Europe. The central panel may represent six of Granada's 14th-century kings; those on the side are scenes of a chivalric court. The artist is believed to have been a visiting Spanish Christian painter, possibly from Seville. From the Sala de las dos Hermanas, steps lead down to the **Patio de Lindaraja** (or Mirador de Daraxa), with its fountain and flowers, Washington Irving's favourite spot in the Alhambra. Originally the inner garden of the palace, it was remodelled for the royal visits of Charles V and Philip V. Irving actually lived in the **Queen's Chamber**, decorated with frescoes of Charles V's expedition to Tunis – in 1829, apartments in the Alhambra could be had for the asking! Just off this chamber, at ground-floor level, is the beautifully decorated **hammam**, the palace baths.

Follow the arrows, out of the palace and into the outer gardens, the **Jardines del Partal**, a broad expanse of rose terraces and flowing water. The northern walls of the Alhambra border the gardens, including a number of well-preserved towers: from the west, the **Torre de las Damas**, entered by a small porch, the **Torre del Mihrab**, near which is a small mosque, now a chapel; the **Torre de los Picos**; the **Torre de la Cautiva** (Tower of the Imprisoned Lady), one of the most elaborately decorated; and the **Torre de las Infantas**, one of the last projects in the Alhambra (*c*. 1400).

Palacio de Carlos V

Anywhere else this elegant Renaissance building would be an attraction in itself. Here it seems only pompous and oversized, and our appreciation of it is lessened by the mind-numbing thought of this emperor, with a good half of Europe to build palaces in, having to plop it down here – ruining much of the Alhambra in the process. Once Charles had smashed up the place he lost interest, and most of the palace, still unfinished today, was not built until 1616. The original architect, Pedro Machuca, had studied in Italy, and he took the opportunity to introduce into Spain the chilly, Olympian High Renaissance style of Rome. At the entrances are intricately detailed sculptural **reliefs** showing scenes from Charles's campaigns and military 'triumphs' in the antique manner: armoured torsos on sticks amidst heaps of weapons. This is a very particular sort of Renaissance fancy, arrogant and weird, and wherever it appears around the Mediterranean it will usually be associated with the grisly reign of the man who dreamt of being Emperor of the World. Inside, Machuca added a pristinely classical circular courtyard, based perhaps on a design by Raphael. For all its Doric gravity, the patio was used almost from its completion for bullfights and mock tournaments. In 1922, Lorca and the painter Ignacio Zuloaga organized a famous festival of flamenco here, with performances in the courtyard that contributed greatly to the revival of flamenco as a serious art.

The Museums

Museo de Bellas Artes, t 95 822 48 43, open Tues 2.30–6, Wed–Sat 9–6, Sun 9–2.30; Museo Nacional, t 95 822 75 27, open Tues–Sat 9–2.

On the top floor of the Palace is the **Museo de Bellas Artes**, a largely forgettable collection of religious paintings from Granada churches. Downstairs, the **Museo Nacional de Arte Hispano-Musulmán** contains perhaps Spain's best collection of Moorish art, including some paintings, similar to those in the Moorish palace's Sala de los Reyes. Also present are original *azulejo* tiles and plaster arabesques from the palace, and some exceedingly fine wooden panels and screens. There is a collection of ceramic ware with fanciful figurative decoration – elephants and lady musicians – and some lovely astronomical instruments. Tucked in a corner of the museum are four big copper balls stacked on a pole, a strangely compelling ornament that once stood atop a Granada minaret. These were a typical feature of Andalucían minarets (as on La Giralda in Seville) and similar examples can be seen in Morocco today; Granada's great mosque had a big one designed to be visible to travellers a day's journey from the city. Behind Charles's palace a street leads into the remnants of the town that once filled much of the space within the Alhambra's walls, now reduced to a small collection of restaurants and souvenir stands. In Moorish times the Alhambra held a large permanent population, and even under the Spaniards it long retained the status of a separate municipality. At one end of the street, the church of **Santa María** (1581), designed by Juan de Herrera, architect of El Escorial, occupies the site of the Alhambra's mosque; at the other, the first Christian building on the Alhambra, the **Convento de San Francisco** (1495) has been converted into a *parador*.

Around the Alhambra

The Generalife

Opening hours same as for the Alhambra; adm incl. in Alhambra ticket.

The Generalife (*Djinat al-Arif*: high garden) was the summer palace of the Nasrid kings, built on the height the Moors called the Mountain of the Sun. Many of the trillions of visitors the Alhambra receives each year have never heard of it, and pass up a

Nights in the Gardens of Spain

The first proper garden in al-Andalus, according to legend, was planted by the first Caliph himself, Abd ar-Rahman. This refugee from Damascus brought with him fond memories of the famous Rusāfah gardens in that city, and he also brought seeds of the palm tree to plant. As Caliph, he built an aqueduct to Cordoba, partly for the city and partly to furnish his new Rusāfah; his botanists sent away for more palms, and also introduced the peach and the pomegranate into Europe.

Following the Caliph's example, the Arabs of the towns laid out recreational gardens everywhere, particularly along the riverfronts. The widely travelled geographer al-Shaqindi wrote in the 11th century that the Guadalquivir around Cordoba was more beautiful than the Tigris or the Nile, lined with orchards, vines, pleasure gardens, groves of citrus trees and avenues of yews. Every city did its best to make a display, and each had its district of villas and gardens. Seville's was in Triana and on the river islands. Valencia too, which had another copy of the Rusāfah, came to be famous for its gardens; poets called the city 'a maiden in the midst of flowers'.

All this gardening was only part of a truly remarkable passion for everything green. Andalucia's climate and soil made it a paradise for the thirsty Arabs and Berbers, and bringing southern Spain into the wider Islamic world made possible the introduction of new crops and techniques from all over: rice, peppers, sugar, cotton, saffron, oranges (*naranja* in Spanish, from the Persian *nārang*), even bananas. In the 12,000 villages of the Guadalquivir valley, Moorish farmers were wizards; they learned how to graft almond branches on to apricot trees, and they refined irrigation and fertilizing to fine arts (one manuscript that survives from the time is a 'catalogue of dung'; pigs and ducks were considered very bad, while the horse was best for almost all fields). Sophisticated techniques of irrigation were practised throughout al-Andalus, and everywhere the rivers turned the wooden water wheels, or *norias* (another Persian word, *nā'urāh*); one in Toledo was almost 200ft tall. No expense was spared in bringing water where it was needed; near Moravilla remains can be seen of a mile-long subterranean aqueduct, 30ft in width. The farmers had other tricks, mostly lost to us; it was claimed they could store grain to last for a century, by spreading it between layers of pomegranate leaves and lime or oak ash.

Flowers were everywhere. On the slopes of Jabal al-Warad, the 'Mountain of the Rose' near Cordoba, vast fields of these were grown for rose water; other blooms widely planted for perfumes and other products included violet, jasmine, gillyflower, narcissus, gentian and tulip. And with all the flowers and gardens came poetry, one of the main preoccupations of life in al-Andalus for prince and peasant alike. When Caliph Abd ar-Rahman saw his palm tree growing, he wrote a lyric in its honour:

In the centre of the Rusāfah I saw a palm tree growing,
born in the west, far from the palm's country.
I cried: 'Thou art like me, for wandering and peregrination,
and the long separation from family and friends.
'May the clouds of morning water thee in thy exile.
'May the life-giving rains that the poor implore never forsake thee.'

chance to see the finest garden in Spain. To get there, it's about a five-minute walk from the Alhambra along a lovely avenue of tall cypresses.

The buildings here hold few surprises if you've just come from the Alhambra. They are older than most of the Casa Real, which was probably begun around 1260. The gardens are built on terraces on several levels along the hillside, and the views over the Alhambra and Albaicín are transcendent. The centrepiece is a long pool with many water sprays that passes through beds of roses. A lower level, with a promenade on the hill's edge, is broken up into secluded bowers by cypress bushes cut into angular shapes of walls and gateways. There is no evidence that the original Moorish gardens looked anything like this; everything here has been done in the last 200 years.

If you're walking down from the Alhambra, you might consider a different route, across the Alameda and down through the picturesque streets below the Torres Bermejas, an outwork of the Alhambra's fortifications built on foundations that date back to the Romans. The winding lanes and stairways around Calle del Aire and Calle Niño del Rollo, one of the most beautiful quarters of Granada, will eventually lead you back down near the Plaza Nueva.

Albaicín

Even more than the old quarters of Cordoba, this hillside neighbourhood of whitewashed houses and tall cypresses has successfully preserved some of the atmosphere of al-Andalus. Its difficult site and the fact that it was long the district of Granada's poor explain the lack of change, but today the Albaicín looks as if it is becoming fashionable again.

From the Plaza Nueva, a narrow street called the **Carrera del Darro** leads up the valley of the Darro between the Alhambra and Albaicín hills; here the little stream has not been covered over, and you can get an idea of how the centre of Granada looked in the old days. On the Alhambra side, old stone bridges lead up to a few half-forgotten streets hidden among the forested slopes; here you'll see some 17th-century Spanish houses with curious painted *esgrafiado* façades. Nearby, traces of a horseshoe arch can be seen where a Moorish wall once crossed the river; in the corner of Calle Baruelo there are well-preserved **Moorish baths** (*open Tues–Sat 10–2*). Even more curious is the façade of the **Casa Castril** on the Darro, a flamboyant 16th-century mansion with a portal carved with a phoenix, winged scallop shells and other odd devices that have been interpreted as elements in a complex mystical symbolism. Over the big corner window is an inscription 'Waiting for her from the heavens'. The house's owner, Bernardo de Zafra, was once a secretary to Ferdinand and Isabella, and he seems to have got into trouble with the Inquisition.

Casa Castril has been restored as Granada's **archaeological museum** (*t 95 822 56 40, open Tues 2.30–8, Wed–Sat 9–8, Sun 9–2.30*) with a small collection of artefacts from the huge number of caves in Granada province, many inhabited since Palaeolithic times, and a few Iberian settlements. There is a Moorish room, with some lovely works of art, and finally, an even greater oddity than Casa Castril itself. One room of the museum holds a collection of beautiful alabaster burial urns, made in Egypt, but found in a Phoenician-style necropolis near Almuñécar. Nothing else like them has ever been discovered in Spain, and the Egyptian hieroglyphic inscriptions on them are provocative in the extreme (translations given in Spanish), telling how the deceased travelled here in search of some mysterious primordial deity.

Farther up the Darro, there's a small park with a view up to the Alhambra; after that you'll have to do some climbing, but the higher you go the prettier the Albaicín is, and the better the views. Among the white houses and white walls are some of the oldest Christian churches in Granada. As in Cordoba, they are tidy and extremely plain, built to avoid alienating a recently converted population unused to religious imagery. **San Juan de los Reyes** (1520) on Calle Zafra and **San José** (1525) are the oldest; both retain the plain minarets of the mosques they replaced. Quite a few Moorish houses survive in the Albaicín, and some can be seen on **Calle Horno de Oro**, just off the Darro; on **Calle Daralhorra**, at the top of the Albaicín, are the remains of a Nasrid palace that was largely destroyed to make way for Isabella's **Convento de Santa Isabel la Real** (1501).

Here, running parallel to Cuesta de la Alhacaba, is a long-surviving stretch of Moorish wall. There are probably a few miles of walls left, visible around the hillsides over Granada; the location of the city made a very complex set of fortifications necessary. In this one, about halfway up, you may pass through **Puerta de las Pesas**, with its horseshoe arches. The heart of the Albaicín is here, around the pretty, animated **Plaza Larga**; only a few blocks away the **Mirador de San Nicolás**, in front of the church of that name, offers the most romantic view imaginable of the Alhambra with the snow-capped peaks of the Sierra Nevada behind it. Note the brick, barrel-vaulted fountain on the *mirador*, a typical Moorish survival; fountains like this can be seen throughout the Albaicín and most are still in use. Granada today has a small but growing Muslim community, and they are beginning to build a mosque just off the *mirador*. Construction hasn't started yet; apparently they are facing some difficulties with the city government.

On your way back from the Albaicín you might consider taking a different route, down a maze of back streets to the **Puerta de Elvira**, one of the most picturesque corners of the neighbourhood.

Sacromonte

For something completely different, you might strike out beyond the Albaicín hill to the **gypsy caves of Sacromonte**. Granada has had a substantial gypsy population for several centuries now. Some have become settled and respectable, others live in trailers on vacant land around town. The most visible are those who prey on the tourists around the Alhambra and the Capilla Real, handing out carnations with a smile and then attempting to extort huge sums out of anyone dumb enough to take one (of course, they'll tell your fortune, too). The biggest part of the gypsy community, however, still lives around Sacromonte in streets of some quite well-appointed cave homes, where they wait to lure you in for a little display of flamenco. For a hundred years or so, the consensus of opinion has been that the music and dancing

> ### Tortilla al Sacromonte
> Regional dishes include cod rissole soup, chick peas and onions, plus, of course, the famous *tortilla al Sacromonte* made from a delightful concoction of brains, lamb's testicles, vegetables and eggs. The name originates from the Sacromonte gypsies. Broad beans Granadine, cooked with fresh artichokes, tomatoes, onions, garlic, breadcrumbs and a smattering of saffron and cumin, may seem less adventurous compared to *tortilla al Sacromonte* but it's just as typical of *granadinas* dishes. If you're in Las Alpujarras, try the fresh goats' cheese, and in Trevélez you'll be hard pushed to avoid its famous ham.

are usually indifferent, and the gypsies' eventually successful attempts to shake out your last peseta can make it an unpleasantly unforgettable affair. Hotels sell tours for around 4,000 pts. Nevertheless, if you care to match wits with the experts, proceed up the Cuesta del Chapiz from the Río Darro, turn right at the **Casa del Chapiz**, a big 16th-century palace that now houses a school of Arab studies, and keep going until some gypsy child drags you home with him. The bad reputation has been keeping tourists away lately so it's now much safer and friendlier as the gypsies are worried about the loss of income. Serious flamenco fans will probably not fare better elsewhere in Granada except during the festivals, though there are some touristy flamenco nightspots – the **Reina Mora** by Mirador San Cristóbal is the best of them. On the third Sunday of each month, though, you can hear a **flamenco mass** performed in the San Pedro Church on the Carrera del Darro.

Central Granada

The old city wall swung in a broad arc from Puerta de Elvira to Puerta Real, now a small plaza full of traffic where Calle Reyes Católicos meets the Acera del Darro. Just a few blocks north of here, in a web of narrow pedestrian streets that make up modern Granada's shopping district, is the pretty **Plaza de Bib-Rambla**, full of flower stands and toy shops, with an unusual fountain supported by leering giants at its centre. This was an important square in Moorish times, used for public gatherings and tournaments of arms. The narrow streets leading off to the east are known as the **Alcaicería**. This area was the Moorish silk exchange, but the buildings you see now, full of tourist souvenir shops, are not original; the Alcaicería burned down in the 1840s and was rebuilt in more or less the same fashion with Moorish arches and columns.

The Cathedral

Pza de Pasiegas, t 95 822 29 59; open Mon–Sat 10.30–1.30 and 4–7, Sun 4–7.

The best way to see Granada's **cathedral** is to approach it from Calle Marqués, just north of the Plaza Bib-Rambla. The unique façade, with its three tall, recessed arches, is a striking sight, designed by the painter Alonso Cano (1667). On the central arch, the big plaque bearing the words 'Ave María' commemorates the exploit of the Spanish captain who sneaked into the city one night in 1490 and nailed up this message up on the door of the great mosque this cathedral has replaced.

The other conspicuous feature is the name 'José Antonio Primo de Rivera' carved on the façade. Son of the 1920s dictator, Miguel Primo de Rivera, José Antonio was a mystic fascist who founded the Falangist Party. His thugs provoked many of the disorders that started the civil war, and at the beginning of the conflict he was captured by the loyalists and executed. Afterwards his followers treated him as a sort of holy martyr, and chiselled his name on every cathedral in Spain. That you can still see it here says a lot about Granada today.

The rest of the cathedral isn't up to the standard of its façade, and there is little reason to go in and explore its cavernous interior or dreary museum. Work was begun in 1521, after the Spaniards broke their promise not to harm the great mosque. As in many Spanish cathedrals, the failure of this one stems from artistic indecision. Two very talented architects were in charge: Enrique de Egas, who wanted it Gothic, like his adjacent Capilla Real, and (five years later) Diego de Siloé, who decided Renaissance would look much nicer. A score of other architects got their fingers in the pie before its completion in 1703. Some features of the interior: the grandiose **Capilla Mayor**, with statues of the apostles, and of Ferdinand and Isabella, by Alonso de Mena, and enormous heads of Adam and Eve by Alonso Cano, whose sculptures and paintings can be seen all over the cathedral; the **Retablo de Jesús Nazareno** in the right aisle, with paintings by Cano and Ribera, and a St Francis by El Greco; the Gothic **portal** leading into the Capilla Real (now closed) by de Egas. At the foot of the bell tower is a **museum**; its only memorable work is a subject typical of the degenerate art of the 1700s – a painted wooden head of John the Baptist.

Capilla Real

Gran Vía de Colón; open daily 10.30–1 and 3.30–6.30, Sun 11–1; adm.

Leaving the cathedral and turning left, you pass the outsized **sacristy**, begun in 1705 and incorporated in the cathedral façade. Turn left again at the first street, Calle de los Oficios, a narrow lane paved in charming patterns of coloured pebbles – a Granada speciality; on the left, you can pay your respects to *Los Reyes Católicos*, in the Capilla Real. The royal couple had already built a mausoleum in Toledo, but after the capture of Granada they decided to plant themselves here. Even in the shadow of the bulky cathedral, Enrique de Egas's **chapel** (1507) reveals itself as the outstanding work of the Isabelline Gothic style, with its delicate roofline of traceries and pinnacles. Charles V thought it not monumental enough for his grandparents, and only the distraction of his wars kept him from wrecking it in favour of some elephantine replacement.

Inside, the Catholic Kings are buried in a pair of Carrara marble sarcophagi, decorated with their recumbent figures, elegantly carved though not necessarily flattering to either of them. The little staircase behind them leads down to the **crypt**, where you can peek in at their plain lead coffins and those of their unfortunate daughter, Juana the Mad, and her husband, Philip the Handsome, whose effigies lie next to the older couple above. Juana was Charles V's mother, and the rightful heir to the Spanish throne. There is considerable doubt as to whether she was mad at all; when Charles arrived from Flanders in 1517, he forced her to sign papers of abdication, and then locked her up in a windowless cell for the last 40 years of her life, never permitting any visitors. The interior of the chapel is sumptuously decorated – it should be, considering the huge proportion of the crown revenues that were expended on it. The iron *reja* by Master Bartolomé de Jaén and the *retablo* are especially fine; the latter is largely the work of a French artist, Philippe de Bourgogne. In the chapel's sacristy you can see some of Isabella's personal art collection – works by Van der Weyden, Memling, Pedro Berruguete, Botticelli (attributed), Perugino and others, mostly in need of some restoration – as well as her crown and sceptre, her illuminated missal, some captured Moorish banners, and Ferdinand's sword.

Across the narrow street from the Capilla Real, an endearingly garish, painted Baroque façade hides **La Madraza**, a domed hall of the Moorish *madrasa* (Islamic seminary); though one of the best Moorish works surviving in Granada, it is hardly ever open to visitors (just walk in if the building is open). The Christians converted it into a town hall, whence its other name, the Casa del Cabildo.

Across Calle Reyes Católicos

Even though this part of the city centre is as old as the Albaicín, most of it was rebuilt after 1492, and its age doesn't show. The only Moorish building remaining is also the only example left in Spain of a *khan* or *caravanserai*, the type of merchants' hotel common throughout the Muslim world. The 14th-century **Corral del Carbón**, just off Reyes Católicos, takes its name from the time, a century ago, when it was used as a coal warehouse. Under the Spaniards it also served time as a theatre; its interior courtyard with balconies lends itself admirably to the purpose, being about the same size and shape as a Spanish theatre of the classic age, like the one in Almagro (La Mancha). Today it houses a government handicrafts outlet, and much of the building is under restoration. The neighbourhood of quiet streets and squares behind it is the best part of Spanish Granada and worth a walk if you have the time. Here you'll see the *mudéjar* **Casa de los Tiros**, a restored mansion built in 1505 on Calle Pavaneras, with strange figures carved on its façade; it houses a **museum** of the city's history. **Santo Domingo** (1512), the finest of Granada's early churches, is just a few blocks to the south. Ferdinand and Isabella endowed it, and their monograms figure prominently on the lovely façade. Just north of here is the Campo de Principe, another delightful square frequented by students and crammed full of restaurants and cafés.

From here various winding streets provide an alternative ascent to the Alhambra. This neighbourhood is bounded on the west by the Acera del Darro, the noisy heart of modern Granada, with most of the big hotels. It's a little discouraging but, as compensation, just a block away the city has adorned itself with a beautiful string of wide boulevards very like the Ramblas of Barcelona, a wonderful spot for a stroll. The **Carretera del Genil** usually has some sort of open-air market on it, and further down, the **Paseo del Salón** and **Paseo de la Bomba** are quieter and more park-like, joining the pretty banks of the Río Genil.

Northern Granada

From the little street on the north side of the cathedral, the Calle de la Cárcel, Calle San Jerónimo skirts the edge of Granada's markets and leads you towards the old **university** district. Even though much of the university has relocated to a new campus half a mile to the north, this is still one of the livelier spots of town, and the colleges themselves occupy some fine, well-restored Baroque structures. The long yellow College of Law is one of the best, occupying a building put up in 1769 for the Jesuits; a small botanical garden is adjacent. Calle San Jerónimo ends at the Calle del Gran Capitán, where the landmark is the church of **San Juan de Dios**, with a rococo façade and a big green and white tiled dome. **San Jerónimo**, a block west, is another of the oldest and largest Granada churches (1520); it contains the tomb of Gonzalo de Cordoba, the 'Gran Capitán' who won so many victories in Italy for the Catholic Kings; adjacent are two Gothic cloisters.

Here you're not far from the Puerta de Elvira, in an area where old Granada fades into anonymous suburbs to the north. The big park at the end of the Gran Vía is the **Jardines del Triunfo**, with coloured, illuminated fountains the city hardly ever turns on. Behind them is the Renaissance **Hospital Real** (1504–22), designed by Enrique de Egas. A few blocks southwest, climbing up towards the Albaicín, your senses will be assaulted by the gaudiest Baroque chapel in Spain, in the **Cartuja**, or Carthusian monastery, on Calle Real de Cartuja (*open daily except Mon, 10–1 and 4–8, t 95 816 19 32*). Gonzalo de Cordoba endowed this Charterhouse, though little of the original works remain. The 18th-century chapel and its sacristy, done in the richest marble, gold and silver, and painted plaster, fairly oozes with a froth of twisted spiral columns, rosettes and curlicues. It has often been described as a Christian attempt to upstage the Alhambra, but the inspiration more likely comes from the Aztecs, via the extravagant Mexican Baroque.

Lorca

Outside Spain Federico García Lorca is popularly regarded as Spain's greatest modern dramatist and poet. The Spanish literati would acknowledge others from the generation of 1925 and from the previous generation of 1898 to have at least equal stature. The Galician dramatist and poet Ramón del Valle-Inclán springs to mind. But Lorca's murder certainly enhanced his reputation outside Spain. Under Franco, any mention of him was forbidden (understandably so, since it was Franco's men who shot him).

Today the *granadinos* are coming to terms with Lorca, and seem determined to make up for the past. Lorca fans pay their respects at two country houses, now museums, where the poet spent many of his early years: the **Huerta de San Vicente**, on the outskirts of town at Virgen Blanca, and the **Museo Lorca** at Fuente Vaqueros, the village where he was born, 17km away to the west near the Cordoba road (*both open for guided tours every hour, 10–1 and 5–8, daily except Mon*).

Day Trips from Granada

The Sierra Nevada and Las Alpujarras

From everywhere in Granada, the mountains peer over the tops of buildings. Until the 20th century they were chiefly known for the so-called icemen who made the gruelling journey to the peaks and back again with chunks of ice to sell in town. Today, Spain's loftiest peaks are more accessible.

Dress warmly, though. As the name implies, the Sierra Nevada is snowcapped nearly all year, and even in late July and August, when the road is clear (*see* 'Getting Around' below) and you can travel right over the mountains to the valley of Las Alpujarras, it's as chilly and windy as you would expect it to be, some 3,300m (10,825ft) above sea level. These mountains, a geological curiosity of sorts, are just an oversized chunk of the Penibetic System, the chain that stretches from Arcos de la Frontera almost to Murcia. Their highest peak, **Mulhacén** (3,481m/11,420ft), is less than 40km from the coast. From Granada you can see nearly all of the Sierra: a jagged snowy wall without any really distinctive peaks. The highest expanses are barren and frosty, but on a clear day they offer a view to Morocco. Mulhacén and especially its sister peak **Veleta** (3,392m/11,125ft) can be climbed without too much exertion. Up until quite recently the area was fairly inaccessible and the facilities – certainly compared to Alpine standards – pretty basic. But the place has come on in leaps and bounds in the last decade – so much so that it was deemed good enough to host the 1995 World Skiing Championships (unfortunately postponed until 1996 owing to lack of snow). The Sierra Nevada cannot compete in terms of scale and variety with Alpine resorts but there are more than enough pistes to detain you for a long weekend.

If you're adventurous, you can continue onwards from Veleta down into **Las Alpujarras**, a string of white villages along the valley of the Río Guadalfeo, between

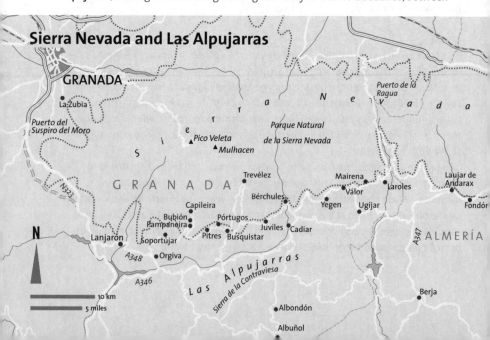

Sierra Nevada and Las Alpujarras

the Sierra Nevada and the little Contraviesa chain along the sea coast. On the way to Las Alpujarras, just outside Granada, you'll pass the spot called **Suspiro de Moro**, where poor Boabdil sighed as he took his last look back over Granada. His mother was less than sympathetic – 'Weep like a woman for what you were incapable of defending like a man,' she told him. It gave Salman Rushdie the title for his novel *The Moor's Last Sigh* (1995). The last 33km (20½ miles) of this route, where the road joins the Guadalfeo valley down to Motril, is one of the most scenic in Spain.

In Moorish times this was a densely populated region, full of vines and orchards. Much of its population was made up of refugees from the Reconquista, coming mainly from Seville. Under the conditions for Granada's surrender in 1492, the region was granted as a fief to Boabdil el Chico but, with forced Christianization and the resulting revolts, the entire population was replaced by settlers from the north.

Though often described as one of the most inaccessible corners of Spain, this region has attracted growing numbers of visitors since Gerald Brenan wrote *South from Granada* and, more recently, Chris Stewart wrote *Driving Over Lemons*, an account of setting up home in one of the remoter corners of this region. The roads wind past stepped fields, cascades of water, high pastures and sudden drops, and when the almond trees are in blossom it is at its most appealing. Unlike the other Andalucían villages with their red-tiled roofs, the *pueblos* of Las Alpujarras are flat-roofed. Though you won't be the only visitors to Las Alpujarras, the region is hardly spoiled; and with the villages relatively close to each other, and plenty of wild country on either side, it's a great spot for hiking or just finding some well-decorated peace and quiet.

Lanjarón, the principal tourist centre in the region, has been attracting visitors to its spas since Roman times and now markets its bottled water all across Spain. There are eight springs in all, each offering a different blend of natural minerals, while shops along the elegant main street offer complementary remedies for whatever ails you. The ruined Moorish castle on the hill saw the Moors' last stand against the Imperial troops on 8 March 1500. Well and truly Catholic today, Lanjarón's *Semana Santa* celebrations are the most famous in the province.

Orgiva was made the regional capital by Isabel II in 1839 and it remains the biggest town of Las Alpujarras today. There are few remains of its Moorish past; the castle of the Counts of Sástago may look the part but it dates from the 17th century. The Renaissance church has a carving by Martínez Montañés and there is a Benizalte mill, just outside the town. Orgiva springs to life on Thursdays, when everyone congregates for the weekly market. The town has become a magnet for New Age travellers and you can't fail to notice them or their beaten-up transit vans passing through the streets. Just outside town they have set up a village, consisting mainly of wigwams.

From here you'll have a choice of keeping to the main road for **Ugíjar** or heading north through the highest and loveliest part of the region, with typical white villages climbing the hillsides under terraced fields. **Soportújar**, the first, has one of Las Alpujarras' surviving primeval oak groves behind it. Next comes **Pampaneira**, a pretty little town of cobbled streets and flowers. In the Plaza de la Libertad there's a museum dedicated to the customs and costumes of Las Alpujarras and a locally run

Getting Around

Sierra Nevada: there are two or three buses a day from the main bus station in Granada, to the main square of the ski resort, Solynieve. Departures during the season are at 8am, 10am and 5pm, returning at 9am, 4pm and 6pm. In summer the bus leaves at 9am, returning at 5.30pm. The buses are operated by Autocares Bonal, t 95 827 31 00. Some 20km before you reach Veleta, you'll enter the Solynieve ski area; from here there are cable cars up to the peak itself.

Las Alpujarras: a few years ago it was still possible to penetrate the white villages of Las Alpujarras by bus over the top of the Sierra Nevada. However, the high road past Mulhacén has been closed to all motorized traffic, even in high summer. If you still wish to take this incredibly scenic route you can walk, cycle, or go by horse, in the summer months.

Tourist Information

Lanjarón: opposite the spa, on the right as you come in from Granada: t 95 877 02 82. Opening times vary.

Pampaneira: Parque Natural de la Sierra Nevada, Plaza de la Libertad s/n, t 95 876 31 27, f 95 876 33 01, www.nevadensis.com. *Open in summer Tues–Sat 10–2 and 4–7, winter 10–2 and 3–6, Mon and Sun all year 10–3.*

For skiing information contact the tourist office in Granada or the Federación Andaluza de Montaña, Pso de Ronda 101, t 95 829 13 40. *Open Mon–Fri 8.30–10.30pm.* Alternatively call t 95 824 91 19 for snow reports in English and Spanish.

Where to Stay and Eat

Most of the ski hotels close from June to December. Ask at the tourist office in Granada for what's available, or contact the Cetursa Reservation Centre in Pradollano, t 95 824 91 11. Among the five modern hotels in the ski resort of Pradollano, none particularly stands out; in the skiing season accommodation at these places means a week's stay on half board for *90,000–120,000 pts per person (instruction extra)*.

In the Las Alpujarras region, Lanjarón has most of the rooms; a score of good bargains in the 3,000–4,000 pts range are to be found on or near the main road into town, the Avenida Andalucia and its continuation, the Avenida de la Alpujarra. It also has the majority of the (limited) upmarket accommodation in the area. Elsewhere, you'll find acceptable accommodation and food in Orgiva, Pampaneira, Capileira and Ugíjar. The area also abounds in self-catering apartments, *casas rurales* and privately rented houses for longer stays. You can pick up lists of these from the numerous tourism offices in the area including Rustic Blue in Bubión (t 95 876 33 81, f 95 876 31 34, www.rusticblue.com) where English is spoken.

Lanjarón ✉ 18420

★★★Nuevo Palas, Avda de Alpujarra 24, t 95 877 00 86, f 95 877 01 11, www.nuevopalas.com *(moderate)*. The best in town; recently refurbished, comfortable rooms with views, pool, gym, games room and a good restaurant.

★★Castillo Alcadima, C/Francisco Tarregas 3, t 95 877 08 09, f 95 877 11 82, www.castillo-alcadima.es *(moderate)*. Just down from the main road and occupying one of the best spots in town, with rooms set round a pool/dining area with views to the castle

office for the **Parque Natural de la Sierra Nevada**. All sorts of activities are on offer here, from horse or donkey rides, through to skiing, hang-gliding, nature walks and caving expeditions. They also sell good maps of the park. If you'd prefer something more contemplative, the **Tibetan Monastery of Clear Light**, the birthplace of a reincarnated Spanish Tibetan lama, Osel, sits above the town on the sides of the **Poqueira Gorge**, complete with a visitor centre (*open daily 3–6*) offering courses in Mahayana Buddhism and retreats. To get there, take the road marked Camino Forestal, on the right just before you approach the turn-off for Pampaneira; it's about 7km along a very poor dirt track.

and across the valley. They also rent apartments for longer stays.

★España, Avda Andalucía 44, t/f 95 877 01 87 (*inexpensive*). Excellent value for what it has, which includes a pool and its own grounds. Situated in the fine-looking building on your left as you enter town on a street lined with other one- and two-star places that are all much of a muchness.

Castillo Alcadima, C/Francisco Tarregas 3, t 95 877 08 09, f 95 877 11 82. This hotel restaurant offers good value and fine views.

El Rincon de Jamon, along the main road just beyond the España. For an altogether earthier experience, come here to enjoy a *copa* of *vino* and a few slices of *jamón* from Trevelez in spit-and-sawdust surroundings; it's also a good place to buy *embutidos*.

Orgiva ✉ 18400

★★★Taray, Ctra Talbate-Albuñol, km 18, t 95 878 45 25, f 95 878 45 31, *tarayalp@teleline.es* (*moderate*). On the road out of Orgiva, this is one of the best places to stay in the whole of this area: comfortable rooms in a *cortijo*-style hotel, set round a large pool, and with a bar and good restaurant.

★★★Hotel Alpujarras, Ctra de Trevélez, t 95 878 55 49 (*inexpensive*). The next best option, on the junction as you go into town; its restaurant does a wonderful roast kid.

Ugíjar ✉ 18480

Hostal Vidaña, Ctra de Almería, t 95 876 70 10 (*inexpensive*). Serves up humungous portions of delicious mountain fare, such as partridge, goat and rabbit; also provides basic accommodation.

Pedro, Fábrica de Sedas s/n, t 95 876 71 49 (*cheap*). Another good-value place to stay.

Pampaneira ✉ 18411

Hostal Ruta de Mulhacén, Avda Alpujarra 6, t 95 876 30 10, f 95 876 34 46 (*cheap*). On the main road as you go through the town, this is simple but comfortable.

Hostal Pampaneira, Jose Antonio 1, t 95 876 30 02. Slightly cheaper and a bit more basic.

For food there are numerous options in the pretty main square, Plaza de la Libertad, none of them outstanding.

Bubión ✉ 18412

Villa Turistica de Poqueira, Barrio Alto s/n, t 95 876 31 11, f 95 876 31 36, *www.ctv.es/alpujarr* (*moderate*). Offers self-catering apartments with the advantages of a hotel. Prices depend on apartment size; this is a good base for families wanting to explore the area and the apartments mostly offer beautiful views.

Terrazas de la Alpujarra, Plaza del Sol s/n, t 95 876 30 34, f 95 876 32 52, *terrazas@teleline.es* (*cheap*). A perfectly acceptable budget option, with en suite rooms in the hostal, or excellent value apartments (*inexpensive*) with open log fires and, as the name suggests, *terrazas* with breathtaking views across the valley.

As a place firmly on the tourist trail, Bubión has a number of good bars and restaurants.

La Artesa, C/Carretera 2, t 95 876 30 82 (*inexpensive*). Perhaps the best restaurant, serving hearty fare at a reasonable price.

Teide, C/Carretera, t 95 876 30 37. Another good restaurant.

Cervecería Fuenfría, C/Carretera. A little further up the road; worth trying for after-dinner drinks.

CiberMonfi, Café Morisco, C/Alcalde Pérez Remón 2 (a street off the Plaza del Sol),

Bubión is a Berber-style village in a spectacular setting with a textile mill and tourist shops. All these villages are within sight of each other on a short detour along the edge of the beautiful (and walkable) ravine called **Barranco de Poqueira**. **Capileira**, the last village on the mountain-pass route over Mulhacén and Veleta, sees more tourists than most. Its treasure, in the church of **Nuestra Señora de la Cabeza**, is a statue of the Virgin donated to the village by Ferdinand and Isabella. North from here a tremendously scenic road takes you up across the Sierra Nevada and eventually to Granada. In winter this pass is snowbound, and even in summer you need to take extra care – it's steep and dangerous with precipitous drops down the ravines.

t 95 876 30 53, *cibermonfi@hotmail.com*. Drink mint tea and surf the web in very stylish surroundings.

Capileira ✉ 18143
***Finca Los Llanos**, Ctra de Sierra Nevada, t 95 876 30 71, f 95 876 32 06 (*moderate*). A luxury option at the top end of town, with a pool; its restaurant is known for its speciality: aubergines in honey (*moderate*).
Mesón Poqueira, Doctor Castilla, 6, t 95 876 30 48 (*cheap*). Rooms with a view, and a good restaurant.
Paco López, Ctra de la Sierra 5, t 95 876 30 76 (*cheap*). Rooms with bath.
Panjuila, on the road just outside the village. Nightlife is fairly limited in Capileira, but if you're here on a Thursday then track down this bar for some flamenco.

Pitres ✉ 18414
Posada La Taha, Bancal de Perico s/n, t/f 95 834 30 41 (*cheap*). Rents out apartments in a typical Alpujarran house.

Pórtugos ✉ 18415
**Nuevo Malagueño, Ctra Orgiva–Trevélez, t 95 876 60 98 (*inexpensive*). Offers comfortable rooms and views over the Alpujarras.
*Mirador de Pórtugos, Pza Nueva 5, t 95 876 60 14 (*inexpensive*). Another reasonable option with views.

Trevélez ✉ 18005
***Alcazaba de Busquistar**, Ctra Orgiva-Láujar, km 37, t 95 885 86 87, f 95 885 86 93 (*moderate*). This is one of the best places to stay in the Alpujarras, despite the indifferent service. Rather confusingly, it is nowhere near Busquistar (but four kilometres beyond Trevélez). It is a new hotel arranged along traditional Alpujarran lines. It has apartments and studios, all with log fires, kitchen, phone and satellite TV. There is a heated indoor pool, squash court, excellent restaurant, three cafés and games room. They also organize activities such as horseriding.
*La Fragua, C/San Antonio 4 (in the Barrio del Medio), t 95 885 85 73 (*inexpensive*). The best in town, with warm rooms and a good restaurant which concentrates on Alpujarras specialities, many dishes featuring mountain-cured ham (*moderate*).
The Hostal Mulhacén, Ctra Ugíjar, t/f 95 885 85 87 (*inexpensive*). Well situated for hill walks and the annual all-night pilgrimage up Spain's highest mountain at midnight on August 4th. The *hostal* is also beside the river, where locals swim during the summer.
Mesón Haraiçel, t 95 885 85 30 (*inexpensive*). Serves Arab-influenced food with plenty of almond sauces and meat dishes. For dessert try a *soplillo* (honey and almond meringue).

Cádiar ✉ 18440
Alqueria de Morayma, C/Alqueria de Morayma, t 95 834 32 21 (*moderate*). A recreated *cortijo* with a pool and good restaurant. The best place to stay in town.
**Almirez, Ctra Laujar-Berja, km 1.6, t 95 051 35 14, f 95 051 35 61 (*inexpensive*). A good second bet for half the price.

Yegen ✉ 18460
El Rincon de Yegen, Camino de las Eras, t 95 885 12 70 (*moderate*). Despite its indifferent service, probably the best place to stay, just east of the village with a pool and a good restaurant. It also lets apartments.
Casas Blancas, in the nearby village of Mecina Bombarón, t 95 885 11 51 (*inexpensive*). A rural hotel which also lets studio rooms.

However, the beautiful scenery makes the risks worthwhile. The road is permanently closed to all motorized traffic, but you can do it on foot (about 5½ hours), or by bike or on horseback. Alternatively, continue on the GR421 to **Pitres**, centre of a Hispano-Japanese joint venture that produces and exports handcrafted ballet shoes, of all things. There is a ruined hilltop mosque, and the remains of a few other Moorish buildings litter the village.

The road carries on through the villages of **Pórtugos**, a pilgrimage centre for Our Lady of Sorrows, and **Busquistar**, before arriving in **Trevélez**, on the slopes of

La Fuente, in the main square, **t** 95 885 10 67 (*cheap*). The budget option, just round the corner from Gerald Brenan's house. Also rents apartments.

Laujar de Andarax ✉ 04470
★★Villa Turistica de Laujar, Cortijo de la Villa (just outside the village), **t** 95 051 30 27, **f** 95 051 35 54, *turrualp@larural.es* (*moderate*). Rents 31 apartments with open fires, satellite TV and terrace. Also has a swimming pool, tennis, good restaurant and kids' play area.

Alhama de Almería ✉ 04400
★★San Nicolás, C/Baños s/n, **t** 95 064 13 61 (*inexpensive*). On the site of the original Moorish baths, offering comfortable rooms on its own grounds at reasonable prices.

Solynieve (Pradollano) ✉ 18196
Most of what you'll need for skiing you can find here: ski hire shops rent out the entire kit (including clothes) for about 7,000 pts. There is also what is reputed to be the biggest covered car park in Spain with space for almost 3,000 cars. Ski passes cost between 2,500 and 3,500pts a day, depending on the season. Nearby are the lifts and cabins to the slopes. Seasoned Alpine skiers will not be hugely challenged by the slopes, but for the beginner the area is a dream, with plenty of wide gentle pistes. There is plenty to keep you occupied for two or three days, and the views from the top of Veleta, across to Morocco on clear days, are unsurpassable.

★★★Kenia Nevada, in town, **t** 95 848 09 11, **f** 95 848 08 07 (*expensive*). Alpine-style, with a jacuzzi, pool, gym and sauna for those stiff days on the slopes.

★★★Hotel Parador, on the main highway, **t** 95 848 06 61, **f** 95 848 02 12 (*expensive– moderate*). An exception to the general rule, this hotel is one of the smaller and newer *paradores* that remains open all year round.

★★★★Melia Sierra Nevada, **t** 95 848 0400, *melia.sierra.nevada@solmelia.es* (*expensive–moderate*). The huge, ugly block back from the square which offers similar luxuries at a slightly higher price.

★★★★Maribel, **t** 95 848 1019, **f** 95 848 2010, *hmaribel@eurocibes.es* (*expensive– moderate*). Prettier and more intimate with just 32 rooms but no pool.

★★★Ziryab, **t** 95 848 0512, **f** 95 848 1415 (*expensive–moderate*). A dramatically situated hotel on the main square, with big, comfortable rooms and lots of warm, chunky wood furniture. Right by the car park.

★Telecabina, Pza de Pradollano, **t** 95 824 91 20, **f** 95 824 91 22 (*moderate*). Over the summer months only, this place offers pleasant but basic doubles.

★★El Ciervo, **t** 95 848 0409, **f** 95 848 0461, *www.eh.etursa.es* (*cheap*). A large *pensione*.

Albergue Universitario, Peñones de San Francisco, **t** 95 848 01 22 (*cheap*). Cheaper accommodation like this can be had in this village at the end of the bus route.

Most restaurants are open only in the skiing season, and most are a little pretentious – but that's ski resorts for you.

Ruta de Veleta, **t** 95 848 12 28 (*moderate*). This restaurant in Edificio Bulgaria is worth a try.

Rincón de Pepe Reyes, in Pradollano (*inexpensive*). Has good *andaluz* cooking.

Borreguiles, halfway up Veleta, **t** 95 848 00 79. You can take the cable car up to this frenetic and none-too-clean café and sit out on the terrace to take in the view.

Mulhacén. Trevélez likes to claim it's the highest village in Europe. It's also famous in Andalucía for its snow-cured hams – Henry Ford and Rossini were fans – and a ham feast is held in their honour every August. Today Trevélez is full of tour buses, and a string of ugly developments has removed any charm it once had. This is the main starting point for climbers heading for the summit of Mulhacén and the other peaks in the Sierra Nevada, but, despite the tacky tourist shops, there's little to detain other visitors. From there the road slopes back downwards to **Juviles** and **Bérchules**, one of the villages where the tradition of carpet-weaving has been maintained since

Moorish times. From here you can go down to **Cádiar**, the 'navel' of Las Alpujarras, as Gerald Brenan described it, a non-descript place with an attractive main square. Otherwize you can move along to **Ugíjar**, or cut down to the coast via **Albondón** and **Albuñol** (both famous for their rosé wines), finishing at **La Rabita**, in Almería.

The C332 from Bérchules takes you to **Yegen**, some 10km further, which became famous as the long-time home of British writer Gerald Brenan. His house is still in the village – ask for 'El Casa del Inglés'. After that come more intensively farmed areas on the lower slopes, with oranges, vineyards and almonds; you can either hit Ugíjar or detour to the seldom-visited villages of **Laroles** and **Mairena** on the slopes of **La Ragua**, one of the last high peaks of the Sierra Nevada. In 1569 Fernando de Cordoba y Válor rallied the last remaining Moors in the area to revolt against the Christians; **Válor** is the site of the Moors' last stand. The events are recreated in the annual 'Moors and Christians' festival in September.

The A337 will take you north over the mountains and towards Guadix. Further east, through countryside that rapidly changes from healthy green to dry brown, the road enters Almería province and the town of **Laujar de Andarax**. It was here that the deposed Boabdil planned on setting up his court to rule the Alpujarras after being expelled from Granada in 1492. But his plans were short-lived and in less than a year the Christian kings had reneged on their promise and expelled him: his last view of Spain was from Adra before he set sail for Africa.

A few kilometres on, the village of **Fondón** is of particular interest; an Australian architect, Donald Grey, and his Spanish partner, José Antonio Garvayo, have set up a school to teach the traditional crafts of ironwork, carpentry, tile- and brick-making, so most of the buildings have been restored, and Fondón is now a model village. The church tower was once a mosque's minaret. The road from here passes through some nondescript villages before arriving in **Alhama de Almería**, a spa town since Moorish times. You can take the waters here or drop down to the coast and Almería.

Around the Sierra Nevada: Guadix

It's a better road entering Granada from the west than that leaving it to the east. Between the city and Murcia are some of the emptiest, bleakest landscapes in Spain. The first village you pass through is **Purullena**, long famous for its pretty ceramic ware; the entire stretch of highway through it is lined with stands and displays.

The poverty of this region has long forced many of its inhabitants to live in caves, and nowhere more so than in Guadix. Several thousand of this city's population, most of them gypsies, have homes, complete with whitewashed façades, chimneys and television aerials sticking out of the top, built into the hillsides. The cave dwellings have their advantages: they're warmer in the winter and cooler in summer than most Andalucían homes, relatively spacious and well ventilated – and when the time comes to build a new room, all you need is a pick and shovel. If you care to venture around the cave area, largely concentrated in the Barrio Santiago, beware of being lured into someone's home and charged an exorbitant fee for the privilege. For a better understanding of troglodyte culture head instead to the **Cave Museum**, Plaza del Beato Poveda s/n (*t 95 866 08 08*).

The centre of Guadix is dominated by a Moorish **Alcazaba**, largely rebuilt in the 16th century; near the arcaded central **Plaza Mayor** stands the huge **cathedral**, begun by Diego de Siloé, builder of Granada's cathedral, and given its magnificent façade in the 1700s by Andalucía's great rococo eccentric, Vicente Acero. The ornate traceries of the church, and the imposing castle, appearing together out of the empty, queerly eroded hills make a striking sight.

Forty-six kilometres northeast on the A92N lies **Baza**, which was important in Moorish times as a centre of silk production, important in Roman times when it was known as Basti and was capital of the area, and also in prehistoric times as a centre for ancient Iberian tribes. Today it is an unassuming market town, worth an afternoon's wander. It too has a cave quarter, though not as extensive as Guadix, and a ruined Alcazaba. More rewarding though are the **Moorish baths** – some of the oldest in Spain, dating from the 10th century or possibly earlier – which are still privately owned but can be visited (check with the *turismo*). But Baza is most famous for its **Dama de Baza**, an Iberian sculpture of a goddess dating from the 3rd or 4th century BC, unearthed nearby but now residing in Madrid; a copy can be seen in the local **archaeological museum** in Plaza Mayor (*t 95 870 06 91*). There are a couple of other buildings worth seeking out, including the 16th-century **cathedral of Santa Maria** (built on the site of a mosque) and the **Palacio de los Enriquez**, just off the main square, which dates from the 15th or 16th century and has many interesting Moorish-influenced designs. The town is bounded by a natural park which has many ancient settlements including cave dwellings found on nearby Mount Jabalcón, accessible from the village of **Zújar**, famous since Roman times for its thermal waters.

Tourist Information

Guadix: situated out of town on the Granada road, t 95 866 26 65. *Open Mon–Fri 8–3.*

Where to Stay and Eat

Guadix ✉ 18500

★★★Comercio, C/Mira de Amezcua 3, t 95 866 05 00, f 95 866 50 72, *www.moebius.es/hotelcomercio* (*inexpensive*). The best place to stay in town, in a refurbished mansion which has seen better days, with all mod cons at a very reasonable price.

★★Mulhacén, Avda Buenos Aires 41, t 95 866 07 50, f 95 866 00 47 (*inexpensive*). An acceptable alternative, near the train station, with a café.

★★Carmen, Avda Mariana Pinenda 61, t 95 866 15 00, f 95 866 01 79 (*inexpensive*). Has a TV and phone in each room and, rather incongrously, a tennis court.

Cuevas Pedro Antonio Alarcón, Avda de Buenos Aires (just out of the centre), t 95 866 49 86, f 95 866 17 21 (*moderate*). For something completely different, you might like to try a night in a cave: the hotel is a series of luxuriously appointed caves complete with pool and a decent restaurant.

Baza ✉ 18800

★★Robemar, Ctra de Murcia 175, t 95 886 07 04, f 95 870 07 98 (*inexpensive*). The best place to stay, out of the centre, but it does boast a pool.

Pension Anabel, C/Maria de Luna 3, t 95 886 09 98 (*inexpensive*). All rooms are en suite with TV and phone; café attached.

Galera ✉ 18840

Casas Cuevas, C/Nicasio Tomás 12, t 95 873 90 68 (*moderate*). Another comfortable hotel set in a system of caves.

From Baza the main highway heads into Almería towards Velez Rubio and Velez Blanco. Alternatively you could make a detour to **Huéscar**, some 37km from Baza along the A92N then north along the A330 at Cullar Baza. Huéscar has a stormy past, stuck as it is at the border of the former Nasrid Kingdom of Granada and the provinces of Albacete, Murcia and Almería. It constantly fell in and out of Moorish and Christian hands through the Middle Ages, suffering terribly in the Moorish uprising of the 16th century. As a result most of its buildings have been damaged and replaced with ugly modern blocks. However, seek out its church, **Santa Maria de la Encarnación**; both Diego de Siloe and Vandelvira had a hand in its construction. Near the village of **Galera**, about 7km to the south, are some hill-top caves which form part of the ancient Iberian settlement of Tútugi (5th to 6th century BC). Orce, to the east, is built round an old Alcazaba, which has been largely reconstructed.

There's not much else to distract you in this corner of Spain. If you're headed for Almería and the coast (N324), you'll pass near **La Calahorra**, with an unusual Renaissance castle with domed turrets, and **Gérgal**.

The Coast South of Granada

Nerja

Approaching this town, the scenery becomes impressive as the mountains loom closer to the sea. Sitting at the base of the Sierra de Tejeda, Nerja itself is pleasant and quiet for a Costa resort. In Moorish times the town was a major producer of silk and sugar, an industry that fell into rapid decline after their departure. An earthquake in 1884 partially destroyed Nerja, and from then to the early 1960s it had to eke a living out of fishing and farming.

Its attractions are the **Balcón de Europa**, a promenade with a fountain overlooking the sea, and a series of secluded beaches under the cliffs – the best are a good walk away on either side of the town. A few kilometres east, the **Cueva de Nerja** (*open daily 10.30–12 and 4–6.30; adm*) is one of Spain's fabled grottoes, full of Gaudiesque formations and needle-thin stalactites – one, they claim, is the longest in the world. The caves were discovered in 1959, just in time for the tourist boom, and they have been fitted out with lights and music, with photographers lurking in the shadows who'll try to sell you a picture of yourself when you leave. The caves were popular with Cro-Magnon man, and there are some Palaeolithic artworks. Occasionally, this perfect setting is used for ballets and concerts.

A scenic 7km drive north of Nerja on the MA105 finds pretty **Frigiliana**, a pristine whitewashed village of neat houses, cobbled streets and a large expat population. There are splendid views down to the eastern coast, especially from the ruins of the Moorish fort. This was the site of one of the last battles between Christians and Moriscos in 1569; the story of the battle is retold on ceramic plates around the village's old quarter. Nowadays, Frigiliana is like an English colony rather than an inland Andalucían village.

Tourist Information

Nerja: Puerto de Mar 1, **t** 95 252 15 31. *Open weekdays 10–2 and 5–7, Sat 10–1.*
Almuñécar: Avda de Europa (in the small Moorish palace), **t** 95 863 11 25, **f** 95 863 15 07. *Open Mon–Sat 10–2 and 5–9.*
Salobreña: Pza de Goya s/n, **t** 95 861 03 14, *salobre@redestb.es. Open Mon–Fri 9.30–1.30 and 4.30–7, Sat 9.30–1.30; closed Sun.*

Eating Out

Nerja ✉ 29780

★★★★Parador de Nerja, Playa de Burriana, Almuñécar 8 (just outside town at El Tablazo), **t** 95 252 00 50, **f** 95 252 19 97, *nerja@parador.es* (*expensive*). A luxurious place; one of Nerja's two fine hotels.
★★★★Balcón de Europa 1, Pso Balcón de Europa, **t** 95 252 08 00, **f** 95 252 44 90, *balconeuropa@spa.es* (*expensive–moderate*). Probably a better choice than the Parador, though not quite as luxurious; the beautiful location on the 'balcony of Europe' in the town centre and the reasonable rates make the difference. Both hotels have lifts down to the beaches under Nerja's cliffs.
★★★Plaza Carana, Plaza Carana, **t** 95 252 40 00, **f** 95 252 40 08, *hotelplazacarana@inforegocio.com* (*moderate*). Just a few minutes walk from the Balcon de Europa, with air conditioning and two swimming pools.
★Portofino, Puerta del Mar 2, **t** 95 252 01 50 (*moderate*). A reasonable option on the beach.
★★Hostal Marissal, Balcón de Europa 3, **t** 95 252 01 99 (*inexpensive*). In an excellent location and good value; sea views, air conditioning and TV, with café attached.
★Carabeo, C/Carabeo 34, **t** 95 252 39 41, **f** 95 252 54 44 (*inexpensive*). Done out in the style of an old English hotel, with suites and doubles; also a tapas bar and restaurant.
Alhambra Antonio Milon, at Chaparil (*inexpensive*). Friendly with attractive rooms and sea-facing balconies.
De Miguel, C/Pintada 2, **t** 95 252 29 96 (*expensive*). Reservations are essential at this restaurant celebrated for its international

meat and fish dishes, and not least for the flambéd strawberries. *Closed Mon and Feb.*
Rey Alfonso (*moderate*). A popular restaurant; there is nothing special about the cuisine but the view is superb, on cliffs directly under the Balcón de Europa.
La Marina, Plaza de la Marina, **t** 95 252 12 19 (*inexpensive*). Serves a wide range of fish and seafood tapas for under 1,000 pts.
El Candil, **t** 95 252 07 97 (*inexpensive*). Has a good selection of Spanish dishes in a lovely setting, in a square just off the Balcón.

Almuñécar ✉ 18690

★★★Hotel Helios, Paseo San Cristobal, **t** 95 863 44 59, **f** 95 863 44 69 (*moderate*). The town's smartest hotel, with a pool.
★★Casablanca, Plaza San Cristobal 4, **f** 95 863 55 75 (*inexpensive*). A family-run pseudo-Moorish affair with rooms looking out to sea or to the castle and the Sierras beyond.
★Hotel San Cristobal, Plaza San Cristobal, **t** 95 863 36 12, **f** 95 83 16 12 (*cheap*). A cheaper option, with sea-facing rooms and balconies.
Los Geranios, Pza Rosa 4a, **t** 95 263 07 24 (*moderate*). A cheerful restaurant full of geraniums and owned by a Hispano-Belgian couple; the menu is international with a Spanish bias. *Closed Sun and Nov.*
Bodega Francisco, C/Real 15, **t** 95 263 01 68 (*inexpensive*). A wonderful watering hole serving inexpensive tapas and the usual *andaluz* staples.

Salobreña ✉ 18680

★★★Salobreña, outside the town on the coastal highway, **t** 95 861 02 61, **f** 95 861 01 01 (*moderate*). Close to the beach with pool and garden. The restaurant is also worth trying; it does excellent barbecues in summer and the views are worth the price alone (*moderate*).
★Mary Tere, Ctra de la Playa 7, **t** 95 882 84 89, **f** 95 861 01 26. One of a number of hostales near the beach with doubles and bath.
Meson de la Villa, Plaza F. Ramirez de Madrid, **t** 95 861 24 14 (*moderate–inexpensive*). The best restaurant in town, serving up local fish dishes and *rabo de toro. Closed Wed.* There are also a number of good *chiringuitos* along the beach during the season.

Almuñécar and Salobreña

The coastal road east of Nerja, bobbing in and out of the hills and cliffs, is the best part of the Costa del Sol, where avocado pears and sugar cane keep the farming community busy; however the next resort, **Almuñécar**, is a nest of dreary high-rises around a beleaguered village. Even so, this former fishing village has a lot to offer, not least the fact that Laurie Lee immortalized it in *As I Walked Out One Midsummer Morning*, describing his experiences just prior to the outbreak of the Civil War, and in *A Rose For Winter*, when he returned some 20 years later. Although the hotel where he stayed, 'a white, square crumbling hotel where I had previously worked as a porter and a minstrel', is long gone and replaced by an apartment block, there is a plaque in the square in front which mentions his books. Lee was careful to disguise Almuñécar, calling it 'Castillo' due to its strong resistance against Franco's forces, so there is no mention of individual bars or restaurants. He does, however, speak of the castle in ruins, a fairly accurate description today. Lee *aficionados* may also like to visit the pretty **Ayuntamiento**, on Plaza de la Constitución (where the peasants raised flags before the town was overcome by fascists), and **Iglesia de la Encarnación**, Plaza Nueva, which the locals set alight during the uprising.

For an idea of the ancient history of the town, visit the **Cueva de los Siete Palacios**, where the town's **archaeological museum** (*open 10.30–1.30 and 6–8*) is based. Almuñecar was founded by the Phoenicians as *Sexi*, which can be confusing for the first-time visitor: the *ayuntamiento* has taken to putting up signs declaring certain areas 'Sexi'. The museum has artefacts from this period through to the Romans and the Moors, as well as an Egyptian vase fired between 1700 and 1600 BC for Pharoah Apophis I, and inscribed with the oldest written text found in Iberia.

The **castillo** is dominated by a huge tower, and used to contain the town's cemetery, which has recently been located out of town. Below it lies the **Parque Ornitológico** (*open daily 11–2 and 4–8; adm*) which holds 1,500 birds from all over the world, and a cactus garden. Despite being the Granadinos' favourite resort, Almuñécar's numerous beaches are pretty dire, consisting of black sand and pebbles, while the nudist stretch is disconcertingly called *El Muerto*, 'the dead'. Outside town are the remains of a Roman aqueduct.

Salobreña, where the road from Granada meets the coast, is much nicer than Almuñecar, though it may not stay that way. The village's dramatic setting, slung down a steep, lone peak overlooking the sea, is the most stunning on the coast, and helps to insulate it just a little from the tourist industry. The beaches, just starting to become built up, are about 2km away.

Seville

Seville

Jardines del Guadalquivir

Puente de la Barqueta

Antiguo Hospital Provincial

Calle de Resolana

Calle San Juan de Ribera

Monasterio de San Clemente

Calle Calatrava

Calle de Santa Clara

Calle Muñoz León

Convento de Capuchinos

Avenida de la Cruz Roja

Avenida de Miraflores

Monasterio Santa Clara

Basilica de la Macarena

Moorish Walls

Calle de San Luis

Ronda Capuchinos

Río Guadalquivir

Monasterio de Santa Maria de las Cuevas

Calle del Torneo

Calle Eslava

Calle de Jesús del Gran Poder

San Lorenzo

Alameda Hércules

Calle de Relator

La Feria

San Luis

Calle Amor de Dios

Avenida de la Enladrillada

Calle de San Vicente

Juan Rabadán

San Vicente

Calle de Baños

CENTRO

Calle Regina

Castellar

Palácio de las Duenas

Calle Gerona

Bustos Tavera

San Marcos

Calle del Sol

Convento de Santa Catalina

EL FONTANAL

Puente de la Cartuja

Calle de Alfonso XII

Plaza Duque Victoria

Plaza de la Encarnación

Plaza San Pedro

Plaza Ponce de León

Calle José Laguillo

Santa Justa Train Station

Puente del Cachorro

Calle Marqués de Paradas

Museo de Bellas Artes

La Magdalena

Calle Tetuan

El Salvador

Plaza Cristo de Burgos

Calle de Rey

San Ildefonso

Casa de Pilatos

Calle de Recaredo

Calle Juan Antonio Cavestany

Calle de Arjona

Calle Las Sierpes

San Pablo

Reyes Católicos

Calle Zaragoza

Ayuntamiento

Plaza Nueva

Santa María Blanca

San Esteban

Calle de Luis Montoto

Bus Station

EL ARENAL

Calle de Adriano

Argote de Molina

Correo

Santa María la Blanca

Calle de Menendez Pelayo

Áqueduct (ruin)

TRIANA

Plaza del Altozano

Plaza de Toros de la Maestranza

Paseo de Cristóbal

Hospital de la Caridad

SANTA CRUZ

Catedral La Giralda

Alcázar

C. Demetrio de los Ríos

SAN BERNARDO

Santa Ana

Pages del Corro

Torre del Oro Museo Maritimo

Santander

Archivo de Indias

Puerta de Jerez

Jardines de Alcázar

Calle de Enramadilla

Puente de San Telmo

Av. Sanjurio

Avenida de Roma

Calle San Fernando

Universidad

Bus Station

Avenida de Carlos V

Plaza de Cuba

Palacio de San Telmo

Av. del Cid

Prado de San Sebastián

Avenida de Portugal

Capitanía General

Avenida de la República Argentina

LOS REMEDIOS

Calle de la Asunción

Paseo Colón

Avenida de María Luisa

Plaza de España

Avenida de Bórbolla

Plaza República Dominicana

Virgen de Luján

Puente del Generalísimo

Parque de María Luisa

Parque de los Remedios

Avenida Santiago Montoto

Las Delicias

Museum of Popular Art and Customs

Calle Felipe II

Archaeological Museum

Puente de Alfonso XIII

N

1 km

1/2 mile

Getting There

By Air
Seville has regular flights from Madrid and Barcelona. San Pablo airport is 12km (7½ miles) east of the city, and the airport bus leaves from Bar Iberia on C/Almirante Lobos. Airport **information** is available on t 95 444 90 00.

By Train
Estación de Santa Justa, in the surreally named Avenida Kansas City in the northeast of town, is the modern Expo showpiece. There are several trains daily to Madrid by AVE in a staggeringly quick 2hrs 15mins, and a daily *talgo* to Barcelona. The central RENFE office is at C/Zaragoza 29, information t 95 454 02 02, reservations t 95 422 26 93. For AVE **information** and reservations, call t 95 454 03 03.

By Bus
There are two bus stations in Seville, one at Plaza de Armas, **information** t 95 490 80 40 or t 95 490 77 37, and one at Prado de San Sebastián, **information** t 95 441 71 11. Buses for the western side of the peninsula, including Madrid, leave from Plaza de Armas. All buses for the eastern side of the country, including Barcelona, leave from Prado de San Sebastián. Information on routes and timetables is available from the tourist office, or from the information office inside the bus stations.

Getting Around
The narrow, twisting streets of old Seville are a delight to stroll around, and most of the main sights are bunched within walking distance of each other.

By Bus
For the footweary, there is a good city bus service; among the most useful lines are buses C4 and C3, which circle the perimeter of the old city, and lines C1 and C2, which make a larger circle and encompass Triana, La Cartuja, the main train station (Estación de Santa Justa) and the bus station on Plaza de Armas. Night bus routes are prefaced with the letter A. The tourist information office has free, comprehensive bus maps with explanations in

English. On the back is a useful table called 'How to Get There', which makes working out the routes at bus stops much simpler. For city bus information, call t 90 071 01 71; for lost property call t 95 455 72 22. Buy single tickets (125 pts) on the bus; 3- or 7-day tourist passes (1,000/1,500 pts) which offer unlimited travel for a set period are available at ticket offices at the Prado de San Sebastián, Plaza Nueva (where there is a little 'Bono-bus' kiosk, open 9–2 and 5–7) and Plaza Encarnación.

By Taxi
Taxis are everywhere and fairly inexpensive; if you do need to call one, try Radio Taxis t 95 458 00 00/95 457 11 11, Tele Taxi t 95 462 22 22/95 462 14 61, or Radio Teléfono Giralda t 95 467 55 55.

By Bicycle
Bicycles can be rented at BiciBike, C/Miguel de Mañara 11B, t/f 95 456 38 38, just behind the main tourist office, near the Reales Alcazares.

By Tour
Sightseeing buses and river cruises depart from the Tower of Gold. Bus tours are offered by Sevilla Tour, t 95 450 20 99 (includes a ride in an old-fashioned tram car), and Sevirama, t 95 456 06 93. River cruises are offered by Cruceros Turisticos Torre del Oro, t 95 421 13 96; Cruseros del Sur, t 95 456 16 72; and Buque El Patio, Paseo de Colon 11, t 95 456 16 92.

Tourist Information
The permanent tourist office is very helpful; it's near the cathedral at Avenida de la Constitución 21, t 95 422 14 04, f 95 453 76 26 (*open Mon–Fri 9–7, Sat 10–2 and 3–7, Sun 10–2*). The municipal information centre is near the María Luisa Park, on Paseo de las Delicias 9, t 95 423 44 65. There's also an information centre at the airport, t 95 444 91 28, and at Santa Julia station, t 95 423 76 26.

Internet and Telephones
It is easy to find Internet access in Seville; these are a few options:

In Situ, Plaza Alameda de Hercules, t 95 490 33 94. Has a pleasant vegetarian and organic café and shop on the ground floor, while upstairs there are Internet and e-mail facilities. The staff are very pleasant and helpful.

Cibercafé, C/Nuñez de Balboa 3, t 95 450 28 09, *www.toredeoro.net*. An unassuming, friendly little place tucked behind the bullring. One hour costs 300 pts.

Cibercenter, C/Julio César 8, t 95 422 88 99, *www.cibercenter.es*. Supplies Internet and e-mail access at the heart of the city, just off C/Reyes Católicos.

Sevilla Internet Center, C/Almirantzago 2–10, t 95 450 02 75, *www.sevillacenter.com*. Offers Internet, e-mail and fax services, and inexpensive telephone calls. *Open Mon–Fri 9am–10pm, weekends 12–10pm*.

The Email Place, C/Sierpes 54, t 95 421 85 92, *www.sevillaonline.com*. Tucked away in the Plaza de las Delicias.

Post Office

The main post office is on Avenida de la Constitución 32, t 90 219 71 97.

Shopping

All the paraphernalia associated with Spanish fantasy, such as *mantillas*, castanets, wrought iron, gypsy dresses, Andalucían dandy suits, *azulejo* tiles and embroidery, is available in Seville. **C/Cuna** is the best place to find flamenco paraphernalia, and several of the convents sell jams and confectionery. **Triana**, of course, is the place to find *azulejo* tiles and all kinds of perfumed soaps. If you want to pick up a First Communion outfit (sailor suits for the boys, meringues for the girls) or any kind of religious kitsch, check out the astonishing number of shops devoted to it around the **Plaza del San Salvador**.

If you want to look the part at Feria, deck yourself out at one of several equestrian shops, including **Jara y Sedal**, C/Adriano 16.

For fashion, there is a branch of the luxurious leather store **Loewe** on the Plaza Nueva, as well as other upmarket designer shops, and the **C/O'Donnell** has a number of fashionable and more affordable boutiques.

There are two branches of **El Corte Inglés**, where the well-heeled *sevillanos* shop and, on Plaza Duque de la Victoria, a branch of Zara

(also to be found at C/Velázquez) and Mango, the perennial fashion favourites.

Vértice is a bookshop, on Mateos Gago near the cathedral, with a small selection of English-language literature and local guidebooks, maps and history books; but for a pleasant wander head for the pedestrianized **C/Sierpes**.

Where to Stay

Seville ✉ 41000

Hotels are more expensive in Seville than in most of Spain and it is advisable to book in advance. High season is March and April; during Semana Santa and the April Feria you should book even for inexpensive *hostales*, preferably a year ahead. Low season is July and August, when the inhabitants flee from the heat, and January to early March.

Luxury–Expensive

★★★★★Alfonso XIII, C/San Fernando 2, t 95 422 28 50, f 95 421 60 33. Built by King Alfonso for the Exposición Iberoamericana in 1929, this is the grandest hotel in Andalucía, attracting heads of state, opera stars, and tourists who want a unique experience, albeit at a price. Seville society still meets around its lobby fountain and somewhat dreary bar. Its restaurant San Fernando is good if pricey – partridge flambé, wheat-fed cock or Beluga caviar.

★★★★★Hotel Colón, C/Canalejas 1, t 95 422 29 00, f 95 422 09 38, *trypcolon@sei.es*. Grand and extremely comfortable. It used to be a haunt of bullfighters and their hangers-on.

★★★★Hotel Doña María, C/Don Remondo 19, t 95 422 49 90, f 95 421 95 46. Charming and superbly located by the cathedral. Among the mostly antique furniture are some beautifully painted headboards and four-poster beds, and there is a rooftop swimming pool with stunning views of La Giralda.

★★★★Los Seises, C/Segovias 6, t 95 422 94 95, f 95 422 43 34. Hidden in the maze of streets that make up the Santa Cruz Quarter, this converted 16th-century archbishop's palace contains Roman artefacts and Arabic columns and tiles which mingle with later antiques; each room is individually styled. The name is derived from *setza*, meaning sixteen, which was the number of young boys who sang and danced at the main altar of the cathedral; the tradition is still maintained on special feast days such as Corpus Christi. There is a rooftop swimming pool here too, surrounded, bizarrely, with astro-turf, and the restaurant is highly acclaimed.

★★★★**Fernando III**, San Jose 21, **t** 95 421 73 07, **f** 95 422 02 46, *www.altor.com*. Superbly located in the Barrio Santa Cruz, offering four-star amenities at much cheaper rates than its competitors.

★★★★**Las Casas del Rey de Baeza**, Plaza Jésus de la Resencion 2, **t** 95 456 14 96, **f** 95 456 14 41, *baeza@zoom.es*. Also in Santa Cruz, with an elegant white and ochre façade and pretty rooms, some overlooking the square.

★★★★**Hotel Taberna de Alabardero**, C/Zaragoza 20, **t** 95 456 06 37, **f** 95 456 36 66. One of Seville's most winning establishments; the former home of the poet J. Antonio Cavestany, who wrote a number of lyrical romantic poems about the city, the building now houses an outstanding restaurant and culinary school. Ten charming and intimate rooms, all with Jacuzzi as well as the usual accoutrements, are set around the light-filled central courtyard. The service is discreet and excellent, and the cuisine, as you might expect, is sublime. Prices include breakfast in the award-winning restaurant.

★★★★**Inglaterra**, Plaza Nueva 7, **t** 95 422 49 70, **f** 95 456 13 36, *www.hotelinglaterra.es*. A gracious and typically *sevillano* hotel, despite its name, with a chic clientele and smart, well-equipped rooms.

★★★★**Meliá Confort Macarena**, C/San Juan de Rivera 2, **t** 95 437 57 00, **f** 95 438 18 03. Situated by the Macarena walls, this is another classy establishment with a beautiful *azulejo*-tiled fountain, a swimming pool, and far-reaching views over the city and the nearby Andalucían parliament from the rooftop terrace.

★★★**Las Casas de la Judería**, Callejón de Dos Hermanos 7, **t** 95 441 51 50, **f** 95 422 21 70, *www.lascasas.zoom.es*. A row of charming and perfectly restored townhouses in the Santa Cruz Quarter, expertly run by the Medina family – well-known and very stylish *sevillano* hoteliers.

★★★**Las Casas de las Mercaderes**, C/Álvarez Quintero 9/13, **t** 95 422 58 58, **f** 95 422 98 84, *www.lascasas.es*. In the Arenal district, the stylish rooms have been sympathetically restored and are arranged around an 18th-century courtyard.

Casa Numero 7, C/Virgenes 7, **t** 95 422 15 81, **f** 95 421 45 27. If you want a slice of England in the heart of Seville – at a price – this converted 19th-century mansion with just four rooms is your place. It's designed in a similar way to an English country house, spotless and modern but slightly stuffy.

Expensive–Moderate

★★★**Hotel San Gil**, C/Parras 28, **t** 95 490 68 11, **f** 95 490 69 39. Near the Andalucían parliament is this beautiful ochre building from the turn of the last century (listed, no less, in Seville's official catalogue of the city's top 100 buildings), with a shady courtyard dotted with palm trees, fabulous mosaics and *azulejo* tiles, and lofty ceilings.

★★**Hotel Baco**, overlooking Plaza Ponce de León 15, **t** 95 456 50 50, **t** 95 456 36 54. A stalwartly old-fashioned place with a wrought-iron entrance and charming, simple rooms.

★**Hostal Plaza Seville**, C/Canalejas 2, **t** 95 421 71 49, **f** 95 421 07 73. Has a beautiful neoclassical façade, the work of Aníbal González, architect of the 1929 Exposición, and is ideally placed near the restaurants and bars of San Eloy.

★**Hostal Monreal**, C/Rodrigo Caro 8, **t** 95 421 41 66. A lively place close to the cathedral with almost too much character and a good cheap restaurant when it's open.

Moderate

★★**Monte-Carlo**, C/Gravina 51, **t** 95 421 75 03, **f** 95 421 68 25, *hmontecarlo@arrakis.es*. Has a bright peachy façade and quiet, recently refurbished rooms. The service is friendly and helpful and they are good sources of local information.

★★**Hostal Sierpes**, Corral del Rey 22, **t** 95 422 49 48, **f** 95 421 21 07. Situated in the pedestrianized shopping area, with pretty archways surrounding an interior courtyard, and spacious, airy rooms. There is also a garage and a reasonable restaurant.

*Hotel Simón, C/García de Vinuesa 19, **t** 95 422 66 60, **f** 95 456 22 41. One of the best-value options in the city, in a fine position just off the Avenida de la Constitución by the cathedral, and in a restored 18th-century mansion.

Hotel de Doña Lina, C/Gloria 7, **t 95 421 09 56, **f** 95 421 86 61. In the Santa Cruz area, a charmingly kitsch place with simple white-washed bedrooms and a terrace.

Moderate–Inexpensive

Hostería del Laurel, Plaza de los Venerables 5, **t 95 422 02 95, **f** 95 421 04 50, *host-laurel@eintec.es*. Less pricey, overlooking a slightly touristy square, this is an engagingly quirky hotel with layered turrets and terraces that once attracted Romantic poets and novelists.

Hotel Murillo, C/Lope de Rueda 9, **t 95 421 60 95, **f** 95 421 96 16, *murillo@nexo.es*. Old-fashioned, family-run and comfortable; the prices are very reasonable for its central location in Santa Cruz, although it can be expensive in season.

Hotel Rabida, C/Castelar 24, **t 95 422 09 60, **f** 95 422 43 75, *hotel-rabida@sol.com*. In the quiet heart of El Arenal, not far from the bullring, with simple, well-equipped rooms set around two courtyards, one of which doubles as a salon with wicker furniture and a pretty stained-glass ceiling.

Hostal Cordoba, C/Farnesio 12, **t 95 422 74 98. Offers clean rooms with fans.

*Hostal Argüelles, C/Alhóndiga 58, **t** 95 421 44 55. Small with a garden and terrace.

*Pensión Fabiola, C/Fabiola 16, **t** 95 421 83 46. Cooler than most in summer, quiet and with a little courtyard.

Inexpensive–Cheap

For inexpensive *hostales*, the Santa Cruz Quarter is surprisingly the best place to look, particularly on the quiet side streets off C/Mateos Gago.

*Hostal Nuevo Picasso, C/San Gregorio 1, **t/f** 95 421 08 64, *hpicasso@arrakis.es*. One of the nicest pensions in this district, with a plant-filled entrance hall and a green interior courtyard hung with bric-a-brac. Rooms are spotless and attractively furnished.

Hostal Atenas, C/Caballerizas 1, **t 95 421 80 47, **f** 95 422 76 90. Quiet and very nice, in a good location between the Plaza Pilatos and the cathedral. Take a cab – it's hard to find.

Hostal Goya, C/Mateos Gago 31, **t 95 421 11 70, **f** 95 456 29 88. Makes up for its slight gloominess by being located on the most animated street in the *barrio*.

*Hostal Bailén, C/Bailén 75, **t** 95 422 16 35. A delightful old building with a garden and courtyard in the Santa Cruz quarter.

Hostal Naranjo, C/San Roque 11, **t 95 422 58 40, **f** 95 421 69 43. Located on a tranquil residential street in a shady old building; also in the Santa Cruz quarter.

Hostal Londres, C/San Pedro Mártir 1, **t 95 421 28 96, **f** 95 421 28 96. Near the Fine Arts Museum, a quiet place with pretty balconies overlooking the street.

*Hostal La Francesa, C/Juan Rabadan 28, **t** 95 438 31 07. Has just three little rooms and no bath in a quiet part of town, close to the river and the St Lorenzo church.

Eating Out

Restaurants in Seville are more expensive than in most of Spain, but even around the cathedral and the Santa Cruz Quarter there are a few places that can simply be dismissed as tourist traps. Remember that in the evening the *sevillanos*, even more than most Andalucíans, enjoy bar-hopping for tapas, rather than sitting down to one meal.

Expensive

Taberna del Alabardero, C/Zaragoza 20, **t** 95 456 29 06, **f** 95 456 36 66. Northwest of La Giralda, you can dine memorably in this grand mansion which once belonged to a *sevillano* poet; it's one of Seville's most celebrated restaurants, with Michelin-stars and is now also home to an illustrious school for chefs. Specialities include wild-boar ragout, fresh artichokes and Jabugo ham in olive oil, and *urta* (a firm-fleshed, white fish caught locally around Rota) cooked in red wine. The staff are friendly and very knowledgeable. Head up the grand marble staircase overhung with an ornate chandelier to a series of wood-panelled dining rooms set around the central courtyard, each with a different ambience. There is also a handful of elegant guest rooms available if you over-indulge and can't make it home (*see* 'Where to Stay', above). The *taberna* is open daily year-round. Its light-filled café in the central glassed-over courtyard serves an excellent set lunch at 1,500 pts, and wonderful cakes and pastries in the afternoons. There is also a sumptuous tile-lined bar with an adventurous range of tapas, such as red peppers stuffed with bull's tail, and octopus served with potatoes and local cheese.

La Albahaca, Plaza Santa Cruz 12, **t** 95 422 07 14. Situated on one of Seville's most delightful small squares. There is a Basque twist to many of the beautifully prepared classic dishes; specialities have included scorpion fish with fennel and peanuts, and mushrooms with green asparagus, but the menu changes with the season. *Closed Sun*.

Corral del Agua, Callejón del Agua 6, **t** 95 422 48 41. Well-seasoned travellers usually steer clear of cutesy wishing-wells, but the garden in which this one stands is a haven of peace and shade, perfect for a lazy lunch or an unashamedly romantic dinner. You will find it next to Washington Irving's garden.

Egaña-Oriza, C/San Fernando 41, **t** 95 422 72 54, **f** 95 441 21 06. Splendidly situated on the corner of the Jardines Alcázar, opposite the university, this is one of Seville's best-loved restaurants. Among its tempting delights are clams on the half-shell, baked *hongos* mushrooms, and a kind of *sevillano* jugged hare. *Closed Sat lunch, Sun and Aug*.

Bar España, C/San Fernando. Attached to the Egaña-Oriza, this tapas bar is chic, bright, cosmopolitan – and the Basque tapas are sensational.

Jaylu, C/Virgen del Águila 8, **t** 95 428 17 36. You can dine here on some of the city's best and freshest seafood. *Closed Sun*.

Casa Nobles, C/Alvarez Quintero 58, **t** 95 456 32 72, *www.arrakis.es*. In a wonderful setting, with dishes combining traditional *andaluz* cooking and the best of new cuisine. It specializes in home-made pastries.

Moderate

La Juderia, C/Caño y Cueto, **t** 95 441 20 52, **f** 95 441 21 06. Tucked away in the old Jewish

quarter, with brick arches and terracotta tiles. There is an almost bewildering range of richly flavoured regional dishes, like *cola de toro* – oxtail stew, the house speciality – game in season, dozens of fish dishes and, to finish up, delicious homemade desserts. *Closed Tues and Aug*.

Marea Grande, C/Diego Angulo Iñiguez 16, **t** 95 453 80 00. Fish-lovers should head slightly out of the centre for this plush establishment, justly considered one of the city's finest seafood restaurants. *Closed end of Aug and Sun*.

La Dorada, Avenida Ramon y Cajal, **t** 95 492 10 66. Serves delicately prepared fish and shellfish. *Closed Sun*.

Rincón de Casana, C/Santo Domingo de la Calzada, **t** 95 453 17 10, **f** 95 453 17 10. Fine traditional cuisine served in rustic surroundings. *Closed Sun from June to Aug*.

Becerrita, C/Recaredo 9, **t** 95 453 37 27, **f** 441 20 57. Run by the affable Jésus Becerra, who serves traditional *andaluz* dishes in small, intimate surroundings. *Closed Sun eves*.

Enrique Becerra, C/Gamazo 2, **t** 95 421 30 49, **f** 95 422 70 93. Enrique followed in his father's footsteps (he is the 5th generation of this family of celebrated *sevillano* restaurateurs), with this prettily tiled restaurant. The menu is based on flavoursome regional dishes accompanied by a variety of delicious breads. For dessert, try the house speciality, *pudding de naranjas Santa Paula*, made with *sevillano* marmalade from the Convent of St Paula. There is also a lively tapas bar. *Closed Sun and the last two weeks of July*.

Los Seises, C/Segovias 6, **t** 95 422 94 95, **f** 95 422 43 34. In the Hotel los Seises, deep in Santa Cruz, you'll find this restaurant with fine classic dishes served in the sumptuous surroundings of an old archbishop's palace at surprisingly reasonable prices.

Hotel Salvador Rojo, C/San Fernando 23, **t** 95 422 97 25. Near Hotel Alfonso XIII and yet virtually hidden. The décor is almost spartan, which is all the more reason to concentrate simply on the food, a selection of very creative *andaluz* dishes deftly prepared by Salvador Rojo himself.

El Bacalao, Plaza Ponce de Léon 15, **t** 95 421 66 70 or 95 422 49 52. For infinite varieties of *bacalao* (dried salted cod), this delightful restaurant and tapas bar is the only place to go; some meat and game dishes are also served. *Closed Sun eves*.

Mesón Don Raimundo, t 95 422 33 55, f 95 421 89 51. By the cathedral, in the narrow Argote de Molina (at No.26), and set in a 17th-century convent with an eclectic décor of religious artefacts and suits of armour. No enforced abstinence here, though. You can pig out on the large selection of traditional *andaluz* dishes based on fish, shellfish and game, to the accompaniment of fine wines from an extensive list. *Closed Sun eves*.

Las Meninas, C/Santo Tomás 3, t 95 422 62 26. Also owned by Don Raimundo; draws big crowds for its hearty but cheap portions.

Río Grande, C/Betis s/n, t 95 427 39 56, f 95 427 98 46. Along the Triana side of the Guadalquivir, you can dine here with a tremendous view of the Tower of Gold and La Giralda, and even join in with the whoops from the bullring opposite if a *corrida* is in progress. The kitchen here specializes in regional cuisine, including braised bull's tail and a good *gazpacho*, but the cuisine usually fails to match the splendid views.

Ox's, C/Betis 61, t 95 427 95 85, f 95 427 84 65. A delightful *asador* (grill room) with novelties from Navarra – cod-stuffed peppers, fish and steaks grilled over charcoal for a delicious smoky piquancy. *Closed Sun eves, Mon and Aug*.

Restaurante San Marco, C/Cuna 6, t 95 421 24 40, f 95 456 40 85. Back in the winding pedestrian and shopping district, and set in an 18th-century palace with an enormous Moorish carved wooden door. The cuisine is Franco-Italian and the desserts are particularly good. *Closed Mon lunchtime and Sun*.

Inexpensive (*see* also 'Tapas Bars' below)

Pizzeria San Marco, Meson del Moro 6–10, t 95 421 43 90. Run by the same family as the Restaurante San Marco (*see* above), with excellent pizzas and a wide range of pasta dishes in an old Arab bath-house. The prices and the relaxed, stylish décor attract a young, chatty crowd.

Bodegón Torre del Oro, C/Santander 15, t 95 421 42 41, f 95 421 66 28. The rafters here are hung with dozens of different hams and the dining room shares the space with the

bar. There's a three-course set meal with wine and the *raciones* are excellent.

Casa Salva, C/Pedro del Toro 12, t 95 421 41 15. A tiny, unassuming and very welcoming restaurant near the Fine Arts Museum. The fresh, simple menu changes daily. *Open Mon–Fri lunchtimes only*.

La Illustre Victima, C/Doctor Letamandi 35 (not far from the Plaza de Alamede de Hércules). A friendly, laid-back and pleasingly chaotic café, bar and restaurant with painted murals and colourful walls. It serves a variety of snacks, including some very reasonable pasta and couscous dishes, *enchiladas* and *fajitas*, some suitable for vegetarians.

Vegetarian

La Mandrágora, C/Albuera 11, t 95 422 01 84. In a country where meat and fish reign supreme, it's a nice surprise to find La Mandrágora, a very friendly vegetarian restaurant with an excellent and wide-ranging menu; everything is home-cooked – even the piquant salsas. *Closed Sun*.

Jalea Real, C/Sor Angela de la Cruz (at the corner of C/Jerónimo Hernandez), t 95 421 61 03. Not far from Plaza de la Encarnación – a delightful place with an excellent, healthy and cheap three-course lunch menu.

In Situ, Plaza de Alameda de Hércules 94. A newish craft shop, organic delicatessen, vegetarian café and Internet centre in one; situated just off the Plaza de Alameda de Hércules. *Closed Sun*.

Ice-cream and *Pastelerías*

La Campana, on C/Sierpes. I head here for delicious cakes, coffee or ice-cream.

Ochoa, on C/Sierpes. Another of the city's prettiest old *pastelerías*.

Horno Santa Cruz, C/Guzmen el Bueno 12. Pretty blue and white tiles and a lovely plant-filled courtyard – the perfect place to buy your bread and pastries.

Il Garibaldi, in the Santa Cruz quarter. Has an incredible range of homemade Italian-style ice creams and frozen yogurts, as well as tiramisu and cheesecake. Try the *horchata*, a delicious almond-flavoured milk drink.

Alfafa 10, at No.10. One of the nicest café-bars on trendy Plaza de Alfalfa, with very untypical but delicious cappuccino and strudel.

Tapas Bars

Tapas bars are an intrinsic part of daily life in Seville, and even the smartest restaurants, such as the Taberna del Alabardero, Egaña-Oriza, El Bacalao and many others, often have excellent tapas bars attached (*see* above).

El Rinconcillo, at C/Gerona 42 (north of the cathedral, between the Church of St Pedro and the Convent of Espíritu Santo). The oldest bar in Seville, this is reputedly where the custom of topping a glass with a slice of sausage or a piece of bread and ham – the first tapas – began. Decorated in moody brown *azulejos*, the place dates back to 1670 and is frequented by lively *sevillano cognoscenti*, who gather to enjoy the tasty nibbles. The staff, oblivious, chalk up the bill on the bar.

Bar Manolo, on buzzing Plaza de Alfalfa. The best of several tapas bars on the square. It's lively at breakfast time as well as in the evening.

Bar El Refugio, C/Huelva 5. Just round the corner, with delicious fried vegetables served with a creamy *béchamel* sauce.

Bar Alicantina, on the Plaza del Salvador. Has great *ensalada rusa* and is a favoured hangout of the young and fashionable.

La Eslava, C/Eslava 3, **t** 95 490 65 68. Many of Seville's most renowned tapas bars also have dining rooms at the back; this is one of the nicest, serving a wide range of excellent tapas, including a delicious version of *salmorejo*, the thick Cordoban gazpacho soup topped with chopped boiled egg and ham. The popular restaurant has a more extensive menu and can get very crowded. *Closed Sun, Mon eve and Aug.*

Casa Morales, C/García de Vinuesa 11, **t** 95 422 12 42. In the Santa Cruz quarter, just a skip away from the cathedral, this is purportedly Seville's second-oldest bar, with old pottery wine casks, sawdust scattered across the tiled floor and a range of simple tapas.

Bar Modesto, C/Cano y Cueto 5, **t** 95 441 68 11. Another well-established favourite with wonderful seafood tapas, and a dining room for full meals.

La Bodeguita de Santa Julia, C/Hernando Colon 1 (near the cathedral). Serves some of Seville's most traditional and tastiest tapas.

Bar Giralda, C/Mateos Gago 1, **t** 95 422 74 35. In an old Moorish bath-house, with a great range to choose from; popular with tourists and locals.

Hostaría del Laurel, Plaza de los Venerables 5, **t** 95 422 02 95. Serves superb tapas in a room filled with hanging *jamon* and beautiful Triana tiles.

Infanta Seville, C/Arfe 36, **t** 95 422 96 89. Heading down towards the river, this is a very stylish bar popular with yuppies who come for the excellent tapas; the range is limited but the quality is outstanding. Try the chorizo sausage or the *bacalao*.

Sol y Sombre, C/Castilla 149–151, **t** 95 433 39 35. Over in Triana, this is an atmospheric place covered in *taurino* memorabilia, with more superb tapas.

Kiosko de las Flores. A pretty and informal café-bar partly overlooking the river, justly celebrated for its *pescaítos fritos*.

Bodega La Albariza, C/Betis 6A, **t** 95 433 20 16. Serves its astonishing range of tapas on empty sherry casks in the bar. There is a little dining area at the back with a very reasonably priced menu.

Las Golondrinas, C/Antillano Campos 26. Come here for great *alcachofa* (artichoke) and tortilla in a charming tiled two-floor bar.

Bodega Santa Cruz, on the corner of C/Rodrigo Caro. Attracts a young university crowd and serves an excellent selection of tapas , which will be chalked up at your place at the bar.

Las Teresas, C/Sta Teresa. A traditional café-bar deep in the heart of the *barrio*, its walls lined with old photos.

Entre Calles, C/Ximenez de Encisco. An old, dark and atmospheric tapas bar.

Casa Placido, C/Meson del Moro. Serves excellent and reasonably priced tapas in an old-style tiled bar.

Entertainment and Nightlife

Bars and Clubs

Red and white signs emblazoned *Cruzcampo* hang from many of the bars; this is Seville's most popular **beer**, a pale brew served ice cold either on draft or in bottles. Other favourites include San Miguel, and you should try Mahon Five Star if you see it.

The Plaza del Salvador fills up quickly in the evenings, so start your night with a chilled sherry at the tiny **Antigua Bodeguita**, or its next-door neighbour, **Los Soportales**, opposite the church. Sip the sherry with the locals out in the square or lounging on the church steps, and ponder your next move. One particular pleasure, in a city which pursues so many, is to set out on a bar crawl, trying different sherries and tapas (see 'Tapas Bars', above).

Many of the liveliest bars are around the Plaza de Alfalfa, which teems with revellers for most of the night; head down C/Boteros for some of the buzziest. C/Peres Galdos is another good street for popular bars, with hordes of youthful *sevillanos* and *sevillanas* spilling out on to the pavement. The Santa Cruz Quarter is equally vibrant, although you'll find more young foreigners here.

Bar Berlin, C/Boteros. Loud, crammed and great fun.

El Garlochi, C/Boteros. Changes decoration with the seasons – before Semana Santa, for example, it is scented with incense and filled with flowers.

Holiday, C/Jésus del Grand Poder. Come here if you want to dance until dawn – but don't even think about arriving before 2 or 3am.

La Subasta, C/Argote de Molina. Whitewashed walls and an old wooden bar, on a road packed with a string of popular bars.

Antigüedes, C/Argote de Molina. Has books suspended, pages flapping, from the ceiling.

Metropol, C/La Florida. A trendy new bar, recently opened as a café by day and a *bar de copas* with a DJ by night.

Flamenco

If you've been longing to experience flamenco, Seville is a good place to do it. The most touristy flamenco factories will hit you for 1,500 pts and upwards per drink. Bars in Triana and other areas do it better for less; C/Salado and environs in Triana, for example, has some good bars. There are more venues across the river in the Santa Cruz Quarter. The tourist office on Avenida de la Constitución has a notice board with up-to-date details of flamenco shows and special deals.

La Caseta, C/Febo 36. Young, vibrant and popular with locals, though a long way from pure flamenco.

El Simpecao, Paseo Nuestra Senora de la O. Youthful and occasionally impromptu, this place is not too far from the real thing.

La Carbonería, C/Levies 18. The king of modern flamenco, the late El Camaron de la Isla, used to play at this bar which is still one of the best venues in the city for extemporaneous performances of all styles. Cheap food such as *chorizo al inferno* (a spicy sausage served in a terracotta dish) is served at the back in the main performance area. The bar attracts a largely young, foreign crowd. Thursday is best for flamenco.

El Tamboril, on Plaza Santa Cruz. Come here for *sevillana* dancing (very similar to flamenco but slightly less tortured and frenetic); it's as popular with *sevillanos* as it is with tourists.

Los Gallos, t/f 95 421 69 81. A few doors away from El Tamboril, though less spontaneous. There's a 3,500 pts entrance charge and *sevillano* and flamenco dancing lit by the flashes of tourist cameras. *Open 9–11.30.*

El Palacio Andaluz, Avenida Maria Auxiliadora 18B, t 95 453 47 20. More formal, with a 1½hr show staged for tourists in an expensive resturant; the *4,000 pts* entrance fee includes drinks. *Open 7.30–10.*

Music, Theatre and Opera

They do play other kinds of music in Seville, and two publications, *El Giraldillo* and *Ocio*, available around town, have listings. Again, the tourist information office is very helpful. For mainstream drama, the best-known theatre is the **Lope de Vega Theatre**, Avenida María Luisa, t 95 459 08 53, built for the 1929 exhibition. The **Maestranza Theatre**, Paseo de Cristóbal Colón, t 95 422 33 44, has quickly established itself as one of the top opera houses in Europe.

Bullfighting

See a bullfight in the famous **Maestranza** if you can, but don't just turn up! Get tickets as far ahead as possible; prices at the box office, C/Adriano 37, t 95 422 35 06, will be cheaper than at the little stands on C/Sierpes.

Apart from in the Alhambra of Granada, the place where the lushness and sensu-
ality of al-Andalus survives best is Andalucía's capital. Seville may be Spain's
fourth-largest city, but it is a place where you can pick oranges from the trees, and
see open countryside from the centre of town. Come in spring if you can, when the
gardens are drowned in birdsong and the air becomes intoxicating with the scent of
jasmine and a hundred other blooms. If you come in summer, you may melt: the
lower valley of the Guadalquivir is one of the hottest places in Europe. The pageant
of Seville unfolds in the shadow of La Giralda, still the loftiest tower in Spain. Its size
and the ostentatious play of its arches and arabesques make it the perfect symbol for
this city, full of the romance of the south and delightful excess.

At times Seville has been a capital, and it remains Spain's eternal city; neither past
reverses nor modern industry have been able to shake it from its dreams. That its
past glories should return and place it alongside Venice and Florence as one of the
jewels in the crown of Europe, a true metropolis with full international recognition, is
the first dream of every *sevillano*. Seville is still a city very much in love with itself.
Even the big celebrations of Semana Santa and Feria – although enjoyable for the
foreigner (anyone from outside the city), with revelry in every café and on every
street corner – are essentially private; the *sevillanos* celebrate in their own *casitas*
with friends, all the time aware that they are being observed by the general public,
who can peek but may not enter, at least not without an *enchufe* ('the right connec-
tion'). Seville is much like a beautiful, flirtatious woman: she'll tempt you to her
doorstep and allow you a peck on the cheek – whether you get over the threshold
depends entirely on your charm.

History: from Hispalis to Isbiliya to Seville

One of Seville's distinctions is its long historical continuity. Few cities in western
Europe can claim never to have suffered a dark age, but Seville flourished after the fall
of Rome – and even after the coming of the Castilians. Roman **Hispalis** was founded
on an Iberian settlement, perhaps one of the cities of Tartessos, and it soon became
one of the leading cities of the province of Baetica, as well as its capital. **Itálica**, the
now ruined city, lies just to the northwest; it is difficult to say which was the more
important. During the Roman twilight, Seville seems to have been a thriving town. Its
first famous citizen, St Isidore, was one of the Doctors of the Church and the most
learned man of the age, famous for his great *Encyclopedia* and his *Seven Books
Against the Pagans*, an attempt to prove that the coming of Christianity was not the
cause of Rome's fall. Seville was an important town under the Visigoths, and after the
Moorish conquest it was second only to Cordoba as a political power and a centre of
learning. For a while after the demise of the western caliphate in 1023, it became an
independent kingdom, paying tribute to the kings of Castile. Seville suffered under
the Almoravids after 1091, but enjoyed a revival under their successors, the Almohads,
who made it their capital and built the **Giralda** as the minaret for their new mosque.

The disaster came for Muslim **Isbiliya** in 1248, 18 years after the union of Castile and
León. Fernando III's conquest of the city is not a well-documented event, but it seems
that more than half the population found exile in Granada or Africa preferable to

Castilian rule; their property was divided among settlers from the north. Despite the dislocation, the city survived, and found a new prosperity as Castile's window on the Mediterranean and South Atlantic trade routes (the River Guadalquivir is navigable as far as Seville). Everywhere in the city you will see its emblem, the word NODO (knot) with a double knot between the O and D. The word recalls the civil wars of the 1270s, when Seville was one of the few cities in Spain to remain loyal to Alfonso the Wise. 'No m'a dejado' ('She has not forsaken me'), Alfonso is recorded as saying; madeja is another word for knot, and placed between the syllables NO and DO it makes a clever rebus, besides being a tribute to Seville's loyalty to medieval Castile's greatest king.

From 1503 to 1680, Seville enjoyed a legal monopoly of trade with the Americas, and it soon became the biggest city in Spain, with a population of over 150,000. The giddy prosperity this brought, in the years when the silver fleet ran full, contributed much to the festive, incautious atmosphere that is often revealed in Seville's character. Seville never found a way to hold on to much of the American wealth, and what little it managed to grab was soon dissipated in showy excess. There was enough to attract great artists such as Velázquez, Zurbarán and Murillo. and the city participated fully in the culture of Spain's golden age – even Don Quixote was born here, conceived by **Cervantes** while he was doing time in a Seville prison for debt.

It was in this period, of course, that Seville was perfecting its charm. Poets and composers have always favoured it as a setting. The prototypes of Bizet's Carmen rolled their cigars in the Royal Tobacco Factory, and for her male counterpart Seville contributed Don Juan Tenorio, who evolved through Spanish theatre in plays by Tirso de Molina and Zorrilla to become Mozart's *Don Giovanni*; the same composer also used the city as a setting for *The Marriage of Figaro*. The historical ironies are profound: amidst all this opulence, Andalucía was rapidly declining from one of the richest and most cultured provinces of Europe to one of the poorest and most back-ward. Over the 17th and 18th centuries the city stagnated.

In 1936, the Army of Africa, under **Franco**'s command, quickly took control of Andalucía. In Seville, a flamboyant officer named Gonzalo Queipo de Llano single-handedly bluffed and bullied the city into submission, and as soon as the Moroccan troops arrived he turned them loose to butcher and terrorize the working-class district of Triana. Queipo de Llano was soon to be famous as the Nationalists' radio propaganda voice, in shrill, grotesque nightly broadcasts full of sexual innuendoes about the Republic's politicians, and explicit threats of what his soldiers would do to the Loyalists' women once they were conquered.

Various industrial programmes, including a new shipbuilding industry, were started up by Franco's economists in the 1950s, stemming the flow of mass emigration and doing something to reduce the poverty of the region. But when **King Juan Carlos** ushered in the return of democracy, the city was more than ready. In the late 1970s, Andalucíans took advantage of revolutionary regional autonomy laws, building one of the most active regional governments in the country. **Felipe González**, a Socialist from Seville, ran Spain from 1982 to 1996 (when the many political scandals of 1995 and economic discontent finally discouraged the electorate from returning him to office).

In 1992, crimped and prinked, Seville opened her doors to the world for **Expo '92**. Fresh romance and excess mingled with the old. New roads, new bridges and a new opera house combined with Moorish palaces and monuments in a vainglorious display that attracted 16 million visitors.

The Cathedral and Around

La Giralda

Open Mon–Sat 11–5, Sun and hols 2–6; adm. Information t 95 421 49 71.

A good place to start your tour of Seville is at one of Andalucía's most famous monuments. You can catch the 319ft tower of **La Giralda** peeking over the rooftops from almost anywhere in Seville; it will be your best friend when you get lost in the city's labyrinthine streets. This great minaret, with its *ajimeces* and brickwork arabesques, was built under the **Almohads**, from 1172 to 1195, just 50 years before the Christian conquest. Two similar minarets, built in the same period, still survive in Marrakesh and Rabat in Morocco, and the trio are known as the **Three Sisters**. The surprisingly harmonious spire stuck on top is a Christian addition. Whatever sort of turret originally existed was surmounted by four golden balls stacked up at the very top, designed to catch the sun and be visible to a traveller one day's ride from the city; all came down in a 13th-century earthquake. On the top of their spire, the Christians added a huge, revolving statue of Faith as a weathervane (many writers have noted the curious fancy of having a supposedly constant Faith turning with the four winds). **La Giraldillo** – the weathervane – has given its name to the tower as a whole. The climb to the top is fairly easy: instead of stairs, there are shallow ramps – wide enough for Fernando III to have ridden his horse up for the view after the conquest in 1248. He was probably not the first to ride up – it is likely that the *muezzin* used a donkey to help him to the top to call the faithful to prayer. For those without equine support, there are plenty of viewing ledges on the way up for a breather, and a handful of glassy chambers exhibiting fragments of La Giralda's past, such as the robust 14th-century door which combines Gothic motifs and verses from the Koran, and the memorial stone of Petrus de la Cera, one of the knights who seized the city in November 1248 and couldn't bear to leave. There are also the remains of the monstrous hooks and pulleys which hoisted the stones into place.

The Biggest Gothic Cathedral in the Whole World

The same opening hours as La Giralda; both are visited with one ticket.

For a while after the Reconquista, the Castilians who repopulated Seville were content to use the great Almohad mosque, built at the same time as La Giralda. But at the turn of the 1400s, in a fit of pious excess, it was decided to build a new cathedral so grand that 'future ages shall call us mad for attempting it'. If they were mad, at least they were good organizers – they got it up in slightly over a century. The architects are unknown, though there has been speculation that the original master was either French or German.

Semana Santa and Feria

The penitential rituals of the medieval *cofradías*, or fraternities, form the basis of the solemn processions at the heart of Seville's Semana Santa (Holy Week), although they owe their current theatrical pizzazz to the Baroque era. Every year between Palm Sunday and Easter Saturday, 57 *cofradías* hoist up their *pasos* (floats) and process through the crowds along the sinuous streets from their church to the great cathedral and back, taking, as decreed by a humane cardinal in the 17th century, the shortest possible route. Even this can take between four and twelve hours, with the occasional pit stop at a bar or local convenience. The musical accompaniment is a solemn and sonorous *marcha*, and, occasionally, a single voice will break in with a *saeta*, a soaring mournful song sung '*a capella*', and closely related to flamenco.

Most of the *cofradías* carry two *pasos*: the first, the Paso de Cristo, depicts a scene between the Last Supper and the Resurrection, and the second, called the Paso Palio, carries the Virgin, weeping at the death of her son. Both are ornately carved and gilded, but it is the second *paso* that draws all eyes as each *cofradía* vies to produce the most beautiful Virgin, resplendent in a richly embroidered cape and covered by a swaying canopy. There are two main contenders in this beauty contest: La Macarena (*see* p.148) and her rival from across the river in Triana, La Esperanza de Trianera (*see* p.144). But, in Seville, everyone has a Virgin, and the crowds will wait for hours to see 'their' Virgin pass.

The most important *cofradías* – El Silencio, El Gran Poder, La Macarena, El Calverio, La Esperanza de Trianera and Los Gitanos – are given top billing and process on Good Friday morning, the high point of Semana Santa. The heavy floats are carried by 20 to 30 *costaleros*, for whom it is a great honour to be chosen and who practise for weeks ahead of time. It's hard, hot and claustrophobic work hidden beneath the *paso*, and it's essential that their moves are synchronized and guided by the black-suited *capataz* (overseer). Around the floats are the Nazarenos in their macabre pointed hats and masks, carrying candles and banners. The Penitents, who follow the Paso de

---

The exterior, with its great rose window and double buttresses, is as fine as any of the Gothic cathedrals of northern Spain – if we could only see it. Especially on the western front, facing the Avenida de la Constitución, the buildings close in; walking around its vast bulk, past the fence of Roman columns joined by thick chains, is like passing under a steep and ragged cliff. Some of the best original sculptural work is on the two portals flanking the main door: the **Door of Baptism** (left) and the **Door of Birth** (right), which are covered with elaborate terracotta figures sculpted by the Frenchman Lorenzo Mercadante de Bretaña and his follower Pedro Millán during the late 15th century. The groundplan of this monster, roughly 400ft by 600ft, probably covers the same area as did the mosque. On the northern side, the **Court of the Orange Trees** (Patio de los Naranjos), planted accordingly, preserves the outline of the mosque courtyard. The Muslim fountain survives, along with some of the walls and arches. In the left-hand corner, the Moorish 'Gate of the Lizard' has hanging from it a stuffed crocodile, said to have been a present from an Egyptian emir asking for the hand of a Spanish infanta. Along the eastern wall is the entrance of the **Biblioteca**

Cristo and bear wooden crosses, are often performing authentic acts of penitence and process barefoot (many others just want to dress up and be in the show). They also wear the long flowing robes and masks of the Nazarenos, but their hoods are not supported by the conical *antifaz* and so hang down at the back. The official procession route, scented with thick clouds of incense, runs along C/Sierpes to Plaza El Salvador and Plaza de San Francisco, and then to the enormous cathedral itself. Boxes are set up for important figures, while the streets and balconies are crammed with up to a million spectators, most men in blue suits and the ladies in black *mantilla* veils. Easter Sunday sees the first bullfight of the year.

After all the gloom and solemnity of Semana Santa, Seville erupts a week or two later in a week-long party – the April Feria. Another medieval institution, it was re-introduced to the city by a Basque and a Catalan in the mid-19th century. Originally a cattle market, nothing remains of its original purpose other than the circus-style striped tents, or *casetas*, which have become increasingly ornate through the years (prizes are awarded for the most beautiful) and are divided into two sections: the front has stalls for food and drink and the back is used for dancing. The drink, of course, is sherry, and calculations suggest that as much is drunk in this one week in Seville as the rest of Spain drinks in a year. Having the right connections, or *enchufe*, is supremely important: to be denied entrance to the most élite tents is to lose considerable face (it helps if you've made some local friends). The Feria now takes place in the *barrio* of Los Remedios, but the council is besieged by so many applications for *casetas* that it may have to move again. The streets are decorated with thousands of lanterns; horses and carriages push through dense, jubilant crowds, many people wearing traditional costume (the women's flamenco costumes are especially dazzling); and the nearby funfair reverberates with screams of laughter. The festivities begin with a ceremonial lighting of the lanterns at midnight on Monday and culminate in a firework extravaganza the following Sunday, which also marks the official opening of the bullfighting season at La Maestranza.

Colombina, a library of ancient manuscripts and an archive of the explorer's life and letters, founded by his son, who obviously inherited his father's itchy feet. He travelled with his father to the Indies, took expeditions to Africa and Asia, and was part of Charles V's entourage in Flanders, Germany and Italy. He collected over 20,000 volumes on his travels, and bequeathed them to the city when he died in 1539.

The cathedral's cavernous interior overpowers the faithful with its size more than its grace or beauty. The main altarpiece is the world's biggest *retablo*, almost 120ft high and entirely covered with carved figures and golden Gothic ornaments; it took 82 years to make, and takes about a minute to look at. Just behind the Large Chapel (Capilla Mayor) and the main altar, the **Royal Chapel** (Capilla Real) contains the tombs of St Fernando, conqueror of Seville, and of Alfonso the Wise; Pedro the Cruel and his mistress, María de Padilla, are relegated to the crypt underneath. Above the iron grille at the entrance to the Royal Chapel, the Moor Axataf hands over the keys of the city to a triumphant Fernando III. The art of the various chapels around the cathedral is lost in the gloom, but Murillo's masterpiece *La Visión de San Antonio* (1656) hangs in the Chapel of St Antonio (in the northern aisle), and a luminous, stark *retablo* depicting the life of St Paul by Zurbarán is fixed in the Chapel of St Pedro (to the left of the Royal Chapel). In the southern aisle, four stern pall-bearers on a high pedestal support the **tomb of Christopher Columbus**, although his bones were shifted, lost and reclaimed with such regularity that it is impossible to know with any certainty whose remains are borne so ceremoniously aloft. The pall-bearers represent the kingdoms of Castile, León, Navarra and Aragón. Columbus has been something of a refugee since his death. In the 16th century his remains were moved from Valladolid to the island of Santo Domingo, and after Dominican Independence from there to Havana cathedral. In 1899, after Cuba became independent, he was brought to Seville, and this idiosyncratic monument was put up to honour him. In the Dominican Republic, they'll tell you Columbus is still buried in Santo Domingo. Of course, most Spaniards are convinced that Columbus was born in Spain, not in Genoa, so it is appropriate that the life of this most elusive character should have mysteries at both ends.

Most of the cathedral's collections are housed in a few chambers near the entrance. In the **Chapter House**, which has an Immaculate Conception by Murillo, Seville's bishop can sit on his throne and pontificate under the unusual acoustics of an elliptical Baroque ceiling. The adjacent **Sacristy** contains paintings by Zurbarán, Murillo, van Dyck and others, most in dire need of restoration. Spare a moment for the reliquaries. Juan de Arfe, maker of the world's biggest silver monstrances, is represented here with one that is almost a small palace, made with 900lbs of silver and complete with marble columns. Spain's most famous, and possibly most bizarre, reliquary is the **Alfonsine Tables**, filled with over 200 tiny bits of tooth and bone. They were said to have belonged to Alfonso the Wise and were made to provide extra-powerful juju for him to carry into battle. (Interestingly, 'Alfonsine tables' also refers to the famous astronomical tables made for the same king by Jewish scholars of Toledo, until the 1600s used all over Europe to calculate eclipses and the movements of the planets.)

The Archive of the Indies (Archivo de Indias)

Open Mon–Fri 10–1, closed Sat–Sun; research, by appointment, 8–3,
t 95 421 12 34.

In common with most of its contemporaries, parts of Seville's cathedral were public ground, and were used to transact all sorts of business. A 16th-century bishop put an end to this practice, but prevailed upon Philip II to construct next to the cathedral an **Exchange** (Lonja), for the merchants. Philip sent his favourite architect, Juan de Herrera, then still busy with El Escorial, to design it. The severe, elegant façades are typically Herreran, and the stone balls and pyramids on top are practically the architect's signature. By the 1780s, little commerce was still going on in Seville, and what was left of the American trade passed through Cadiz. Also, two foreigners, a Scot and a Frenchman, had had the gumption to publish histories of the Indies unflattering to the Spanish, so Charles III converted the lonely old building to hold the **Archive of the Indies**, the repository of all the reports, maps and documents that the Crown had collected during the age of exploration. Inside, a glorious staircase of rosy jasper marble leads handsomely to the upper floors, where the artefacts and treasures are stored in almost six miles of 18th-century Cuban mahogany and cedarwood shelves.

The Alcázar

Open summer Tues–Sat 9.30–7, Sun and hols 9.30–5; winter Tues–Sat 9.30–5, Sun and hols 9.30–1.30; closed Mon; adm.

It's easy to be fooled into thinking this is simply a Moorish palace; some of its rooms and courtyards seem to come straight from the Alhambra (*see* pp.99–104). Most of them, however, were built by Moorish workmen for **King Pedro the Cruel** of Castile in the 1360s. The Alcázar and its king represent a fascinating cul-de-sac in Spanish history and culture, and allow the possibility that Al-Andalus might have assimilated its conquerors rather than been destroyed by them.

Pedro was an interesting character. In Froissart's *Chronicle*, we have him described as 'full of marveylous opinyons...rude and rebell agaynst the commandements of holy churche'. Certainly he didn't mind having his Moorish artists, lent by the kings of Granada, adorn his palace with sayings from the Koran in Kufic calligraphy. Pedro preferred Seville, still half-Moorish and more than half-decadent, to Old Castile, and he filled his court here with Moorish poets, dancers and bodyguards – the only ones he trusted. But he was not the man for the job of cultural synthesis. The evidence, in so far as it is reliable, suggests he richly deserved his honorific 'the Cruel', although to many underdog *sevillanos* he was Pedro the Just. Long before Pedro, the Alcázar was the palace of the Moorish governors. Work on the Moorish features began in 712 after the capture of Seville. In the 9th century it was transformed into a palace for Abd ar-Rahman II. Important additions were made under the Almohads, since the Alcázar was their capital in al-Andalus. Almost all the decorative work you see now was done under Pedro, some by the Granadans and the rest by Muslim artists from Toledo; altogether it is the outstanding production of *mudéjar* art in Spain.

The Alcázar is entered through the little gate on the Plaza del Triunfo, on the southern side of the cathedral. The first courtyard, the **Court of León**, has beautiful arabesques, with lions amid castles for Castile and León; this was the public court of the palace, where visitors were received, corresponding to the Mexuar at the Alhambra. At the far end of the courtyard is the lovely façade of the interior palace, decorated with inscriptions in Gothic and Arabic scripts.

Much of the best *mudéjar* work can be seen in the adjacent halls and courts; their seemingly haphazard arrangement was in fact a principle of the art, to increase the surprise and delight in passing from one to the next. Off the Court of León is the **Hall of Justice**, with a stunning star-shaped coffered ceiling, where Pedro I passed the sentence of death on his brother, who had had the temerity to have an affair with Pedro's wife (*see* Convent of Santa Clara, p.148). Behind it, the secluded **Court of Plaster** is largely a survival of the Almoravid palace of the 1170s, itself built on the site of a Roman *praetorium*. The **Court of the Maidens**, entered through the gate of the palace façade, is the largest of the courtyards and is named for the young Christian maidens who were given as brides as peace offerings to the Moors. The Islamic motto 'None but Allah conquers' is entwined with the heraldic devices of the Kingdom of

Castile and León, and the gallery was added during the reign of Charles V. The court-yard leads to the **Hall of the Ambassadors**, a small domed chamber that is the finest in the Alcázar despite the jarring addition of carved balconies from the time of Philip II. In Moorish times this was the throne room. Another small courtyard, the **Court of the Dolls**, once the hub of the palace's domestic life, takes its name from two tiny faces on medallions at the base of one of the horseshoe arches – a little joke on the part of the Muslim stone-carvers; to find them will bring luck (look on the right-hand arch of the northern gallery). The columns come from the ruins of Medinat az-Zahra.

Spanish kings couldn't leave the Alcázar alone. Ferdinand and Isabella spoiled a large corner of it for their **Casa de Contratación**, a planning centre for the colonization of the Indies. There's little to see in it: a big conference table, Isabella's bedroom, a model of the *Santa María* in wood, and a model of the royal family (Isabella's) in silver.

Charles V, who was married here in 1526 to Isabelle of Portugal, added a **palace** of his own, as he did in the Alhambra. This contains a spectacular set of **Flemish tapestries** showing finely detailed scenes of Charles' campaigns in Tunisia. Within its walls, the Alcázar has extensive and lovely **gardens**, with reflecting pools, avenues of clipped hedges, and lemons and oranges everywhere. The park is deceptively large, but you can't get lost unless you find the little **labyrinth** near the pavilion built for Charles V in the lower gardens. Outside the walls, there is a formal promenade called the **Plaza Catalina de Ribera** with two monuments to Columbus, and the extensive **Jardines de Murillo**, bordering the northern wall of the Alcázar.

From the Cathedral to the River: El Arenal

Avenida de la Constitución, passing the façade of the cathedral, is Seville's main street. Between it and the Guadalquivir is the neighbourhood of El Arenal, once the city's bustling port district, thronged with sailors, shopkeepers, idlers and prostitutes. Those colourful days have long passed – even its old name, 'Baratillo' meaning 'sham-bles', was changed in the 18th century by writers in search of a more romantic past. El Arenal means, poetically, 'expanse of sand', referring to its isolation outside the old Arabic city perimeter, when only a slim stretch of wall along the river protected it from invaders. Now it is a quiet, tranquil district with small shops and cafés, without the distinction of the Santa Cruz Quarter, but with an earthy charm all of its own. Heading down to the river, you will pass through one of the few surviving rampart gates leading to the old port area, the Gate of Olive Oil (Postigo del Aceite), a 16th-century remodelling of an old Moorish gate, with long vertical grooves for slotting in flood barriers when the river sporadically burst its banks. The city's coat of arms was added in the refurbishment, along with a little chapel.

Hospital de la Caridad

Open Mon–Sat 9–1 and 3.30–6.30, Sun 9–1; adm.

Behind a colourful façade on C/Temprado is the **Charity Hospital**, built in 1647 in the old warehouse area which used to back on to the port. This piece of ground was used for hanging criminals until the 15th century, when the Cofradía de la Caridad sought permission to give the dead a Christian burial and provide shelter for the poor. The original hospital was established in the docklands Chapel of St Jorge, before its reconstruction in infinitely grander style during the 17th century. The new, improved hospital's benefactor was a certain Miguel de Mañara, a reformed rake who has been claimed (erroneously, as the dates just won't add up) as the prototype for Tirso de Molina's Don Juan.

The Worst Man in the World

Life does imitate art, sometimes, and it seems that rather than serving as a model for Tirso de Molina, Miguel de Mañara saw the play, *El Burlador de Seville*, in 1641 when he was fourteen years old, and decided that he himself would become Don Juan. His story is as *sevillano* as anyone could ask, but this Mañara was in fact a Corsican, the son of a wealthy landowner living in Spain. The Corsicans are almost as proud of him as they are of Napoleon.

Like Napoleon, he wasn't the most amazing of physical specimens, with unprepossessing features arranged around a big Corsican nose, but his intensity and force of character were always enough to get him in the door, and usually well beyond it. The first notorious scandal he caused in Seville was taken right out of the play. He seduced a woman named Dona Teresita Sanchez who was legendary for her chastity and virtue, and then killed her father when he caught them together in her bedroom. With the police on his heels, he managed to escape and joined the Spanish army fighting in the Netherlands, where he performed with such conspicuous bravery that eventually the charges against him were dropped, and he returned to Seville.

There were bigger escapades to come. Mañara travelled to Corsica, where he was not known, and seduced his own cousin. Then he went back to Seville and had another go at Dona Teresita, who after her father's murder had become a nun. God, apparently, had had enough of Miguel de Mañara, and He sent him a vision of his own death and funeral, late at night on the corner of Seville's Calle del Ataud and Calle de la Muerte (Street of the Coffin and Street of Death) and the old rake – he had reached the ripe old age of 21 – was frightened sufficiently to send a letter to Dona Teresita explaining his designs, and how he had planned to abandon her. The shock of learning that he had never really loved her was too much, and she died that night.

Mañara resolved to reform, and because this is Seville his redemption took a form as extreme as his former life of evil. At first he married, and behaved himself, but the visions of his own funeral kept recurring, and he eventually joined the fraternity of the Santa Caridad and took it over as prior. Here Mañara became a local legend. He spent his entire fortune on this hospital, and was known for personally caring for the sick during a plague, feeding the poor and comforting the afflicted; he even extended his pity to Seville's dogs, building the low trough in the convent wall to give them a drink. His confessions are still kept at the hospital's archive, and he is buried near the chapel entrance in a tomb, where he himself ordered the inscription: 'Here lie the ashes of the worst man the world has ever known.' There was a movement to make Mañara a saint, but so far he has only reached the title of Venerable.

Though it still serves its intended purpose as a charity home for the aged, visitors come to see the art in the hospital chapel. The entrance is through a shadowy magenta and ochre courtyard with a double gallery, palms, fountains and panels of 17th-century Dutch Delft tiles brought from a convent in Cadiz. Much of the chapel's art has gone, unfortunately – in the lobby they'll show you photographs of the four Murillos stolen by Napoleon. The remaining eight in the series still hang here, a cosy group of saints and miracles, among them St Isabel of Hungary tending the poor, and a wild-eyed Moses drawing water from the rock. Murillo, a close friend of Mañara, and a prominent lay brother, was also responsible for the *azulejo* panels on the chapel façade depicting a rampant St Jorge, St James and three, overwrought virtues, Faith, Hope and Charity. Among what remains inside are three works of art, ghoulish even by Spanish standards, that reflect the funereal obsessions of Miguel de Mañara, who commissioned them. Juan de Valdés Leal (1622–90) was a competent enough painter, but warmed to the task only with such subjects as you see here: a bishop in full regalia decomposing in his coffin, and Death snuffing out your candle. Even better than these is the anonymous, polychrome bloody Jesus, surrounded by smiling Baroque *putti*, who carry, instead of harps, whips and scourges. Murillo's reported judgement on these pictures was that 'one has to hold one's nose to look at them'.

The Mint (Casa de la Moneda) and the Tower of Gold (Torre del Oro)

On C/Santada stands the renovated **Tower of Silver** (Torre de la Plata) and, along from it on C/Hubana, the **Mint**, rebuilt in the 16th century from a 13th-century Muslim edifice, to cope with the flood of precious metals pouring in from the Indies. Here, the gold and silver marks of the Spanish empire were minted in dizzying quantities. Picture the scene when the annual silver fleet came in; for over a century the fleet's arrival was the event of the year, the turning point of an annual feast-or-famine cycle when debts would be made good, and long-deferred indulgences enjoyed.

The Moorish **Tower of Gold** (*t 95 422 24 19; open Tues–Fri 10–2, weekends 11–2; closed Aug; adm*), which takes its name from the gold and *azulejo* tiles that covered its 12-sided exterior in the days of the Moors, stands on the banks of the Guadalquivir. The tower, built by the Almohads in 1220, was the southernmost point of the city's fortifi-cations. In times of trouble a chain would be stretched from the tower and across the Guadalquivir; in 1248 the chain was broken by an attacking fleet led by Admiral Ramon de Bonifaz, the supply route with Triana was cut off and Seville fell. The inte-rior now houses the small **Museo Marítimo** (*open Tues–Sat 10–2, Sun 10–1*), with plans, models, documents, weapons and maps of the golden age of the explorers.

The Cathedral of Bullfighting

On the river, just north of the tower, is another citadel of *sevillano* charm. **La Maestranza bullring**, with its blazing white and ochre arches, is not as big as Madrid's, but it is still a lovely building, and perhaps the most prestigious of all *plazas de toros*. It was begun in 1760 under the auspices of the aristocratic equestrian society of the

Real Maestranza de Caballería (who still own it) in order to practise equestrian displays, including bullfights, and it was largely responsible for raising the profile of an otherwise dying and insalubrious neighbourhood. The Carlist Wars got in the way and the bullring was, amazingly, not finished until 1880, which is why it took on its characteristic oval shape – to squeeze itself in among the surrounding buildings. Today it is known as the 'cathedral of bullfighting' and is particularly celebrated for its extraordinary acoustics; it is said that every rustle of the matador's cape can be heard. From April until September, it carries a packed schedule; if you like to watch as your *rabo de toro* (oxtail) is prepared, you may be fortunate enough to see a *corrida* while in town (*see* 'Bullfights', pp.58–60). Inside is the **Museo Taurino** (*t 95 422 45 77; open daily 9.30–2 and 3–6, or 9–3 when a bullfight is being held; adm*), with a small shop, and displays of antique posters, portraits of celebrated bullfighters, the mounted heads of famous bulls, elaborate costumes and other memorabilia. Carmen stands haughtily outside, hand on hip, surveying the bullring which saw her tragic end in Bizet's opera.

The large, modern, circular building on the Paseo del Cristóbal Colón which echoes the shape of La Maestranza is the **Theatre of Maestranza** (*information t 95 422 33 44*), a grand opera house built for Expo '92. It displays a 19th-century grille from the local Maestranza de Artillería, or arsenal, which gave its name to the two buildings which have outlived it.

Triana

Across the Guadalquivir from the bullring is the neighbourhood of Triana, an ancient suburb that takes its name from the Emperor Trajan. Until the mid-19th century it was joined to the city centre by a pontoon, a flimsy string of boats which would get washed away by the frequent floods; finally, in 1852, the first fixed bridge was constructed, officially named the Bridge of Isabel II, but known to all as the **Bridge of Triana**. Even now, some people quickly glance at the carved lion's head at the Triana end of the bridge: an old superstition warns that, if the water rises to the lion's mouth, Seville will be flooded again. The bridge culminates in Plaza del Altozano, with a stern figure of the famous bullfighter Juan Belmonte (1892–1962), whose motto was purportedly 'stop, pacify and control'. He looks as if he could still manage it now.

The neighbourhood has a reputation for being the 'cradle of flamenco'. Queipo de Llano's troops wrecked a lot of it at the beginning of the Civil War, but there are still picturesque white streets overlooking the Guadalquivir.

On the riverbank on the right-hand side of the Bridge of Triana (with the bridge at your back) is the Paseo Nuestra Senora de la O, a charming avenue where a colourful and cheap produce market is now held. On the same spot, five centuries ago, the Castle of St Jorge, originally built by the Moors, became the infamous **Castle of the Inquisition**, a prison for those accused of Judaism, heresy and witchcraft. Seville's first auto-da-fé was held here in 1481 and the castle was destroyed only in 1820, when the Inquisition was finally abolished. The air used to be thick with fumes from the kilns which clustered around this part of town, and the streets around C/Castilla and C/San Jorge are still some of the best for finding Triana ceramics. The area's workmen make all Seville's *azulejo* tiles.

C/Betis, right on the river on the left-hand side of the Bridge of Triana, is one of the liveliest streets, with a string of popular bars and restaurants with wonderful views. The Feria de la Velá is held here in July, in honour of Triana's patron saint, Santa Ana, with dancing, buskers and street vendors. A gunpowder factory once stood here, until it exploded, catapulting dozens of people into the river.

The C/Pureza, behind it, leads to the Plaza de Santa Ana and one of the oldest Christian churches in the city. Towards the end of the 13th century, Alfonso X was miraculously cured of a strange disease of the eye and ordered the construction of a church in thanks. Built around 1276, the simple, Gothic church of **Santa Ana** holds a 16th-century *retablo* by Pedro de Campaña, and a fabulous *azulejo*-tiled tomb by Niculoso Pisano. The most famous treasure is the enormous silver monstrance which forms part of Triana's Corpus Chico procession. The square around the church becomes especially animated during big festivals, particularly around Corpus Christi and Christmas, when it erects a huge nativity scene.

Back on C/Pureza, there stands the lovely **Chapel of the Virgen de la Esperanza** (*open Mon–Sat 9–1 and 5.30–9, Sun 9–1*), home to Triana's celebrated weeping figure of the Virgin of Hope, main rival to the equally famous figure in the *barrio* of La Macarena (*see* p.148) during the Semana Santa processions and celebrations. The chapel is also known as the Chapel of Sailors (Capilla de los Marineros), who would come here to pray for a safe return from the new lands being discovered across the seas, and from where mass used to be bellowed, so that all the sailors in the galleons moored along the river could hear.

Triana was traditionally a rich recruitment area for the ships setting out to discover new lands and fabulous treasures. C/Rodrigo de Triana is named after a local sailor who voyaged to the Indies with Columbus and first spied the New World. Another chapel popular with seafarers is the chapel of the **Convent of Remedios** in the Plaza de Cuba; sailors would blast their cannons in homage to the Virgen de Los Remedios (Virgin of Redemption) as they passed in their galleons, and pray for her protection on their Atlantic voyages. The convent later became the Hispano-Cuban Institute for the History of America, but Franco closed it down after a tiff with Fidel Castro.

The street leading off the Plaza de Cubana into the relatively new suburban quarter of Los Remedios is named after **Juan Sebastián Elcano**, who sailed with Magellan on his fateful voyage round the world. Two hundred and sixty-five sailors left Seville in 1519 and, after they had battled their way around the Cape of Good Hope, Magellan was killed in the Philippines; Elcano took command of the last remaining ship and limped home with just 18 sailors three years later. Also near the Plaza de Cubana is **C/Salado**, undistinguished by day but the best place for dancing traditional *sevillanas* by night.

Northwest of the Cathedral: Art and the Auto-da-fé

Back across the river, over the Bridge of Triana, you'll approach the **San Eloy** district, full of raucous bars and hotels. On C/San Pablo is **La Magdalena** (1704), rebuilt by Leonardo de Figueroa on the ruins of the Dominican Convent of St Pablo, itself fused with an even older mosque. The eccentric Baroque façade is decorated with sundials, and the colourful dome is supported by long-suffering South American Indians. Among the art inside are two paintings of the Life of St Dominic by Zurbarán, and gilded reliefs by Leonardo de Figueroa. Above the door is a hint of the church's nefarious past: the shield of the Inquisition. Heresy trials took place in this church and the condemned were led through the Door of the Jews, since closed up and hidden behind a chapel. Heretics were then burned in the Prado de San Sebastián or in the Plaza de San Francisco, expressly remodelled for the purpose. Many of the paintings and frescoes celebrate the triumph of the Catholic faith and the suppression of heresy, including a mural by Lucas Valdés, son of Valdés Leal, depicting an auto-da-fé; the face of the accused was scratched out by his outraged descendants, and restorers had to fill in the blank.

Fine Arts Museum (Museo de Bellas Artes)

Open Tues 3–8, Wed–Sat 9–8, Sun 9–2, closed Mon.

This excellent collection is housed in the **Convent of Merced** (1612), on C/San Roque, expropriated for the state in 1835. It is set around three courtyards, the first of which is handsomely decorated with lustrous tiled panels taken from Seville's convents. There are some fine medieval works: some naïve-looking virgins, and an especially expressive triptych by the Master of Burgos from the 13th century. **Pedro Millán**, one of the most influential sculptors of the period, is well represented; the *Burial of Christ* is haunting and, in another sculpture, a mournful Christ stares in disbelief at the gash in his side. The Italian sculptor **Pietro Torrigiano** (the fellow who broke Michelangelo's nose, and who died here, in the Inquisition's prisons) has left an uncanny, barbaric wooden **St Jerome**. This saint, Jerónimo in Spanish, is a favourite in Seville, where he is pictured with a rock and a rugged cross instead of his usual lion. Torrigiano's *Virgen de Belén* (*c.* 1525) has a luminous clarity and stillness. There is a comprehensive collection of altarpieces and *retablos* from this period, with fiery scenes of hell and damnation, set off by the decapitated head of John the Baptist leering through a glass case. Through another of the lovely courtyards planted with orange trees, the main staircase, known as the Imperial Staircase, richly decorated in the Mannerist style with swarms of angels, leads to a room full of the works of the most mannered of them all, **Murillo** (a *sevillano*, buried in Santa Cruz). Among the paintings is an Immaculate Conception and many other artful missal-pictures, accompanied by a number of pieces by the prolific painter Valdés Leal. Much more interesting are the works of **Zurbarán**, who could express spirituality without the simpering of Murillo or the hysteria of the others. His series of female saints is especially good, and the *Miracle of St Hugo* is perhaps his most acclaimed work. An altarpiece he sculpted for the Monasterio Cartujo de Santa

Maria de las Cuevas (*see* p.152) has also found its way here. Occasionally even Zurbarán slips up; you may enjoy the *Eternal Father* with great fat toes and a triangle on his head, a *St Gregory* who looks like the scheming Church executive he really was, and the wonderful *Apotheosis of St Thomas Aquinas*, in which the great scholastic philosopher rises to his feet as if to say 'I've got it!' The room is dominated by an astounding *Cristo Crucifado* (*c.* 1630–40). Don't miss El Greco's portrait of his son Jorge, or the wonderful stark portraits by Ribera. There are also works by Jan Brueghel, Caravaggio and Mattia Preti, and a less interesting section of 19th- and 20th-century works, mainly portraits of coy *sevillanas*, fluttering their fans or dandling pooches, and dashing dandies, swaggering in their finery.

North of the Cathedral: the Heart of the City

Seville's business and shopping area has been since Moorish times the patch of narrow streets north of La Giralda. **Calle Sierpes** ('Serpent Street') is its heart, a sinuous pedestrian lane lined with every sort of old shop, named after an ancient inn sign which depicted the jaws of a snake – or perhaps just because it was so winding. It was once the heart of the city's nightlife and home to its most animated cafés. Just to the north, **El Salvador** is the city's second-biggest religious building after the cathedral, a fine Baroque church by Leonardo de Figueroa. It is picturesquely mouldering, its once-vibrant 'bull's blood' plasterwork now faded to a dusky rose. On the left is a door leading to the **Patio de los Naranjos**, with dilapidated Roman columns and arches that are all that remain of what was once the city's principal mosque (and before that a Visigothic cathedral and before that a Roman basilica) in a neat patchwork of pragmatic expropriation across two millennia and at least four sets of religious belief. The old minaret was turned into the belfry. The square in front of the church is one of Seville's liveliest, with *movida* kids sprawling on the church steps, and throngs of people sipping chilled sherry from the tiny *bodeguitas* opposite.

East of the Plaza del Salvador is little **Plaza Alfalfa**, now another vibrant nightspot, along with **Plaza de la Encarnación** a couple of streets to the north. The Plaza Alfalfa, once the site of the Roman forum and medieval markets selling meat and *alfalfa*, is at the heart of the city's oldest merchant district, with narrow half-timbered houses jostling for space. Many of the narrow streets and squares in this district are named after the trades that were once carried out here, like the C/de la Pescadería, once the scene of a busy fishmarket, and tiny Plaza del Pan, where the bakers plied their trade.

Not far from the Plaza de la Encarnación, on bustling C/Cuna, is the **Palace of the Countess of Lebrija** (Palacio de la Condesa de Lebrija; *open Mon–Fri 11–1 and 5–8, Sat 10–1, closed Sun; adm, special guided visits available, call* **t** *95 421 81 83*). It is worth a visit for its fine Roman mosaics brought from Itálica (*see* p.156), copies of which cover the entire first floor, while the original pieces hang, framed, on the walls. The vestibule glows with thousands of brightly coloured *azulejo* tiles, painted in Triana in the 18th century. A collection of tiny artefacts, also gleaned from Itálica, includes a handful of engraved signet rings made from cornelian, agate and glass, and shards of pottery (the prettiest are from Moorish pots which gleam like mother-of-pearl). Back out on C/Cuna are a number of Seville's fanciest flamenco shops, with all kinds of dresses and accessories.

On the **Plaza Nueva**, Seville's modern centre, you can see the grimy **City Hall** (Ayuntamiento), with a fine, elaborate Plateresque façade, built as the brand-new home for the town councillors in 1564, after Charles V complained at the shabbiness of their former home. The **Plaza de San Francisco**, which spreads out on the other side of the City Hall, was remodelled at the same time in order to serve as a suitably grand backdrop for the city's processions and its executions. On the Plaza Nueva façade, a barely discernible grimy old notice calls the faithful to mass at 8am on weekdays and 12.30pm on Sundays; this is all that remains of the Friary of San Francisco, once one of the oldest and most important in Seville, which stood next to the City Hall. From here, Avenida de la Constitución changes its name to C/Tetuán. Seville has found a hundred ways to use its *azulejos*, but the best has to be in the **billboard** on this street for 1932 Studebaker cars – so pretty that no one's had the heart to take it down.

La Macarena and Around

The northern end of Seville contains few monuments, though most of its solid, working-class neighbourhoods are clustered around Baroque parish churches. The **Alameda de Hércules** has been adorned since the 16th century with statues of Hercules, the mythical founder of the city, and Julius Caesar, credited with building the city's walls. This is the centre of one of the shabbier, yet most appealing, parts of the city, with a smattering of laid-back bars, music shops and cafés now paving the way for a new wave of gentrification. A fashionable promenade until the late 19th century, it nose-dived into shabby disrepute when the *bordellos* and gambling dens took over at the end of the 19th century, and then had another brief flicker of glory as one of the foremost flamenco venues in Andalucía in the early 1900s. Statues of two of flamenco's finest performers, Aurora Pavón and Monold Caracol, stand at either end of the avenue. Pick up a flouncy secondhand flamenco frock at the atmospheric **flea market**, held here on Thursdays and Sundays, with an eccentric collection of tat from faded books and paintings to old machinery from every conceivable era and occupation, bicycles of dubious origin, and several kitchen sinks. The square was built over the dried-out riverbed of a tributary of the Guadalquivir and was plagued with flooding until relatively recently; rowing boats had to ferry the marooned residents between their homes and it became known as La Laguna de Feria after the neighbouring popular district of **La Feria**, which abuts it. The earthy *barrio* of La Feria is a delightfully old-fashioned, mercantile quarter, once the district of artisans and wool craftsmen, made up of a patchwork of crooked streets around the wide boulevard of C/de la Feria itself. Thursday mornings are particularly lively, animated by **El Jueves**, the celebrated antiques and bric-a-brac market, which has been going strong since the 13th century.

Santa Clara and **San Clemente** are two interesting 13th-century monasteries in this area, both established soon after Fernando III's victory over the Muslims in 1289; the former includes one of Seville's best *artesonado* ceilings and a Gothic tower built by Don Fadrique. There were two Don Fadriques, both of whom came to sticky ends, and both of whom are responsible for the tower according to separate legends. The first was Fernando III's son, who built his palace on this spot and carried on an affair with his widowed stepmother, to the disgust of his brother, who had him executed; the second was Pedro the Cruel's brother, who began an affair with Doña Blanca, Pedro's abandoned wife, for which he too lost his head. This isn't the only dramatic tale which clings to the convent: Pedro I, an infamous womanizer, pursued a terrified gentlewoman named Doña Maria, stripped her husband of his lands and property and executed him. Doña Maria took refuge in the convent and disfigured herself by throwing burning oil on her face. At least this story doesn't have an entirely sad ending: eventually her lands were returned to her and she founded the Convent of Santa Ines in 1374. Her tomb is opened annually on 2 December and her body is said never to have decomposed. The **Convent of San Clemente** is the city's oldest, built on the remains of a Moorish palace; once a rich convent which enjoyed royal patronage, it was stripped of its lands during the Napoleonic occupation, when the nuns were ousted and the buildings were seconded for use as a warehouse and prison. A beautiful 16th-century *mudéjar* coffered ceiling and handsome frescoes by Valdés Leal and his son managed to survive the sacking. The city has just approved a plan to turn the two convents into an interactive audiovisual museum of Seville's history, with, among other things, the scent of orange blossom exuding at the touch of a button.

Also near the Alameda de Hércules is the imposing **Basilica of Jesús de la Grand Poder**, a favourite spot for *sevillano* weddings. The basilica contains a celebrated and much revered 17th-century statue of the same name by Juan de Mesa. It is solemnly paraded through the streets on Good Friday morning.

North of C/San Luis, some of the city's **Moorish walls** survive, near the **Basilica of La Macarena** (*open daily 9–1 and 5–9; adm for museum*), which gives the quarter its name. The basilica, a garish 1940s neo-Baroque construction luridly frescoed with puffs of fluorescent angels, is the home of the most worshipped of Seville's idols, a delicate Virgin with glass tears on her cheeks who always steals the show in the Semana Santa parades. Like a film star she makes her admirers gasp and swarm around her, crying '*¡O la hermosa! ¡O la guapa!*' ('O the beautiful! O the handsome!'). Fleets of veiled old ladies jostle for the closest position to her feet, and twitter over the thousands of photographs laid out in the shop. The small adjacent **museum** (*entrance inside the chapel*) is devoted to her costumes, a breathtaking giant-sized Barbie wardrobe of superbly embroidered robes encrusted with gold and jewels, and solid gold crowns and ceremonial paraphernalia. Also here are the elaborately carved and gilded floats which take part in the Semana Santa parades; the first depicts the moment when Pontius Pilate passed the sentence of death on Christ, and the second carries the Virgin herself, weeping for the death of her son.

South from here, along C/San Luis, you'll pass another Baroque extravaganza, Leonardo de Figueroa's **San Luis**, built for the Jesuits (1699–1731), with twisted columns and tons of encrusted ornament. Lovely **San Marcos**, down the street, has an elaborate façade with a graceful combination of Gothic and Moorish elements, and one of Seville's last surviving *mudéjar* towers. The austere interior, with its soaring wooden roof supported by beautifully carved and decorated supporting beams, is adorned with elegant, white, Moorish horseshoe-shaped arches. Just east is the **Convento de Santa Paula**, with a finely detailed doorway with pink and blue inlaid tiles by Francisco Pisano and Pedro Millán (1504), and a pretty, much embellished openwork bell tower. Inside is a little museum and shop selling jams and confectionery made by the nuns. Another post-1492 palace with *mudéjar* decoration, west on C/Bustos Tavera, is the huge **Palace of the Ladies** (Palacio de las Dueñas; *admission by prior application only; ask at the tourist office*).

Santa Cruz and Beyond

If Spain envies Seville, Seville envies **Santa Cruz**, a tiny, exceptionally lovely quarter of narrow streets and whitewashed houses. It appears to be the true homeland of everything *sevillano*, with flower-bedecked courtyards and iron-bound windows, though there is something unnervingly pristine about it. This is hardly surprising given that it was calculatedly primped up between 1912 and 1920 by the Ministry of Tourism. Before 1492, this was the Jewish quarter of Seville; today it's the most aristocratic corner of town (and the most touristy). In the old days there was a wall around the *barrio*; today you may enter through the Murillo Gardens, the C/Mateos Gago behind the cathedral apse, or from the **Patio de las Banderas**, a pretty Plaza Mayor-style square next to the Alcázar. In the heart of this area lies the **Hospital de los Venerables** (*information t 95 456 26 96; open daily 10–2 and 4–8; adm*), a former home for the elderly and now an art gallery set around a delightful courtyard. On the eastern edge of the *barrio*, **Santa María la Blanca** (on the street of the same name) was a pre-Reconquista church; some details remain, but the whole was rebuilt in the 1660s, with spectacular rococo ornamentation inside and paintings by Murillo. His former home, near little Plaza Alfara and the Murillo Gardens, has become a small **museum** devoted to his life and art.

On the eastern fringes of the old town, Santa Cruz fades gently into other peaceful, pretty areas – less ritzy, though their old streets contain more palaces. One of these, built by the Dukes of Medinaceli (1480–1571), is the **House of Pilate** (Casa de Pilatos; *t 95 422 52 98; open daily 9–7; Tues 1–5*) on Plaza Pilatos, one of Seville's loveliest hidden corners. The site once belonged to a judge who was condemned to death for heresy and had his lands confiscated by the Inquisition. They were snapped up by Don Pedro Enrique, the Governor of Andalucía, who began construction of a palace in 1481, of which only the dauntingly named Chapel of Flagellation remains. His son, yet another Don Fadrique, was responsible for the present pleasing jumble of *mudéjar* and Renaissance work, with a lovely courtyard and lots of *azulejos* everywhere. It was constructed just after his return from a pilgrimage to Jerusalem, where, so the story goes, he was so struck by the Praetorium, Pontius Pilate's official residence, that he decided to model his palace at home on it. The entrance, a mock-Roman triumphal arch done in Carrara marble by sculptors from Genoa, is studded with Crusaders' crosses in commemoration of the pilgrimage. Each year in March, a Via Crucis, following the Stations of the Cross, takes place between the House of Pilate and the Cruz del Campo, apparently the same distance as that between Pontius Pilate's house in Jerusalem and Mount Calvary. The entrance arch leads through a small courtyard into the **Patio Principal**, with 13th-century Granadan decoration, beautiful coloured tiles, and rows of Roman statues and portrait busts. These form a perfect introduction to the dukes' excellent collections of antique sculpture in the surrounding rooms, many with splendid pine-cone-coffered ceilings, including a Roman copy of a Greek *herm* (boundary marker, with the head of the god Hermes), imperial portraits, and a bust of Hadrian's boyfriend, Antinous. There is a series of delightful **gardens and courtyards**, inhabited by nymphs and cherubs, and cooled with trickling fountains and bowers; the rose garden is especially lovely, particularly in spring, when the walls erupt in a blaze of purple bougainvillea. There is an optional tour of the **private apartments** upstairs (*tours in Spanish only*), for a voyeuristic taste of how the other half live. You can see 18th-century furniture (particularly impressive in the sumptuous dining hall), paper-thin porcelain from England and Limoges, fanciful Japanese vases and a rather humdrum collection of paintings ranging from portraits of stolid dukes and duchesses to a bullfight (set in Madrid) by Goya.

Behind the House of Pilate, **San Esteban**, rebuilt from a former mosque, has an altar-piece by Zurbarán. Farther up on Avenida de Luis Montoto are the forlorn remains of an Almoravid **aqueduct**.

Nudging up against the House of Pilate is the **Convento de San Leandro**, founded in 1295, although this building dates from 1369, and has been considerably embellished and refurbished since. The original convent stood in the Field of Martyrs outside the city walls, but was brought in from the cold when the nuns complained of constant attacks from bandits and appealed to the king; Pedro I magnanimously donated them a piece of land confiscated from a 'disloyal' subject. Only the entrance courtyard can be viewed most of the year, but the richly endowed church, with two beautiful *retablos* by Juan Martínez Montañés, opens on the 22nd of each month, when hordes of supplicants descend to petition Santa Rita de Casia, the enormously popular patron saint of lost causes.

On C/Águilas, **San Ildefonso** has a pretty polychrome 18th-century façade, and two perky towers.

South of the Cathedral

Seville has a building even larger than its cathedral – twice as large, in fact, and probably better known to the outside world. Since the 1950s it has housed parts of the city's **university** and it does have the presence of a college building, but it began its life in the 1750s as the state **Tobacco Factory** (Fábrica de Tabacos). In the 19th century, it employed as many as 12,000 women to roll cigars. (One of its workers, of course, was Bizet's Carmen.) These sturdy women, with 'carnations in their hair and daggers in their garters', hung their capes on the altars of the factory chapels each morning, rocked their babies in cradles while they rolled cigars, and took no nonsense from anybody. Next to the factory, the **Hotel Alfonso XIII** (under scaffolding for another refurbishment at the moment), built in 1929, is believed to be the only hotel ever commissioned by a reigning monarch – Alfonso literally used it as an annexe to the Alcázar when friends and relations came to stay. This landmark is well worth a visit, if you're not put off by an icy doorman. To the west of the hotel lies the Baroque **Palacio de St Telmo**, originally a naval academy, which became the court of an offshoot of the royal family in the mid-19th century. The dowager duchess María Luisa Fernanda de la Bourbon donated the elegant 19th-century ornamental gardens, the Delicias Gardens, to the city in 1893, and they formed the basis of the stunning city park which would bear her name.

María Luisa Park

For all its old-fashioned grace, Seville has been one of the most forward-looking and progressive cities of Spain in the 20th century. In the 1920s, while they were redirecting the Guadalquivir and building the new port and factories that are the foundation of the city's growth today, the *sevillanos* decided to put on an exhibition. In a tremendous burst of energy, they turned the entire southern end of the city into an expanse of gardens and grand boulevards. The centre of it is the **Parque de María Luisa**, a paradisiacal half-mile of palms and orange trees, covered with flowerbeds and dotted with hidden bowers and pavilions, one of the loveliest parks in Europe. Two of the largest pavilions, built by Aníbal Gonzalez, on the **Plaza de América** have been turned into museums. The **Archaeological Museum** (*Museo Arqueológico; information t 95 423 24 01; open Tues 3–8, Wed–Sat 9–8, Sun and hols 9–2, closed Mon and Aug*), with an impressively dour neo-Plateresque façade, has an excellent collection of pre-Roman jewellery and icons, and some tantalizing artefacts from mysterious Tartessos. The Romans are represented, as in every other Mediterranean archaeology museum, with copies of Greek sculpture and oversized statues of emperors, but also with a mosaic of the Triumph of Bacchus, another of Hercules, architectural fragments, some fine glass, and finds of all sorts from Itálica and other nearby towns. Across the plaza, the **Museum of Popular Art and Customs** (*Museo de Artes y Costumbres Populares; information t 95 423 25 76; open Tues 3–8, Wed–Sat 9–8, Sun and hols 9–2, closed Mon*), in the Mudéjar Pavilion, with a gleeful motif of tiny unicorns and griffons dancing across blue tiles, is Andalucía's attic, with everything from ploughs and saucepans to flamenco dresses and exhibits from the city's two famous celebrations, Semana Santa and the April Feria.

The Plaza de España

In the 1920s at least, excess was still a way of life in Seville, and to call attention to the **Exposición Iberoamericana** they put up a building even bigger than the Tobacco Factory. With its grand Baroque towers (stolen gracefully from Santiago de

Compostela), fancy bridges, staircases and immense colonnade, the Plaza de España is World's Fair architecture at its grandest and most outrageous. Much of the fanciful neo-Spanish architecture of 1930s Florida and California may well have been inspired by this building. The Fair, as it turned out, was a flop; attendance proved disappointing, and when it was over Seville was left nearly bankrupt. The dictator, Primo de Rivera, who was himself from Jerez, and who had put a lot of money and effort into this fair to show off his native region, died while it was still running, at the lowest depths of unpopularity. For all that, the *sevillanos* are glad they at least have this building and its park to show for the effort. They gravitate naturally to it at weekends, to row canoes in the Plaza's canals and nibble curious pastries. One of the things Seville is famous for is its painted *azulejo* tiles; they adorn nearly every building in town, but here on the colonnade a few million of them are devoted to maps and historical scenes from every province in Spain.

La Cartuja and Contemporary Art

The Isle of La Cartuja was part of the Expo '92 site, but it has become seedy and rundown since and nothing seems to work, including the rusting cable car which once hoisted visitors across the river. Some of the original Expo pavilions are now devoted to holding business fairs and conferences, and another section has become the **Isla Mágica** funfair (*open March–Oct daily 11–11; adm expensive*).

Infinitely more interesting is the **Monasterio Cartujo de Santa Maria de las Cuevas** (*St Mary of the Caves; aka Centro Andaluz de Arte Contemporaneo; open summer Tues–Sun 11–9, winter Tues–Sat 11–7, closed Mon; guided visits at noon and 5pm, t 95 503 70 70*), the partially restored Carthusian monastery where Columbus once stayed while he mulled over his ambitions and geographical theories. Pottery kilns proliferated here from the 12th century, and the Virgin is said to have appeared in one of the workshops. A Franciscan hermitage was established in honour of the vision and, in 1399, Gonzalo de Mena, the Archbishop of Seville, founded the Cartuja monastery. It grew to become a virtually self-sufficient walled city, giving refuge to spiritual figures such as Teresa de Jésus as well as all the Spanish monarchs who passed through Seville. At the peak of its affluence, the monastery was richly endowed with masterpieces by great artists from Zurbarán to Murillo. Since then, sadly, the building has suffered numerous lootings and indignities; the monks were driven out by Maréchal Soult, who used it as a garrison during the Napoleonic occupation of 1810–12 and is responsible for the damage to the extraordinary *artesonado* ceiling in the refectory – his troops used the gable for target practice. As if this wasn't enough, the city sold it off to wealthy Liverpudlian Charles Pickman in the 1830s, who turned it into a ceramics factory. The brick kilns still soar above the monastery garden, which is full of orange trees.

Now the monastery is home to the **Andalucían Centre of Contemporary Art** (*opening times as above*), the only contemporary arts centre in Andalucía and one of the most singular and absorbing anywhere. The atmospheric ruins of the monastery itself serve as a palimpsest of the waves of invaders who have stripped it bare of most of its treasures, and yet, despite them, it retains a hushed and reverent stillness; among the art now displayed on the ruined walls is a series of eight blazing paintings by José Manuel Bioto, in hazy, dreamy ochres and indigoes, in the main chapel, and a limpid collection of Japanese-inspired panels in St Anne's Chapel, where Columbus was once laid to rest. Attached to the monastery complex are the main exhibition galleries, in an unobtrusive, light-filled, modern building entered through a courtyard draped in a forest of vines and fronds filled with birdsong. These are devoted to temporary exhibitions which focus on both emerging and established Andalucían artists and international artists who develop projects designed specifically for the space; this is definitely one of the most engaging and vibrant places in Spain to see contemporary art and it shouldn't be missed.

Day Trips from Seville

Villages South of Seville

Alcalá de Guadaira, off the N334, is jocularly known in Seville as Alcalá de los Panaderos ('of the bakers'), as it used to supply the city with its daily bread. Its **castle** is the best-preserved Almohad fortress in Andalucía. Just outside Utrera, the tiny village of **Palmar de Troya** received a visit in 1968 from the Virgin Mary (to little girls, as usual) which led to the founding of a new church, the Orden de la Santa Faz, a vast

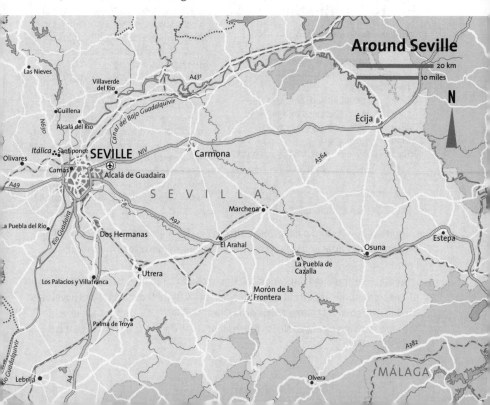

Getting There

There are two ways to travel, both of approx-imately equal length. The **train**, and most of the **buses**, unfortunately take the duller route through the flat lands along the Guadalquivir. The only landmark here is the Spanish-Moorish castle of Almodóvar del Río, perched romantically on a height planted with olive trees, overlooking the river. The southern route (the NIV) also follows the Guadalquivir valley, but the scenery is a little more varied, and the road passes through two fine towns, Carmona and Écija. There are regular buses from Seville to these towns, from where you can easily find connecting buses for Cordoba.

Getting Around

There is no train service for the villages around Seville, but plenty of **buses**. Itálica is on the Ctra Menda, with local buses leaving every half-hour from the Plaza de Armas, near the Puerto del Cachorro; the main highway east and south is the NIV.

Tourist Information

Carmona: Oficina Municipal de Turismo, Alcazar de la Puerta de Seville s/n, **t** 95 419 09 55, **f** 95 419 00 80, *carmona@andal.es*, *www.andal.es/carmona. Open Mon–Sat 10–6, Sun 10–3.*

Osuna: Casa de la Cultura, Pza Mayor s/n, **t/f** 95 582 14 00. *Open 10–2 and 5–7.*

Estepa: C/Saladillo 12, **t** 95 591 27 71. *Open Mon–Fri 9–2 and 3–10.*

Écija: Palacio de Benamaje, **t/f** 95 590 29 33. *Open summer 9–2, closed Mon; winter Tues–Fri 9.30–1.30 and 4.30–6.30, Sat–Sun 9–2, closed Mon.*

Where to Stay and Eat

Carmona ✉ 39554

★★★★★**Palacio Casa Carmona**, Pza de Lasso 1, **t** 95 414 33 00, **f** 95 414 37 52 (*luxury*). Lovingly restored by Marta Medina and her artist son Felipe, this 16th-century palace is the last word in refined good taste, and a stay here will delight all the senses.

★★★★**Parador Alcázar del Rey Don Pedro**, Alcázar s/n, **t** 95 414 10 10, **f** 95 414 17 12, *carmona@parador.es* (*expensive*). Occupying a section of Cruel Pete's summer palace, the finest in Andalucía for style and comfort. It has superlative views, a garden, pool and luxurious furnishings; good value.

★★★★**Hotel Alcazar de la Reina**, Pza de Lasso 2, **t** 95 419 62 00, **f** 95 414 01 13, (*moderate*). Set in a beautiful old house which has been tastefully restored, with a well-designed communal area and bedrooms, and one of the best restaurants in town, La Ferrara (*see* below).

★**Pensión Comercio**, C/Torre del Oro, **t** 95 414 00 18 (*inexpensive*). One of the many *pensiones* and *hostales* in town.

San Fernando, Pza San Fernando, **t/f** 95 414 35 56 (*moderate*). This restaurant has the best reputation in town, although Carmona is not known for culinary excellence. *Closed Sun eve, Mon and Aug.*

La Ferrara, Pza de Lasso 2, **t** 95 419 62 00, **f** 95 414 01 13, *www.alcazar-reina.es* (*moderate*). This restaurant in the Alcazar de la Reina Hotel rivals San Fernando for the quality of its cuisine. Specials include game, lamb and duck, all served in a lovely setting.

Molino de la Nomera, C/Pedro, **t** 95 414 20 00. Just down from the Parador and set in a historic 15th-century building, which can be visited separately. Offers superb food and

complex of towers and pillars which can be seen for miles around. They have their own 'pope' in Palmar and include among their saints Franco, José Antonio and Ramon Llull.

Lebrija, near the Guadalquivir off the main road to Jerez, goes back to the civilization of Tartessos; some important finds from here now grace the museums of Seville and Madrid. The church of **Santa María de la Oliva** is really a 12th-century Almohad mosque, with a typical Middle Eastern roof of small domes and a tower that is a some of the best views in town. Specializes in local meats *al horno* or *a la paradilla*.

El Ancla, Bonifacio 4, t 95 414 38 04 (*moderate*). A full fish meal with wine will set you back around *3,500 pts*. *Closed Mon and Sun nights*.

La Cueva, Barbacan Baja 2, t/f 95 419 18 11 (*inexpensive*). Situated just below the city walls, this cavernous place has a heavy emphasis on pork and an extensive vegetable menu.

Marchena ✉ 39554

★★Ponce, Pza Alvarado 2, t 95 584 60 88 (*inexpensive*). A *hostal* with rooms for *5,200 pts*.

★★Hostal Los Ángeles, on the Ctra Sevilla–Granada, Km 67, t 95 484 70 88 (*inexpensive*). Basic but quite lively.

Los Muleros, Travesía de San Ignacio, t 95 484 31 99 (*inexpensive*). Try local specialities here.

Casa Canillo, C/Las Torres 39 (*inexpensive*). Serves excellent cheap tapas.

Osuna and Estepa ✉ 41640

★★★★Palacio Marques de la Gomera, C/San Pedro 20, t 95 481 22 33, f 95 481 02 00 (*expensive*). Recently opened conversion of one of the town's more impressive mansions dating from the 18th century. There is a good restaurant attached with an emphasis on traditional Mediterranean cooking.

Pensión Caballo Blanco, C/Granada 1; t 95 481 01 84 (*inexpensive*). Centrally located, clean and comfortable, with a garage.

Pensión Esmerelda, C/Tesoreno 7, t/f 95 582 10 73 (*inexpensive*). In a good spot near the historic town centre, with a pleasant café.

★★Los Angeles, Avda. Andalucía 21, t 95 482 09 84 (*cheap*). An adequate base in Estepa.

Doña Guadaloupe, C/Pza Guadaloupe, t 95 481 05 58. A restaurant with a very good reputation – if you can find it.

Écija ✉ 41400

The hotels are mostly motels on the outskirts, serving traffic on the Madrid–Cadiz highway.

★★Hotel Platería, C/Garcilópez 1-A, t 95 590 27 54 (*inexpensive*). Just off the main square with a lovely marble courtyard and helpful service; probably the best in town.

★★Ciudad del Sol, C/Cervantes 50, t 95 483 03 00, f 95 483 58 79 (*inexpensive*). A friendly place with air-conditioned rooms.

★★Astigi, Ctra. Mardid-Cadiz, km 450, t 95 596 50 55 (*moderate*). An alternative, if the others are full.

Fonda Santa Cruz, Romero Gordillo 8, t 95 483 02 22 (*moderate*). A minute's walk from the main plaza, in a back street behind the fabulously named Gasolina Bar – try the veal; they cook it at your table – you will find this delightful little place with simple rooms that open out to the tiled courtyard.

Las Ninfas, in the Palacio de Benameji, t 95 590 45 92 (*expensive*). The setting is stylish and subtle, the food fresh and light with an emphasis on fish. You may also spot the four marble nymphs (hence the name) which once stood in the Pza de España.

Bodegón del Gallego, C/A. Aparicio 3, t 95 483 26 18 (*moderate*). One of the best places to eat in town, serving stylish *andaluz* dishes.

Pasareli, Pasaje Virgen del Rocío, t 95 483 20 24 (*inexpensive*). Looks like any modern cafeteria in the heart of town, but there's a surprisingly efficient little restaurant tucked away in the corner, where you can eat well from a large selection of meat and fish for under *2,000 pts*.

El Bistori, t 95 483 10 66. Situated back on the main plaza and specializing in food from across Spain – shellfish from Huelva, meat from Avila and *pulpo a la callega*.

miniature version of La Giralda, built by a Basque architect in the 19th century. The main altarpiece is a work of Alonso Cano – but Lebrija is better-known for its wine and ceramics, and as a lively centre of flamenco, with an annual festival called the Caracol. Take care before you start any rambles in the countryside; this area south of Seville contains some of the best-known ranches where fighting bulls are bred, and the bulls are always allowed to run free.

Itálica

*Open Tues–Sat 9–5.30, Sun 10–4, closed Mon; **t** 95 599 73 76.*

Eight kilometres (5 miles) north of Seville, in the direction of Mérida, the only significant Roman ruins in Andalucía are at Itálica. The first Roman colony in Spain, this city was founded in the 3rd century BC by Scipio Africanus as a home for his veterans after their victory in the Punic Wars; a Tartessian town may have originally occupied the site. Itálica thrived in the Imperial age. The Guadalquivir had a reputation for constantly changing its course in the old days, and this may explain the presence of two important cities so close together. Three great emperors, Trajan, Hadrian and Theodosius, were born here, as were the poet Lucan and the moralist Seneca. The biggest ruins are an **amphitheatre**, with seating for 40,000, some remains of temples, and a street of villa foundations.

The village of **Santiponce**, near the ruins, has a fine Gothic-*mudéjar* monastery built for the Cistercians in 1301, using surviving columns and other materials from the ruins. **San Isidoro del Campo** has a gruesome St Jerome on the altarpiece, carved in the 1600s by Juan Martínez Montañés (1566–1649).

Northeast Towards Cordoba

Carmona

The first town along the NIV, Carmona, seems like a miniature Seville. It is probably much older. Remains of a Neolithic settlement have been found around town; the Phoenician colony that replaced it grew into a city and prospered throughout Roman and Moorish times. Pedro the Cruel favoured it and rebuilt most of its **Alcázar**. Sitting proudly on top of the town, with views over the valley, this fortress is now a national *parador*.

Carmona is well worth a day's exploration. Its walls, mostly Moorish fortifications built over Roman foundations, are still standing, including a grand gateway on the road from Seville, the **Puerta de Seville** (*t* 95 419 09 55; *open Mon–Sat 10–6, Sun 10–3; adm*). Continue through the arch and up to the palm-decked Plaza de San Fernando, where the under-16s and over-60s gather; the Ayuntamiento here has a Roman mosaic of Medusa in its courtyard. Next door is the **Casa Palacio des Marques de la Torres** (*t* 95 414 01 28; *open daily 11–7; adm*) which is now the town's archaeological museum. Next, take Calle Martín López up to the lofty 15th-century church of **Santa María** (*open daily 9–12 and 6–9*), built on the site of an old mosque. The old quarters of town have an ensemble of fine palaces, and *mudéjar* and Renaissance churches. On one of these, **San Pedro** (1466) (*open Thurs–Mon 11–2 and 5–7; adm*), you'll see another imitation of La Giralda, La Giraldilla – though not as fussily ornate as her big sister, she has a cleaner exterior. Carmona's prime attraction is the **Roman necropolis**, a series of rock-cut tombs off the Avenida Jorge Bonsor. Some, like the 'Tomb of Servilia', are elaborate creations with subterranean chambers and vestibules, pillars, domed ceilings and carved reliefs (*open Tues–Fri 9–5; Sat and Sun 10–2; t* 95 414 08 11).

Near the entrance to the site are remains of the Roman amphitheatre, forlorn and unexcavated.

Twenty-eight kilometres south of Carmona on the C339, **Marchena** still retains many of its wall defences dating from Roman times, with later Moorish and Christian additions. Of its gates, the arch of **La Rosa** is best, and in the **Torre del Oro** there is a new archaeological museum. The Gothic church of **San Juan Bautista** has a *retablo* by Alejo Fernández and a sculpture by Pedro Roldán. There's also a small museum with a collection of paintings by Zurbarán. Nearby **El Arahal** is a bleached white town well worth visiting for its Baroque monuments, notably the church of **La Victoria** of *mudéjar* origin.

Osuna and Estepa

From here, you can continue on the N333 back towards Écija and Cordoba, or take a detour eastwards on the N334 to **Osuna**. Founded by a busy, go-ahead governor named Julius Caesar, this was an important Roman military centre for the south of Spain, and survives as an attractive little city of white houses with characteristic *rejas* over every window. Osuna was an aristocratic town after the Reconquista, home of the objectionable Dukes of Osuna who lorded it over much of Andalucía. Their 'pantheon' of tombs may be seen in the fine Renaissance **Colegiata** church (*open Oct–April 10.30–1.30 and 3.30–6.30; May–Sept 10–1.30 and 4–7; adm*) on a hill on the west side of town. Inside is a memorable Crucifixion by José Ribera, and four other works of his in the high altar *retablo*. Behind the church is the old university building, founded in 1548 and now serving as a school. Several decorative façades of 16th-century mansions can be seen along the **Calle San Pedro**. Osuna has a little **archaeology museum** (Plaza de la Duquesa) in the **Torre del Agua**, part of the old fortifications, and a museum of dubious art in La Encarnación convent, a Baroque work of the late 18th century; the cloister is done out in ceramic tiles (*both open daily except Mon, 10–1.30 and 3.30–6.30; in summer 10–1.30 and 4–7; adm*).

Back on the N334 you'll come to **Estepa**, a smaller version of Osuna known for its Christmas biscuits (*polverones* and *mantecado*), and the mass suicide of its inhabitants who preferred not to surrender to the Roman enemy in 208 BC. Above the town are the remains of a castle with a well-preserved Almohad keep; the two Baroque showpieces are the churches of **El Carmen**, in the main square, with a spectacular façade, and the 18th-century **Virgen de los Remedios**.

Écija

Écija makes much of one of its nicknames, the 'city of towers', and tries to play down the other – the 'frying pan of Andalucía', which isn't exactly fair. Any Andalucían town can overheat you thoroughly on a typical summer's day and, if Écija is a degree hotter and a little less breezy than most, only a born Andalucían could tell the difference. Ask one and you'll soon learn that the Andalucíans are the only people yet discovered who talk about the weather more than the English.

Nowadays you'll be put off by the clinical outskirts of the town and by the ill-concealed gas-holders; all was once forgiven when you reached the **Plaza de España**, which was one of the loveliest in Andalucía, charmingly framed by tall palms with an exquisite fountain at its centre (now in safe-keeping). However, the local council have taken it upon themselves to construct an underground car park beneath the plaza – a project unlikely to be completed for a few years. In the meantime the square lies hidden behind a 6ft-high concrete wall. The Ayuntamiento stands at one end and, if you ask politely, you may be able to look at a Roman mosaic in the council chamber, lovingly described by Laurie Lee in *A Rose For Winter*. The façade of the 18th-century **Santa María** wouldn't look out of place in a Sergio Leone movie. Most of the **towers** are sumptuously ornate, rebuilt after the great earthquake of 1755 – the one that flattened Lisbon. Santa María has one, along with **San Juan Bautista**, gaily decorated in coloured tiles, and **San Gil**. This last is the highest of the towers, and within are paintings by Alejo Fernández and Villegas Marmolejo (*all monuments open 10–1; free*).

Écija also has a set of Renaissance and Baroque palaces second in Andalucía only to those in Úbeda; most of these showy façades can be seen on or near the **Calle de los Caballeros**. Worth visiting is the **Mudéjar Palace**, dating from the 14th century, where you can find some interesting archaeological remains, part *mudéjar*, part Baroque, some Roman mosaics, and various reliefs, coins and glass. The town is also rediscovering its equestrian roots, and there is a horse-riding school nearby, **Tierra de Caballos** (*t 95 590 36 54, www.ecija.org*), which offers riding for non-beginners.

The **Peñaflor Palace** (1728) on Calle de Castellar – now a five-star hotel – is one of the outstanding works of Andalucían Baroque, with its grandiose façade and lovely patio. In the evening the town buzzes. After the big-city crush of Seville, you might find that this is the perfect place to spend a couple of days – busy enough to be interesting, but not too frantic.

Cordoba

11

Getting Around

By Train

Cordoba is on the major Madrid–Seville rail line, so there are about 12 trains a day in both directions by AVE, with a journey time of 43mins from Seville and 1hr 40mins from Madrid. There are also frequent *Talgo* services to Malaga (about 2hrs 15mins), Cadiz, Valencia and Barcelona, and regular trains to Huelva, Algeciras and Alicante. Trains for Granada and Algeciras pass through Bobadilla Junction, and may require a change. Cordoba's station is off Avenida de América, 1.6km (1 mile) north of La Mezquita, **t** 95 749 02 02, and there is a ticket office in town at Ronda de los Tejares 10.

By Bus

Buses for Seville (three plus daily), Granada, Cadiz and Malaga and most nearby towns leave from the Alsina Graells terminal on Avenida Medina Azahara 29, **t** 95 723 64 74. Buses for Madrid (one daily), Valencia (three daily) and Barcelona (two daily), leave from the Ureña office, Avenida de Cervantes 22, **t** 95 747 23 52. The train is probably a better bet for Seville and for Malaga.

The Cordoba bus network is complicated and it's best to check with tourist information as to times and departure points. Otherwise call the bus information line, **t** 95 740 40 40. If you want to go to Medinat az-Zahra, take bus No.01 for Villarubia or Veredón (from Republica Argentina at Azahara); it will drop you off short of the site, and you will have to walk about 2km (1.3 miles).

Tourist Information

The very helpful regional tourist office is on C/Torrijos 10 next to the Mezquita, **t** 95 747 12 35, **f** 95 749 17 78, (*open 9.30–6, Nov–Feb until 7, March–April until 8*). The municipal office is in the Judería on Plaza Judá Levi, **t** 95 720 05 22. It's worth a visit to get a map – Cordoba has the biggest and most labyrinthine old quarter in Spain containing monuments with changeable opening times. To arrange personal guides to the mosque and other sights, call **t** 95 748 69 97, ask at the tourist offices, or turn up at the mosque itself.

Shopping

Cordoba is famous for its silverwork – try the shops in C/José Cruz Grande, where you'll get better quality than in the old quarter round the mosque. Handmade **crafts** are made on the premises at Meryan, C/de las Flores 2, where they specialize in embossed wood and leather furniture. For **antiques**, there's one shop with a very good selection of Spanish art and furniture in Plaza San Nicolás, and they'll arrange packing and shipment. High-quality ladies' and gents' suede and **leather goods** are sold at Sera, on the corner of Rondo de los Teares and Cruz Conde. The mainstream shopping areas are along Calle Conde de Gondomar and Calle Claudio Marcelo on either side of the Plaza de las Tendillas.

Where to Stay

Cordoba ✉ 14000

Near La Mezquita, of course. Even during big tourist assaults the advantages outweigh the liabilities. However, if this area is full, or if you have a car and do not care to brave the old town's narrow streets and lack of parking, there are a few hotels worth trying in the new town and on the periphery.

Luxury

★★★★NH Amistad Cordoba, Pza de Maimónides 3, **t** 95 742 03 35, **f** 95 742 03 65. Sensitively converted from an old *palacio*, with a main entrance fronting the Plaza de Maimónides, and a back entrance neatly built into the old wall of the Judería. Thoughtful management makes it a comfortable and extremely convenient place to stay. The double-room price includes an excellent breakfast buffet. Underground parking is available for a small supplement.

Expensive

★★★★Meliá Córdoba, **t** 95 729 80 66, **f** 95 729 81 47. A big and ugly modern hotel right in the middle of the Jardines de la Victoria. It has every conceivable luxury the chain is known for, including a pool and TV. A double room will set you back *19,000 pts* – worth it for the car park alone, some would consider.

****El Conqistador**, C/Magistral González Francés 15, **t** 95 748 11 02. Recently refurbished, with rooms that look out on to the floodlit walls of La Mezquita, literally just a few metres from your balcony. The breakfasts are somewhat meagre, though, and service is old-fashioned in the worst sense; but there is an underground car park.

***Posada de Vallina**, C/Corregidor Luis de Cerda 83, **t** 95 749 87 50, **f** 95 749 87 51. One of the nicest new hotels to have sprung up in the past year or so, directly opposite La Mezquita. An old inn dating from Roman times, there are just 15 rooms, all sparkling clean and tastefully designed, some with mosque views, others facing the patio. Attached is a good restaurant (*see* below).

Lola, C/Romero 3, **t** 95 720 03 05, **f** 95 742 20 63, *hotellola@terra.es*. Even newer, this hotel sits right in the heart of the old Jewish quarter in a lovingly restored old house with many of the original fittings and furniture, including old Bakelite phones. There are just eight rooms, each individually designed, all doubles, but varying in size. Avoid the cheaper, smaller ones and go for the suite which has a view of the tower of the Mezquita and a tiny terrace. Breakfast is served on the roof terrace or below. Parking arrangement with the El Conquistador.

****Las Adelfas**, Avda de la Arruzafa s/n, **t** 95 727 74 20, **f** 95 727 27 94. A modern hotel five minutes north of the train station, set in spacious gardens with a pool and beautiful views over Cordoba; definitely worth considering if you visit in summer, and a bargain at present for its rates in this category.

****Parador de la Arruzafa**, Avda de la Arruzafa, **t** 95 727 59 00, **f** 95 728 04 09. In common with much of the chain, service in this hotel on the outskirts of town seems to be improving. It isn't in an historic building, but offers a pool, tennis courts and air-conditioned rooms with a view.

Al-Mihrab, Avda del Brillante, km 5, **t** 95 727 21 98. Situated just 5km from the centre of town, this agreeable hotel, which is a listed building, offers peace and a view of the Sierra Morena; another bargain in this category (*moderate* in low season).

Hesperia Córdoba, Avda Confederación s/n, **t** 95 742 10 42, **f** 95 729 99 97,

nnes.cordoba@adv.es. Well placed just over the Roman bridge with pool, parking and fine views across the river to the city, but it's a pretty soulless upmarket establishment.

***Maimónides**, Torrijos 4, **t** 95 747 15 00, **f** 95 748 38 03. A slightly gloomy place next to the mosque, very much catering to the package-tour market, though with underground parking.

Moderate

Hotel Mezquita, Pza Santa Catalina, 1, **t** 95 747 55 85, **f** 95 747 62 19. Right next to the El Conquistador, a recently converted 16th-century mansion sympathetically restored and with many of the original paintings and sculptures, this is fantastic value for its location. The only drawback: no garage.

Albucasis, C/Buen Pastor 11, **t/f** 95 747 86 25. Situated in the Judería, near La Mezquita, this former silversmith's is an attractive, affordable and immaculate place with a charming flower-filled courtyard; it's one of the prettiest hotels in Cordoba. *Closed Jan–mid-Feb*.

Marisa, C/Cardinal Herrero 6, **t** 95 747 31 42, **f** 95 747 41 44. A simple but well-run establishment opposite the Patio de los Naranjos. The location is the only real amenity, but it will just do for the price.

Hotel González, on the edge of the Judería, **t** 95 747 98 19, **f** 95 748 61 87. Rooms contain family antiques and the arabesque patio houses a popular restaurant.

Inexpensive–Cheap

Hostal El Triunfo, C/Corregidor Luis de Cerda 79, **t** 95 749 84 84, **f** 95 748 68 50. Right by the mosque, this is a perfectly decent no-frills option with a pleasant restaurant on its patio; at the top end of this price category.

*Hotel Los Patios**, C/Cardenal Herrero 14, **t** 95 747 83 40, **f** 95 748 69 66. Fantastic value for its location, directly opposite La Mezquita. Brand new and sparkling clean, the 24 rooms set round the hotel's patio come with TV, phone and nice bathrooms.

Hostal Magdalena, C/Munices, 35, **t** 95 748 37 53. Good for those who don't mind a 10-minute walk through the picturesque back streets into town. It's in a quiet location where there's no trouble parking.

*Hostal Seneca, C/Conde y Luque 5 (just north of La Mezquita), **t** 95 747 32 34. A real find among the inexpensive *hostales*, with a beautiful patio full of flowers, nice rooms and sympathetic management. Not surprisingly, it's hard to get a room.

La Fuente, C/Fernando, 51, **t** 95 748 14 78, **f** 95 748 78 27. A very pleasant budget option on the way to the Plaza del Potro, with rooms set round a large patio. The only drawback is that it's on a noisy road.

Plenty of other inexpensive *fondas* can be found on and around Calle Rey Heredia – also known as the street with five names – so don't be thrown by all the different signs.

Fonda Agustina, on nearby Calle Zapatería Vieja, **t** 95 747 08 72. Clean and central.

*Boston, C/Málaga 2, **t** 95 747 41 76. Situated off the Plaza de las Tendillas, with clean modern rooms that are air-conditioned at night; popular with a young Americans.

Hostal Maestre, C/Romero Barros 16, **t/f** 95 747 53 95. Has a range of rooms from doubles to small apartments; all have private bathrooms and those in the hotel have air-conditioning; popular with backpackers (so make a reservation if you want to stay).

Hostal Martínez Rücker, C/Martínez Rücker 14, **t** 95 47 25 62. The cheapest place in town with tiny box-like rooms around a pleasant Moorish courtyard.

Eating Out

Don't forget that Cordoba is the heart of a wine-growing region; there are a few *bodegas* in town that appreciate visitors, including Bodega Campos, C/Colonel Cascajo; and Bodega Doña Antonia, Avda Virgen Milagrosa 5, a small restaurant serving its own wines.

Expensive

El Churrasco, C/Romero 16, **t** 95 729 08 19. Located in an old town house in the heart of the Jewish quarter, this is Cordoba's best-loved restaurant. For food and atmosphere it is perhaps the finest restaurant in southern Spain – but it's not a grand restaurant; it's actually rather small, very intimate, and just a little bit cliquey. It specializes in grilled meats – *churrasco* is the name of the grill

the meat is cooked on, and by extension the piece of grilled meat itself – and unless you're vegetarian or a mad fish-lover, a *churrasco* is your obvious choice here. In winter braziers are put under tables making it possible to dine on the patio all year round, and there's even valet parking if you need it. Additionally, El Churrasco has the best cellar in Andalucía, now so large it is housed in a separate building along the street – ask at the restaurant if you would like to visit. *Closed Aug.*

El Caballo Rojo, Cardenal Herrero 28, **t** 95 747 53 75. Another of Cordoba's best-known restaurants, its menu is supposed to be based on traditional *andaluz* cooking and old Arab recipes – *salmorejo* with cured ham, artichokes in Montilla wine, Mozarabic angler fish – but it has rather lost its way. Dreary-looking tourists sporting bumbags have hardly a word to say to each other and the restaurant is ugly and modern.

Almudaina, Jardines de los Santos Mártires 1, **t** 95 747 43 42. Set in an attractive old house dating from the 16th century, this would be a sophisticated spot to eat, but it has sold out to coachloads of Japanese. Its menu varies from day to day, depending on market availability, and special attention is paid to local produce. Look out for *ensalada de pimientos, alcachofas a la Cordobés*, and *lomo relleno a la Pedrocheña*, which are above average. *Closed Sun from June to Sept, and Sun evening the rest of the year.*

Moderate

Posada de Vallina, C/Corregidor Luis de Cerda 83, **t** 95 749 87 50, **f** 95 749 87 51. Has fine service and offers *finos* and nibbles for free as aperitifs. The setting is lovely, around the hotel patio, but the food lacks subtlety. It will fill you up though: great hunks of meat or a whole partridge with a smattering of chips.

El Burlaero, C/La Hoguera 5, **t** 95 747 27 19. Adjoining El Caballo Rojo and inevitably trippery, but with the advantage of a courtyard. Specialities include run-of-the-mill *rabo de toro, Paloma Torcaz, perdiz, jabalí*.

Rincón de Carmen, C/Romero 4, **t** 95 729 10 55. Family-run, noisy and full of atmosphere. The local dishes are prepared as well as at any establishment in the city, and the prices are low. It also has a very pleasant (and slightly more peaceful) café attached.

Bar Restaurante Millan, Avda Doctor Fleming 14, t 95 729 09 19. Close to the Alcazar, and defiantly non-touristy despite its location, this restaurant serves up a good selection of tapas as well as full meals, including house specials, *merluza al jerez* and *rape millan*, and *charrascos* and *barbacoas*.

El Somontano, Plaza del Escudo, t 95 748 65 54, *joseansg@eremas.com*. A modern place way off the tourist trail in the new part of town, serving a fine selection of reasonably priced fare, including lamb, rabbit and venison.

Inexpensive

Cordoba is famous for its *bodegas* and there are a number dotted around the city.

El Tablón, Cardenal González 79, t 95 747 60 61. Just around the corner from La Mezquita, this characterful restaurant offers one of the best bargains in the city, with a choice of *menús del día* or *platos combinados* at *around 1,500 pts*, glass of wine included.

Los Patios, Calle Cardenal Herrero 18. The best of several good options on Calle Cardenal Herrero, right by the Mezquita.

Taberna San Miguel, Plaza San Miguel 1. Better known as El Pisto, or the barrel, this is perhaps the best known *bodega* in town. It's a big old barn of a place with good honest tapas, lots of little rooms and *montilla*. A tapa will set you back about 300 pts.

Bodega Guzman, C/Judios 7. Another good *bodega* worth seeking out; it's a shrine to bullfighting with a collection of memorabilia inside.

Bodegón Rafaé, on the corner of Calle Deanes and Buen Pastor. Take it or leave it, this place has true *bodega* food and atmosphere. Sausages drape from barrels, religious figurines hang next to fake bulls' heads, the radio and TV are on simultaneously; *cola de toro* with a glass of wine at one of the vinyl-topped tables will cost next to nothing.

Taberna San Miguel, Plaza San Miguel 1. Better known as El Pisto, or the barrel, this is perhaps the best known drinking hole in town. It's a big old barn of a place with good honest tapas and lots of little rooms.

El Campeón, C/Munda 8, t 95 747 02 07. For the young, or young at heart, a lively spot in one of the narrow streets near Plaza de las Tendillas. Here students gather amid the dotty décor to order enormous tankards of beer and *sangría*, and enjoy the loud music and snack food in one of the half-dozen tiny rooms with wooden benches.

Bar Sociedad de Plateros, C/San Francisco 6. Another popular place with good tapas and cheap wine. It started out in the mid-19th century as a society to help struggling silversmiths and has since branched out into the *bodega* business; there are now nine dotted across the city.

Entertainment

Cordoba is the birthplace of Paco Peña – one of Spain's most famous modern flamenco maestros, though his flamenco academy in Cordoba has recently closed down. Paco Peña is part of a long tradition of Cordoba flamenco and the city is a good place to catch some great players and dancers in more authentic venues than, say, Seville. If you love flamenco, June is the best time to visit the city, during the guitar festival, when flourishes and trills drift out of every other room in Cordoba's White Neighbourhood and there are several concerts every night. At other times, wait until midnight and then head for one of the secluded little flamenco bars tucked away throughout the city. These include:

Peña Flamenca Fostorito, C/Ocaña 4 (near the Plaza de San Agustín).

Peña Flamenca Las Orejas Negras, Avda Carlos III 18 (in Fatima Barrio).

Tablao Cardenal, C/Torrijos 10 (strategically positioned next to the tourist office).

Though flamenco may be more authentic in Cordoba than in Seville, the bar nightlife is less lively. The most popular bars with locals are the street bars (*terrazas*) in Barrio Jardín, northwest of the Jardines de la Vitoria, on the Avenida de Republica end of Camino de los Sastrés. **El Loro Verde** and the **Albaicín** are two of the busiest. Barrio El Brillante, northwest of the Plaza Colon is full of upper-middle class Spanish in the summer, particularly the nightclubs and bars around Plaza El Tablero.

The Río Guadalquivir was al-Andalus's great highway, lined with tall water wheels and prosperous farms, while its barges carried the luxuries of the East up to the Caliphs and their court. For all the noise on the Costas, this valley remains the heart of real Andalucía. Right in the centre of it lies a marvel, Cordoba, a citadel of pure Andalucían *duende* that guards at its heart one of the most fascinating buildings on the planet. North of Cordoba are the Sierra Morena, famous for good hunting and cured hams, as well as Belalcázar with its remarkable castle. To the south it's mostly endless rows of olive trees.

There are a few spots around the Mediterranean where the presence of past glories becomes almost tangible, a mixture of mythic antiquity, lost power and dissipated energy that broods over a place like a ghost. In Istanbul you can find it, in Rome, or among the monuments of Egypt, and also here on the banks of the Guadalquivir at Cordoba's southern gate. Looking around, you can see reminders of three defunct empires: a Roman bridge, a triumphal arch built for Philip II and Cordoba's Great Mosque, more than a thousand years old. The first reminds us of the city's beginnings, the second of its decline; the last one scarcely seems credible, as it speaks of an age when Cordoba was one of the most brilliant metropolises of all Europe, city of half a million souls, a place faraway storytellers would use to enthral audiences in the rude halls of the Saxons and Franks. The little plaza by the bridge concentrates melancholy like a magnet; there isn't much left for the rest of the town. Cordoba's growth has allowed it a chance to renovate its sparkling old quarters and monuments. With the new prosperity has come a contentment the city hasn't known since the Reconquista.

Everyone who visits Cordoba comes for the Great Mosque, but you should spare some time to explore the city itself. Old Cordoba is one of the largest medieval quarters of any European city, and certainly the biggest in Spain. More than Seville, it retains its Moorish character, in a maze of whitewashed alleys opening into the loveliest courtyards in all Andalucía.

History

Roman **Corduba**, built on a prehistoric site, was almost from the start the leading city of interior Spain, capital of the province of Hispania Ulterior, and later of the reorganized province of Baetica. Cordoba had a reputation as the garden spot of Hispania; it gave Roman letters Lucan and both Senecas among others, testimony to its prominence as a city of learning. Cordoba became Christianized at an early date. Ironically, the True Faith got its comeuppance here in 572, when the Arian Visigoths under Leovigild captured the city from Byzantine rule. When the Arabs conquered, they found it an important town still, and it became the capital of al-Andalus when Abd ar-Rahman established the Umayyad emirate in 756.

For 300 years, Cordoba enjoyed the position of unqualified leader of al-Andalus. It is impossible to take the chronicles at face value – 3,000 mosques and 80,000 shops, a library of 400,000 volumes, in a city stretching for 16km (10 miles) along the banks of the Guadalquivir. We could settle for half these totals, and still be impressed. Beyond doubt, Cordoba was a city without equal in the West as a centre of learning; it would be enough to mention two 12th-century contemporaries: **Averroës**, the Muslim scientist and Aristotelian philosopher who contributed so much to the rebirth of classical learning in Europe, and **Moses Maimonides**, the Jewish philosopher (and later personal physician to Saladin in Palestine) whose reconciliation of faith and reason were assumed into Christianity by Thomas Aquinas. Medieval Cordoba was a great trading centre, and its luxury goods were coveted throughout western Europe; the old word *cordwainer* is a memory of Cordoba's skill in leatherwork. At its height, picture Cordoba as a city of bustling international markets, great palaces, schools, baths and mosques, with 28 suburbs and the first street lighting in Europe. Its population, largely Spanish, Moorish and Arab, included students and merchants from all over Europe, Africa and Asia, and an army and palace secretariat made up largely of slaves and black Africans. In it Muslims, Christians, and Jews lived in harmony, at least until the coming of the fanatical Almoravids and Almohads. We can sense a certain decadence; street riots in Cordoba were an immediate cause of the break-up of the caliphate in 1031, but here, as in Seville, the coming of the **Reconquista** was an unparalleled catastrophe.

When **Fernando III** 'the Saint' captured the city in 1236, much of the population chose flight over putting themselves at the mercy of the priests, although history records that he was unusually tolerant of the Jews. It did not last. Three centuries of Castilian rule sufficed to rob Cordoba of all its glories and turn it into a depressed backwater. Only in the last hundred years has it begun to recover; today Cordoba has also become an industrial city, though you wouldn't guess it from its sympathetically restored centre. It is the third city of Andalucía, and the first and only big town since Franco's death to have elected a communist mayor and council.

La Mezquita

Open Mon–Sat 10–7, Sun 1.30–7 in summer; 10–5.30 in winter; adm;
t 95 747 05 12.

La Mezquita is the local name for Abd ar-Rahman's **Great Mosque**. Mezquita means 'mosque' and even though the building has officially been a cathedral for more than 750 years, no one could ever mistake its origins. **Abd ar-Rahman I**, founder of a new state, felt it necessary to construct a great religious monument for his capital. As part of his plan, he also wished to make it a centre of pilgrimage to increase the sense of divorce from eastern Islam; Mecca was at the time held by his Abbasid enemies. Islam was never entirely immune to the exaltation of holy relics, and there is a story that Abd ar-Rahman had an arm of Mohammed to legitimize his mosque as a pilgrimage site. The site, at the centre of the city, had originally held a Roman temple of Janus, and later a Visigothic church. Only about one-third of the mosque belongs to the original. Successive enlargements were made by Abd ar-Rahman II, al-Hakim, and al-Mansur. Expansion was easy; the plan of the mosque is a simple rectangle divided into aisles by rows of columns, and its size was increased to serve a growing population simply by adding more aisles. The result was one of the largest of all mosques, exceeded only by the one in Mecca. After 1236, it was converted to use as a cathedral without any major changes. In the 1520s, however, the city's clerics succeeded in convincing the Royal Council, over the opposition of the Cordoba city government, to allow the construction of a choir and high altar, enclosed structures typical of Spanish cathedrals. Charles V, who had also opposed the project, strongly reproached them for the desecration when he saw the finished work – though he himself had done even worse to the Alhambra and Seville's Alcázar.

Most people come away from a visit to La Mezquita somewhat confused. The endless rows of columns and red and white striped arches make a picture familiar to most of us, but actually to see them in this gloomy old hall does not increase one's understanding of the work. They make a pretty pattern, but what does it mean? It's worth going into some detail, for learning to see La Mezquita the way its builders did is the best key we have to understanding the refined world of al-Andalus.

Before entering, take a few minutes to circumnavigate this massive, somewhat forbidding pile of bricks. Spaced around its 685m of wall are the original entrances and windows, excellent examples of Moorish art. Those on the western side are the best, from the time of al-Mansur: interlaced Visigothic horseshoe arches, floral decorations in the Roman tradition, and Islamic calligraphy and patterns, a lesson in the varied sources of this art.

The only entrance to the mosque today is the **Puerta del Perdón**, a fine *mudéjar* gateway added in 1377, opening on to the **Patio de los Naranjos**, the original mosque courtyard, planted with orange trees, where the old Moorish fountain can still be seen. Built into the wall of the courtyard, over the gate, the original minaret – a legendary tower said to be the model for all the others in al-Andalus – has been replaced by an ill-proportioned 16th-century bell tower. From the courtyard, the mosque is entered through a little door, the **Puerta de las Palmas**, where they'll sell you a ticket and tell you to take off your hat. Inside, it's as chilly as Seville cathedral.

Now here is the first surprise. The building is gloomy only because the Spanish clerics wanted it that way. Originally there was no wall separating the mosque from the courtyard, and that side of the mosque was entirely open. In the **courtyard**, trees were planted to continue the rows of columns, translating inside to outside in a remarkable *tour-de-force* that has rarely been equalled in architecture. To add to the effect, the entrances along the other three walls would have been open to the surrounding busy markets and streets. It isn't just a trick of architecture, but a way of relating a holy building to the life of the city around it. In the Middle East, there are many medieval mosques built on the same plan as this one; the pattern originated with the first Arabian mosques, and later in the Umayyad Mosque of Damascus, one of the first great shrines of Islam. In Turkey they call them 'forest' mosques, and the townspeople use them like indoor parks, places to sit and reflect or talk over everyday affairs. In medieval Christian cathedrals, whose doors were always open, it was much the same. The sacred and the secular become blurred, or rather the latter is elevated to a higher plane. In Cordoba, this principle is perfected.

In the aesthetics of this mosque, too, there is more than meets the eye. Many European writers have seen it as devoid of spirituality, a plain prayer-hall with pretty arches. To the Christian mind it is difficult to comprehend. Christian churches are modelled after the Roman basilica, a government hall, a seat of authority with a long central aisle designed to humble the suppliant as he approaches the praetor's throne (altar). Mosques are designed with great care to free the mind from such behaviour patterns. In this one, the guiding principle is a rarefied abstraction – the same kind of abstraction that governs Islamic geometric decoration. The repetition of columns is like a meditation in stone, a mirror of Creation where unity and harmony radiate from innumerable centres. Another contrast with Christian churches can be found in an obscure matter – the distribution of weight. The Gothic masters of the Middle Ages learned to pile stone upwards from great piers and buttresses to amazing heights, to build an edifice that aspires upwards to heaven. Cordoba's architects amplified the height of their mosque only modestly by a daring invention – adding a second tier of arches on top of the first. They had to, constrained as they were by the short columns they were recycling from Roman buildings, but the result was to make an 'upside-down' building, where weight increases the higher it goes, a play of balance and equilibrium that adds much to the mosque's effect. There are about 580 of these columns, mostly from Roman ruins and Visigothic churches the Muslims pulled down; originally, legend credits La Mezquita with a thousand. Some came from as far as Constantinople, a present from the emperors. The same variety can be seen in the capitals – Roman, Visigothic, Moorish and a few mysteries.

The *Mihrab* and Later Additions

The surviving jewel of the mosque is its *mihrab*, added in the 10th century under al-Hakim II, an octagonal chamber set into the wall and covered by a beautiful dome of interlocking arches. A Byzantine emperor, Nikephoras Phokas, sent artists to help with its mosaic decoration, and a few tons of enamel chips and coloured glass cubes for them to work with. That these two states should have had such warm relations isn't that surprising; in those days, any enemy of the Pope and the western Christian states was a friend of Constantinople. Though the *mihrab* is no longer at the centre of La Mezquita, it was at the time of al-Hakim II; the aisle extending from it was the axis of the original mosque.

Looking back from the *mihrab*, you will see what once was the exterior wall, built in Abd ar-Rahman II's extension, from the year 848. Its gates, protected indoors, are as good as those on the west façade, and better preserved. Near the *mihrab* is the **Capilla de Villaviciosa**, a Christian addition of 1377 with fancy convoluted *mudéjar* arches that almost succeed in upstaging the Moorish work. Behind it is a small chapel, usually closed off. Fortunately, you can see most of the **Capilla Real** (Royal Chapel) above the barriers; its exuberant stucco and *azulejo* decoration are among the greatest works of *mudéjar* art. Built in the 14th century as a funeral chapel for Fernando IV and Alfonso XI of Castile, it is contemporary with the Alhambra and shows some influence of the styles developing in Granada. Far more serious intrusions are the 16th-century **Coro** (choir) and **Capilla Mayor** (high altar). Not unlovely in themselves, they would not offend anywhere but here. Fortunately, La Mezquita is so large that from many parts of it you won't even notice them. Begun in 1523, the **Plateresque Coro** was substantially altered in the 18th century, with additional stucco decoration, as well as a set of Baroque choir stalls by Pedro Duque Cornejo. Between the Coro and Capilla Mayor is the **tomb of Leopold of Austria**, Bishop of Cordoba at the time the works were completed (and, interestingly, Charles V's uncle). For the rest of the Christian contribution, dozens of locked, mouldering chapels line the outer walls of the mosque. Never comfortable as a Christian building, today the cathedral seems to be hardly used at all, and regular Sunday masses are generally relegated to a small corner of the building.

Around La Mezquita

The masses of tatty souvenir stands and third-rate cafés that surround La Mezquita on its busiest days unwittingly do their best to recreate the atmosphere of the Moorish *souks* that once thrived here, but walk a block in any direction and you'll enter the essential Cordoba – brilliant whitewashed lanes with glimpses into dreamily beautiful patios or courtyards, each one a floral extravaganza. One of the best is a famous little alley called **Calle de las Flores** ('street of the flowers') just a block northeast of La Mezquita, although sadly its charms are diminished by the hordes of tourists who flock to see it.

Below La Mezquita, along the Guadalquivir, the melancholic plaza called **Puerta del Puente** marks the site of Cordoba's southern gate with a decorative **arch** put up in 1571, celebrating the reign of Philip II. The very curious Churrigueresque monument next to it, with a statue of San Rafael (the Archangel Raphael), is called the **Triunfo** (1651). Wild Baroque confections such as this are common in Naples and southern Italy (under Spanish rule at the time); there they are called *guglie*. Behind the plaza, standing across from La Mezquita, is the **Archbishop's Palace**, built on the site of the original Alcázar, the palace of Abd ar-Rahman.

The **Roman bridge** over the Guadalquivir probably isn't Roman at all any more; it has been patched and repaired so often that practically nothing remains of the Roman work. Another statue of Raphael can be seen in the middle – probably replacing an old Roman image of Jupiter or Mercury. The stern-looking **Calahorra Tower** (*t* 95 729 39 29), built in 1369 over Moorish foundations, once guarded the southern approaches of the bridge and has been in its time a girls' school and a prison; now it contains a small **museum** of Cordoba's history (*open daily 10.30–6*), with old views and plans of the city, and the armour of Gonzalo Fernández de Cordoba, the 'Gran Capitán' who won much of Italy for Ferdinand and Isabella. It also has an historical multivision spectacle, which is probably only of interest to the dedicated tourist.

Just to the west, along the river, Cordoba's **Alcázar de los Reyes Cristianos** was rebuilt in the 14th century and used for 300 years by the officers of the Inquisition. There's little to see, but a good view of La Mezquita and the town from the belvedere atop the walls. The **gardens** (*open daily 10 till dusk*) are peaceful and lovely, an Andalucían amenity much like those in Seville's Alcázar. The gigantic stone figures of Columbus and the Catholic Kings are impressive. On the river's edge you'll see an ancient **waterwheel**. At least some of the Moors' talent for putting water to good use was retained for a while after the Reconquista. This is the mill that disturbed Isabella's dreams when she stayed at the Alcázar; it was rebuilt only in the early 1900s. If you continue walking along the Guadalquivir, after about a kilometre you'll come to Parque Cruz Conde and the new **Cordoba zoo**, currently being renovated. When it reopens (*check with the tourist office*) there is word that you'll be able to see a rare black lion, who probably doesn't enjoy being called 'Chico'.

The Judería

How lovely is Thy dwelling-place O Lord of Hosts!
My soul grows weak and longs for Thy courtyards.
Hebrew inscription on synagogue wall

As in Seville, Cordoba's ancient Jewish quarter has recently become a fashionable area, a nest of tiny streets between La Mezquita and Avenida Dr Fleming. Part of the Moorish walls can be seen along this street, and the northern entrance of the Judería is the old **Almodóvar gate**. The streets are tricky, and it will take some effort to find Calle Maimonides and the 14th-century **synagogue** (*t 95 720 29 28, open daily except Mon 10–1.30 and 3.30–5.30; Sun 10–1.30*), after which you will find yourself repeatedly back at this spot, whether or not you want to be there.

The diminutive Cordoban synagogue is one of the two oldest and most interesting Jewish monuments in Spain (the other is the Tránsito in Toledo). Set back from the street in a tiny courtyard, it was built in the Granadine style of the early 14th century and, according to Amador de los Rios, dates from 1315. After the expulsion, it was used as a hospital for hydrophobes, and later became the headquarters of the cobblers' guild. There is an interesting plasterwork frieze of Alhambra-style arabesques and Hebrew inscriptions. The recess for the Ark (which contained the holy scrolls) is clearly visible, and the ladies' gallery still intact. Despite few obvious signs of the synagogue's original function, its atmosphere is still charged; it is somehow easy to imagine this small sanctum as a focus of medieval Jewry's Golden Age, a centre of prayer and scholarship spreading religious and moral enlightenment. While modern Cordoba has no active Jewish community, several *marrano* families live in the city and can trace their ancestry to the pre-expulsion age. Some have opened shops in the *Judería* selling 'Judaica', which ranges from tacky tourist trinkets and tapes of Israeli folk songs, to beautiful Jewish artefacts worked from Cordoban silver.

On Calle Ruano Torres, the 15th-century **Casa del Indiano** is a palace with an eccentric façade. On Plaza Maimonides is the **Museo Municipal de Arte Cordobés y Taurino** (*t 95 720 10 56, open Tues–Sat 10–2 and 4.30–6.30, Sun 9.30–2.30; adm*) with its beautiful courtyard – not surprisingly it's a museum dedicated to the bullfights. Manolete and El Cordobés are the city's two recent contributions to Spanish culture; here you can see a replica of Manolete's sarcophagus, the furniture from his home and the hide of Islero, the bull that did him in, along with more bullfight memorabilia than you ever thought existed. The Art Nouveau posters are beautiful, and among the old prints you can pay homage to the memory of the famous taurine malcontent Moñudo, who ignored the *toreros* and went up into the stands after the audience.

White Neighbourhoods

From the mosque you can walk eastwards through well over a mile of twisting white alleys, a place where the best map in the world wouldn't keep you from getting lost and staying lost. Though it all looks much the same, it's never monotonous. Every little square, fountain or church stands out boldly, and forces you to look at it in a way different from how you would look at a modern city – another lesson in the Moorish aesthetic. These streets have probably changed little since 1236, but their best buildings are a series of **Gothic churches** built soon after the Reconquista. Though small and plain, most are exquisite in a quiet way. Few have any of the usual Gothic sculptural work on their façades, to avoid offending a people accustomed to Islam's prohibition of images. The lack of decoration somehow adds to their charm. There are a score of these around Cordoba, and nothing like them elsewhere in the south of Spain. **San Lorenzo**, on Calle María Auxiliadora, is perhaps the best, with a rose window designed in a common Moorish motif of interlocking circles. Some 15th-century frescoes survive around the altar and on the apse. **San Pablo** (1241), on the street of the same name, is early Gothic (five years after the Christian conquest) but contains a fine *mudéjar* dome and ceiling. **San Andrés**, on Calle Varela, two streets east of San Pablo, **Santa Marina** on Calle Morales, and the **Cristo de los Faroles** on Calle Alfaros are some of the others. Have a look inside any you find open; most have some Moorish decoration or sculptural work in their interiors, and many of their towers (like San Lorenzo's) were originally minarets. **San Pedro**, off Calle Alfonso XII, was the Christian cathedral under Moorish rule, though largely rebuilt in the 1500s.

The neighbourhoods have other surprises, if you have the persistence to find them. **Santa Victoria** is a huge austere Baroque church on Calle Juan Valera, modelled after the Roman Pantheon. Nearby, on Plaza Jerónimo Páez, a fine 16th-century palace houses the **National Archaeological Museum**, (*t 95 747 10 76, open Tues–Sat 9–8, Sun 9–3*), the largest in Andalucía, with Roman mosaics, a two-faced idol of Janus that probably came from the temple under La Mezquita, and an unusual icon of the Persian *torero*-god Mithras; the museum also holds some Moorish-looking early Christian art, and early funeral steles with odd hieroglyphs. The large collection of Moorish art includes some of the best work from the age of the caliphate, including finds from Medinat az-Zahra.

East of the Calle San Fernando, the wide street that bisects the old quarter, the houses are not as pristinely whitewashed as those around La Mezquita. Many parts are a bit run down, which does not detract from their charm. In the approximate centre of the city is the **Plaza de la Corredera**, which is an enclosed 'Plaza Mayor', like the famous ones in Madrid and Salamanca. This ambitious project, surrounded by uniform blank façades (an echo of the *estilo desornamentado*) was never completed. Now neglected and a bit eerie, the city is apparently being rehabilitated a little at a time. Continuing south, the **Museo de Bellas Artes** (*t 95 747 33 45, open Tues–Sat 9–8, Sun 9–3*) is on the lovely Plaza del Potro (mentioned by Cervantes, along with the little *posada* that still survives on it); its collections include works of Valdés Leal, Ribera, Murillo and Zurbarán, two royal portraits by Goya, and works by Cordoban artists of the 15th and 16th centuries. Beware the 'museum' across the plaza, dedicated exclusively to the works of a local named Julio Romero de Torres, the Spanish Bouguereau. Much prized by the Cordobans, this turn-of-the-last-century artist's *œuvre* consists almost entirely of naked ladies. Eastwards from here, the crooked whitewashed alleys continue for almost a mile, as far as the surviving stretch of **Moorish walls** along Ronda del Marrubial.

Plaza de las Tendillas

The centre of Roman Corduba has, by chance, become the centre of the modern city. Cordoba is probably the slickest and most up-to-date city in Andalucía (Seville would beg to differ), and it shows in this busy district of crowded pavements, modern shops, cafés and wayward youth. The contrast with the old neighbourhoods is startling, but just a block off the plaza on Calle Gondomar the beautiful 15th-century **Church of San Nicolás** will remind you that you're still in Cordoba.

In the other direction, well-preserved remains of a collapsed **Roman temple**, one of the most complete Roman monuments in Spain, have been discovered on the Calle Nueva near the *ayuntamiento*. The city has been at work reassembling the walls and columns and already the front pediment is partially complete, though its setting, in the middle of what looks like an abandoned building site, makes it a far from captivating sight.

Next to the **Plaza de Colón**, a park a few blocks north of the Plaza de las Tendillas, the **Torre de Malmuerta** ('Bad Death') takes its name from a commander of this part of the old fortifications who murdered his wife in a fit of passion; it became the subject of a well-known play by Lope de Vega, *Los Comendadores de Córdoba*.

Across the plaza is a real surprise, the rococo **Convento de la Merced** (1745), an enormous building that has recently been restored to house the provincial government and often hosts cultural exhibitions on various subjects. Don't miss it. The façade has been redone in its original painted *esgrafiado*, almost decadently colourful in pink and green, and the courtyards and grand staircases inside are incredible – more a palace than a monastery.

Medinat az-Zahra

Open Tues–Sat 10–2 and 4–6.30, Sun 10–2, **t** *95 723 40 25*
(check summer hours with the tourist office).

Eight kilometres (5 miles) northwest of the centre of Cordoba, Caliph Abd ar-Rahman III began to build a palace in the year 936. The undertaking soon got out of hand and, with the almost infinite resources of the caliphate to play with, he and his successors turned Medinat az-Zahra ('city of the Flower', so named after one of Abd ar-Rahman's wives) into a city in itself, with a market, mosques, schools and gardens, a place where the last caliphs could live in isolation from the world, safe from the turbulent street politics of their capital. Hisham II was kept a virtual prisoner here by his able vizier, al-Mansur.

The scale of it is pure *Arabian Nights*. One chronicler records an ambassador, being taken from Cordoba to the palace, finding his path carpeted the entire 8km (5 mile) route and lined from end to end with maidens to hold parasols and refreshments for him.

Stories were told of the palace's African menageries, its interior pillars and domes of crystal, and curtains of falling water for walls; another fountain was filled with flowing mercury. Such carrying-on must have aroused a good deal of resentment; in the disturbances that put an end to the caliphate, Medinat az-Zahra was sacked and razed by Berber troops in 1013.

After having served as a quarry for 900 years it's surprising anything is left at all; even under Muslim rule, columns from the palace were being carted away as far as Marrakesh. But in 1944 the royal apartments were discovered, with enough fragments to permit a restoration of a few arches with floral decorations. One hall has a roof on, and more work is under way, but as yet the rest is only foundations.

Day Trips from Cordoba

Villages of the Sierra Morena

The N432 out of Cordoba leads north to the Sierra Morena, the string of hills that curtain the western part of Andalucía from Extremadura, Castilla and La Mancha. This area is the **Valle de los Pedroches**, fertile grazing land for pigs, sheep and goats and an important hunting area for deer and wild boar – though it's a sad fact that most Spaniards are still irresponsible sportsmen and the Andalucían hunter, a mild-mannered plumber or tobacconist during the week, will take a gun in his hand on Sunday and kill anything that moves. Thousands of these animals are stalked and shot in the numerous annual hunts, or *monterías*. The Valle de los Pedroches is also healthy hiking territory, but keep yourself visible at all times – you don't want to be mistaken for someone's supper.

A road winds 73km (46 miles) up to **Bélmez**, with its Moorish castle perilously perched on a rock, from which there are panoramic views over the surrounding arid countryside. **Peñarroya-Pueblonuevo** is a dull industrial town that has fallen into

decline, but is useful here as a reference point. Sixteen kilometres (10 miles) west on the N432, the village of **Fuente Ovejuna** is best remembered for the 1476 uprising of its villagers, who dragged their tyrannical lord from his palace and treated him to a spectacularly brutal and bloody end. His sacked palace was replaced by a church, which still has its original polychromed wooden altar and painted altarpiece. The event is the subject of the drama *Fuente Ovejuna* by Lope de Vega. The village also has an Art Nouveau mansion, **Casa Cardona**, which would be more at home in Barcelona than here. Now sadly in a bad state of disrepair, its flourishes and cornices and multi-coloured windows hint at a more prosperous time. Near the village are some excavations of Roman silver mines.

It's well worth making the trip 40 km (26 miles) north of Peñarroya to **Belalcázar** and one of the most extraordinary castles in Andalucía. **El Castillo de Sotomayor** stands just outside the village and bears down on it like some malevolent force. In any other part of Europe this would be a high point on the tourist trail, but here, in one of the least visited corners of the province, it stands decayed and forlorn. Situated on an outcrop of rock and built on the ruins of an old Moorish fortress, work began on the castle early in the 15th century on the orders of Gutierre de Sotomayor, who controlled the whole of this area. A palace was added in the 16th century, but its dominant feature is the 150ft-high **Torre del Homenaje**, and its wonderfully ornate carvings. The castle remained in the family until the Peninsular War when it was badly damaged. Sadly, it is not open to the public, but can be tramped around to get an idea of its size; all around lie remnants of the earlier fortress. The present owner has declined various offers to sell to an Arab buyer or to turn it into a *parador*, a shame really as it would surely be one of the most spectacular in Spain. The village

Getting Around

Although **buses** do run from Cordoba up into the Sierra Morena and villages of Los Pedroches, they are infrequent and very time-consuming. To explore the best parts, you really need a **car**.

Where to Stay

North of Cordoba there's nothing in the way of deluxe accommodation, but the area has a reasonably wide selection of one- and two-star hotels.

**San Francisco, Ctra Villanueva de la Serena–Andújar, km 129, t 95 710 14 35 (*moderate*). A quiet place in a listed building with tennis courts; situated 2½ kilometres out of Pozoblanco.

***Finca del Rio, near Badajoz, t 92 463 66 01, f 92 463 67 70 (*inexpensive*). This old *cortijo* on the borders of Badajoz has been converted into a lovely hotel with all the amenities, including a swimming pool; open in the summer only, but at a very reasonable rates.

**Sierra de Cardeña, C/Modesto Aguilera 29, off the main square in Cardeña, t/f 95 717 44 55 (*inexpensive*). Offers decent rooms and a restaurant.

Hostal Cardeña, on the main square in Cardeña, t 95 717 41 07, f 95 717 44 84 (*inexpensive*). Slightly cheaper than the Sierra de Cardeña.

*El Comendador, C/Luis Rodríguez 25, Fuente Ovejuna, t 95 758 52 22 (*inexpensive*). An adequate place to stay in Fuente Ovejuna; the rooms are pretty basic and there is a damp feel about it, but the building itself, with a pretty patio, is lovely.

Hostal Javi, C/Córdoba 31, Bélmez, t 95 757 30 99, f 95 758 04 98 (*cheap*). An excellent value *hostal* in Bélmez which has sparkling modern rooms of hotel quality with TV, minibar and large bathrooms, set round a delightful vine-covered staircase; with parking and a pretty patio.

Siena, C/Negrillos 1, Bélmez, t 95 758 00 34 (*cheap*). A less salubrious alternative in Bélmez, which also does food.

La Bolera, C/Padre Torrero 17, Belalcázar, t 95 714 63 00 (*cheap*). A basic place in Belalcázar; food is available in the numerous bars around the main square.

Volao, C/Perralejo 2, Villanueva de Córdoba, t 95 712 01 57. Offers no frills for its very *cheap* rooms.

*Sevilla, C/Miguel Vigara 15, Peñarroya-Pueblonuevo, t 95 756 01 00, f 95 756 23 07 (*inexpensive*). Though there's no reason to stay in Peñarroya-Pueblonuevo, you may like to use it as a base for your day trip. This is the most comfortable place to stay, offering rooms with bath.

*El Sol, C/El Sol 24, Peñarroya-Pueblonuevo, t 95 756 20 50 (*cheap*). Has basic rooms at bargain rates.

Eating Out

This area is famed throughout Andalucía for its supreme quality *jamón ibérico* (locally cured ham) and sucking pig; the excellent *salchichón* from Pozoblanco; and the strong, spicy cheese made from ewes' milk. Sadly it is often difficult for visitors to the region to sample them. There are no outstanding restaurants around, and even indifferent ones are pretty thin on the ground. Driving off into the countryside in search of gastronomic delight can be a risky business; and, though it's true that it occasionally pays rich dividends, to be sure of eating really well you should head for the tapas bars in the villages or, better still, grab some goodies from a supermarket and have a picnic out on the slopes.

Bar Lucas, Pza de la Independencia, in Cardeña (*inexpensive*). If you are in Cardeña, this bar is a good place to eat and drink, with a very reasonably priced menu.

Gran, C/Córdoba. The best restaurant in Bélmez. *Closed Mon.*

La Jaula, in Pedroche (*inexpensive*). The best of a number of eateries just up from the main square on the way to the church. (Should you have an urge to stay in Pedroche, and it is an inviting place, there is only one place, but be warned: it is basic, next to the disco and above a bar; call t 95 713 74 17.)

itself has a pretty main square dominated by 15th-century **Iglesia de Santiago El Mayor**, with its later Gothic facade. Just outside the village is the convent of **Santa Clara de Columna**, founded in 1476 and still in use, though it is open to visits. The ruins of an old monastery, San Francisco, are nearby.

The CP236 heads east from here across an unremarkable landscape to the tiny village of **Santa Eufemia**, some 26km (17 miles) away. The ruins of a medieval castle stand just outside the village, nestling in a cleft in the rocks which rise spectacularly above it. There's a 15th-century Gothic-*mudejár* church, **La Encarnación**, and a well-preserved gate in the main square, as well as some good walking routes available from the *ayuntamiento*, in Plaza Mayor.

From here you could head down to the village of **Pozoblanco** (take the N502 then the A420), famous for the last *corrida* of the renowned bullfighter Francisco Rivera, better known as Paquirri. Gored, he died in the ambulance on the way to Cordoba; presumably bouncing around on those roads didn't help. Paquirri's widow, the singer Isabel Pantoja, soared to even greater heights of popularity on his death, with the Spanish public obsessed as ever by the drama of life and mortality.

Pedroche, 10km (6 miles) away, is a sleepy little village with a fine 16th-century Gothic church with a proud, lofty spire, and a Roman bridge. This place too has had its fair share of drama – in 1936 Communist forces shot nearly a hundred of the menfolk; their deaths are commemorated by a plaque on the side of the church. Just outside the village lies the **Ermita de Piedras Santas**, a non-descript 16th-century building with some pretty atrocious art inside; it becomes the scene of a pilgrimage on 8 September. As many as 50,000 people from the villages around Pedroche come here to pay their respects to their *patronada*. Beyond the villages of **Villanueva de Cordoba** and **Cardeña** to the east is the **Parque Natural de Sierra Cardeña** – rolling hills forested in oak, more stag-hunting grounds and ideal rambling terrain.

East towards Úbeda

East of Cordoba, it's a slow, leisurely journey up the valley of the slow, leisurely Río Guadalquivir, endless rolling hills covered with olive trees and, in places, endless miles of sunflowers, a grand sight in the early summer. The three large towns along the way, Andújar, Bailén and Linares, are much alike, amiable industrial towns still painted a gleaming white, though the main attractions are two lovely, out-of-the-way towns with exceptional ensembles of Renaissance architecture: Baeza and Úbeda.

The Gateway to Andalucía

This area is Andalucía's front door. The roads and railways from Madrid branch off here for Seville and Granada. Many important battles were fought nearby, including Las Navas de Tolosa near La Carolina, in 1212, which opened the way for the conquest of al-Andalus; and Bailén, in 1808, where a Spanish-English force gave Napoleon's boys a sound thrashing and built up Spanish morale for what they call their War of Independence.

Montoro

The NIV snakes along the Guadalquivir valley, and 42km (26 miles) east of Cordoba it brings you to the delightfully placed town of Montoro, sitting on a bend in the river. The facetious-looking tower that rises above the whitewashed houses belongs to the Gothic church of **San Bartolomé** in Plaza de España. Also in the square is the 16th-century **Ducal Palace**, now the *ayuntamiento*, with a Plateresque façade. The beautiful 15th-century bridge that connects Montoro to its suburb, Retamar, is known as the **Puente de Las Doñadas**, a tribute to the women of the village who sacrificed their jewellery to help finance its construction. Seek out the kitsch **Casa de las Conchas**, C/Criado 17 (signposted from the Plaza de España), a house and courtyard done out in hundreds of thousands of sea shells gathered from the beaches of Spain by Francisco del Rio over the past forty or so years. He will show you round for a small fee and flog you a postcard.

Andújar

Approaching Andújar, a further 35km (22 miles) down the NIV, you'll find the countryside dominated by huge, blue sunflower-oil refineries like fallen space stations. Sunflowers, like olives, are a big crop in the region. Nothing remains of Andújar's Moorish castle, but there are a couple of surprises in this town which might tempt you to linger a while. The church of **Santa María**, in the plaza of the same name, has in one chapel the *Immaculate Conception* by Pacheco, Velázquez's teacher, and in another the magnificent *Christ in the Garden of Olives*, by El Greco. What on earth is an El Greco doing here? One reason given is that the Río Guadalquivir, upon which the town stands, was once navigable as far as Andújar and as result the town grew rich through trade with the Americas. Many merchants and nobility settled here, one of whom, so legend has it, donated the painting to the church in lieu of a cash gift. This also accounts for the large number of palaces and mansions – though, due to shortage of funds, many are falling into disrepair and are not open to the public.

The **Casa de Albarracín**, which dates from the 16th century and used to be the town hall, stands opposite the church of **Santa Maria**. The coat of arms has long since disappeared – pulled down by a departing nobleman or ordered off by an angry king. Nearby stands the **Torre del Reloj**, where the minaret of the Moorish mosque once stood. It was finished in 1534 and sports a fabulous imperial coat of arms symbolizing the town's loyalty to the then king, Charles V. The *torre* now houses the *turismo*, which has a mountain of information about the town and offers free walking tours if you ring ahead.

From here it's a short walk to the Plaza de España, which is dominated by the current *ayuntamiento*, housed in what was the town's playhouse. Beside it is **San Miguel**, the oldest church in town, dating from Visigothic times. Inside is a beautiful choir with wrought iron balustrades, the front carved in walnut. The tower outside the church leans slightly, a result of the Lisbon earthquake of 1755. The pink building on the other side of the square is the post office, with an arch leading through to the Plaza de la Constitución.

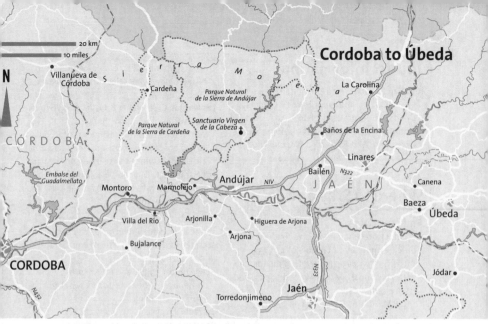

Andújar also has a small **archaeological museum** (*open Tues–Fri 7–9; Sat–Sun 11–1*) housed in another fine building, the Palacio Niños de Don Gome, which stands just behind a part of the Moorish city wall. Inside are a number of local ceramics and artefacts dating from Roman times. The exterior of the palace is decorated with two incongruous, and rather camp, figures, which are supposed to represent South American Indians.

Around Andújar

Just before Andújar, off the NIV, lies the tiny spa village of **Marmolejo**, where the mineral water of the same name is bottled. There is little there to detain you, but a good hotel (*see* under 'Andújar' in 'Where to Stay' overleaf) and the spa itself, which lies 2km into the mountains and is open from May to the end of October. From Marmolejo you could rejoin the NIV or take a detour through endless olive groves to two pretty villages: **Arjonilla**, a production centre of olive oil, which you can smell on the way into town, and **Arjona** a few kilometres on. This village was once topped by a Moorish castle complex, but all that remains today is the heavily restored church of Santa Maria, and the 17th-century chapel opposite. The walk up is worth it, however, for the wonderful views. Below is a pretty square, Plaza de la Constitución, where you can get a drink at Café Campos.

Another possible diversion, 30km (19 miles) north of Andújar on the J501, is the **Santuario de la Virgen de la Cabeza**. It's worth packing a picnic and enjoying the drive; when you get there you'll be rewarded with panoramic views, though there is very little left of the 13th-century sanctuary, which was blown to bits by Republicans after being seized by pro-Franco guards near the start of the Civil War. The present building and surrounds are a grotesque mish-mash of fascistic architecture, similar in style to El Valle de Los Caidos, Franco's tomb outside Madrid. In the crypt below there is a bizarre collection of photos and walking aids hanging from the walls, representing

Tourist Information

Andújar: Torre del Reloj/Pza Santa Maria s/n, t 95 350 02 79, *andujar_turismo@terra.es.
Open Tues–Sat 10–2 and 5–8.*
Montoro: Plaza de España 8, t 95 716 00 89.
Open Mon, Wed, Fri 8.30–3; Tues and Thurs 10–2 and 5–6.30; Sat 10–1; closed Sun.

Where to Stay and Eat

Andújar ✉ 23740
***Gran Hotel Balneario, Calvario 101 (10km outside Andújar at Marmolejo), t 95 354 09 75, f 95 351 74 33 (*moderate*). Probably the area's best hotel, with a swimming pool and its own grounds.
***Del Val, C/Hnos del Val 1, t 95 350 09 50, f 95 350 66 06 (*moderate*). Just outside town, on the corner of the road up to the sanctuary, with a swimming pool and its own grounds.
**Don Pedro, C/Gabriel Zamora 5, t 95 350 12 74, f 95 350 47 85 (*inexpensive*). The best place to stay in Andújar itself, situated in the centre of town, with pleasant rooms and a tavern-style restaurant that specializes in game dishes (*moderate*). It also has a disco attached.
La Fuente, C/Vendederas, t 95 350 42 69, f 95 350 19 00 (*inexpensive*). Clean and friendly with a garage and a good restaurant attached.
*Logasasanti, C/Doctor Fleming 5, t 95 350 05 00, f 95 350 50 05 (*inexpensive*). Another respectable, central option, though slightly more basic.
**Montoro, Madrid–Cadiz road, km 358, t 95 316 07 92 (*cheap*). A basic option on the main road.
Restaurante Madrid–Sevilla, Plaza del Sol 4, t 95 350 05 94 (*expensive*). Patronized by the King and Queen of Spain, and so called for its position on the old road. Run by the indefatigable Manuel Gómez Sotoca, it's a favourite with the hunting fraternity, as well as the royals. Fresh fish is brought in daily and game features heavily on the menu, which changes according to Snr Sotoca's mood. Choose what you want and he'll whip out to the kitchen to create it for you

himself. Your meal is complemented by an extraordinary wine selection from all over the country.
Las Perolas, C/Serpiente 6, t 95 350 67 26 (*inexpensive*). Another great character, Ana Domínguez, runs this restaurant. She cooks up all her specials – venison, rabbit and quail – in big pots which sit steaming on the bar.
Los Naranjos, C/Guadalupe 4. This place looks at first like a café, but it's in fact quite a smart restaurant.

If you have the desire to stay up by the shrine at Nuestra Virgen de la Cabeza there are a few options, all of which have restaurants attached.
*La Mirada, t 95 354 91 11 (*inexpensive*). As its name suggests, has a good view of the shrine, and a pool.
Cofradia, t 95 354 90 50 (*inexpensive*).
Pensión Virgen de la Cabeza, t 95 312 21 65 (*cheap*).
Los Pinos, t 95 354 90 79. A good restaurant on the road up to the sanctuary; also rents out a rural retreat.
El Rancho, opposite Los Pinos, t 95 354 91 10. Serves a good selection of game and fish at reasonable prices.

Bailén ✉ 23710
***Hotel Bailen, Ctra NIV, km 296, t 95 367 01 00, f 95 367 25 30 (*moderate*). Just outside Bailén in an old *parador* and with pleasant gardens, air-conditioning and a swimming pool. It also houses a restaurant and tapas bar.
**Cuatro Caminos, C/Sebastián Elcano 40, t 95 367 02 19, f 95 367 30 38 (*inexpensive*). Better placed near the centre and half the price, with a café attached, but no pool.

Baños de la Encina ✉ 23710
***Hotel Baños C/Cerro Llamada s/n, t 95 361 40 68 (*moderate*). The only hotel in town; neat and newly opened.
Mesón Buenos Aires, Cateyana, t 95 361 32 11. A reliable restaurant with good country cooking, including wild boar and venison in season.
La Encina, Consultorio 3, t 95 361 40 98 (*inexpensive*). Has views of the castle and does a good *menú* for 1,100 pts.

Mesón del Duque, t 95 361 30 26 (*inexpensive*) At the top of town, opposite the Ermita Jesús del Llano; its rather grand name belies its simple and reasonably priced country cooking.

Mirasierra, Bailén s/n, t 95 361 31 20 (*inexpensive*). This restaurant just down from the *turismo* is worth trying.

La Carolina ✉ 23200

****Perdiz**, Ctra NIV, km 268, t 95 366 03 00, f 95 368 13 62, www.nh-hoteles.com (*moderate*). A classic stopover for travellers between Andalucía and northern Spain with an appealing, coaching-inn ambience. It's got a pretty good restaurant too and, as its name ('partridge') implies, it serves seasonal game dishes as well as traditional favourites (*moderate*).

****Orellane Perdiz/Orellana Perdiz II**, Ctra NIV, km 265, t 95 366 12 51, f 95 366 21 70 (*moderate*). Although more or less devoid of character, has good facilities including parking and tennis.

El Retorno, C/General Sanjurjo, 5, t 95 366 16 13 (*cheap*). The best of the budget options in town with an attractive flower-fringed patio, clean, quiet rooms, and a very friendly proprietor.

Los Jardineros, C/General Sanjurjo, t 95 366 88 12 (*cheap*). Next door, and slightly more basic.

Gran Parada, Avda Lindez Vilches 9, t 95 366 02 75 (*cheap*). If everything else is booked, try here as a last resort.

La Toja, Avda Juan Carlos 1, t 95 366 10 18 (*moderate–inexpensive*). Set back from the main street behind steel doors, this large, open-plan restaurant serves good local fare (game) at a reasonable price.

Linares ✉ 23700

*****Aníbal**, C/Cid Campeador 11, t 95 365 04 00, f 95 365 22 04 (*moderate*). The jumbo hotel in town.

*****Victoria**, C/Cervantes 7–9, t/f 95 369 25 00 (*moderate*). Rather characterless, but clean and friendly with large rooms.

****Cervantes**, C/Cervantes 23, t 95 369 18 01, f 95 369 05 08 (*moderate*). Although slightly old-fashioned, it is probably better value

than the Victoria, with spotlessly clean rooms set round a pretty patio.

Baviera, C/Virgen 25, t 95 365 69 10 (*cheap*). Basic rooms, all with bath, for those on a budget.

Mesón Castellano, C/Puente 5, t 95 369 00 09 (*moderate*). The place to go for dinner. *Closed Sun, July and Aug.*

Entertainment and Nightlife

Andújar ✉ 23740

Habana, C/Emperador Trajano. A café-bar that attracts a young crowd; the place to come for a late-night *copa*.

Escena, Pso del Castillo (in the old cinema). A more sophisticated spot.

OTK Cheroly, C/Emperador Adriano. The big disco in town, attracting a pretty young crowd.

Los Romeros, Alto Santo Domingo. Flamenco can be found here – ask at the bar nearby, Memphis, for times.

Baños de la Encina ✉ 23710

There are a small number of places to try for after-dinner drinks and more.

Lipika, Pso de Llana s/n. A pub/disco.

Pub La Colmena, C/Valdeloshuertos 12.

Discoteca El Pinar, C/Migaldías 15.

La Carolina ✉ 23200

Taberna del Arte, C/Real 5 (just down from Pza de Ayuntamiento), t/f 95 368 12 27. For late-night drinking, especially at the weekends; adorned with bullfighting posters and photos. The bar breaks into song every Friday and Saturday in celebration of the local pilgrimage to Nuestra Virgen de la Cabeza. A wide selection of reasonably priced tapas and *raciones* are served.

Linares ✉ 23700

For a few late-night *copas*, C/Cervantes has two good options.

Long Rock, C/Cervantes 13.

Mas Tomate. A disco next door.

those who the Virgin has cured or those who have promised to make a pilgrimage if the Virgin helps them out of a sticky situation.

One of Andalucía's biggest fiestas is the annual *romería* to the sanctuary on the last Sunday in April, when half a million pilgrims trek up on foot, horseback, carts and donkeys. The celebrations begin the week before with various competitions held in the town centre. On the Thursday, thousands of Andújarans dress up in traditional Andalucían dress and layer the ground outside the Capilla del Virgen de la Cabeza, in C/Ollerias, with a blanket of flowers. The next day the streets, resonant with music, fill with people parading in costume on horseback. The pilgrimage proper begins early on the Saturday morning, leaving Andújar for the sanctuary along various routes, including the old Roman road. The halfway point is **Lugar Nuevo**, near an old Roman bridge, where pilgrims stop for a giant picnic, before arriving at the sanctuary that night where an hourly mass begins. Finally, on Sunday morning the Virgin is brought out of the sanctuary and paraded down the hill, where she has various objects – including young children – thrown at her to be blessed. Of course all this means big business, and the sanctuary is spawning a village at its feet, with restaurants, bars and hotels to cater for the pilgrims.

Bailén

Back on the NIV, 27 kilometres (17 miles) further east is the modern, unprepossessing town of **Bailén**. The tomb of the Spanish general Francisco Javier Castaños (1756–1852), who so cleverly whipped the French troops and sent Napoleon back to the drawing board, is in the Gothic parish church of the **Encarnación**, which also has a sculpture by Alonso Cano. But don't dally here – the real treat is to be found 11km (7 miles) to the north on the NIV at **Baños de la Encina**, where the 10th-century oval Moorish castle is one of the best preserved in all Andalucía. Dominating the town, the castle has 14 sturdy, square towers and a double-horseshoe gateway, scarcely touched by time, and from the walls you get a sweeping vista of the olive groves and distant peaks beyond Úbeda. The castle has no set opening hours – enquire at the *turismo* (*t* 95 361 41 85) for the key.

An arduous hour's trek from Baños, through difficult, hilly terrain, lies the natural refuge of **Canforos de Peñarrubia**, with its remarkably preserved Bronze Age paintings of deer and scenes of animal-taming. Serious hikers should ask for a guide at the *ayuntamiento* in the town (*t* 95 361 30 04).

La Carolina

Twenty kilometres (12½ miles) north of here on the NIV is **La Carolina**, a model of 18th-century grid planning. The village owes its existence to forward-thinking Carlos III, who imported a few thousand German artisans in the late 1700s and set them to work excavating the lead and copper mines, tilling the fields and herding sheep. A side effect of this colonization was supposed to be the decline of banditry in the then wild and unpopulated hills. But within two generations almost all the Germans had died off or fled. The town and surrounding area are best known now as a large game-hunting reserve, particularly for partridge.

Linares

From Bailén the N322 heads eastward to the mining town of **Linares**, birthplace of the guitarist Andrés Segovia, who later moved on; others weren't so lucky – in 1947 the great bullfighter Manolete had an off day and met his end on the horns of a bull in the ring here. If things had gone well for him, he might have gone to view the finds from the Roman settlement of nearby Castulo, housed in the town's **archaeology museum**, but unfortunately the last thing he saw was probably the ornate Baroque portal of the hospital **San Juan de Dios**.

From Linares it's a 27km (17 mile) run to Úbeda; a little more than halfway you'll pass an elegant castle at **Canena**.

Baeza

Campo de Baeza, soñaré contigo cuando no te vea
(Fields of Baeza, I will dream of you when I can no longer see you)

Antonio Machado (1875–1939)

Sometimes history offers its recompense. The 13th-century Reconquista was especially brutal here; nearly the entire population fled, many of them moving to Granada, where they settled the Albaicín. The 16th century, however, when the wool trade was booming in this corner of Andalucía, was good to Baeza, leaving it a distinguished little town of neatly clipped trees and tan stone buildings, with a beautiful ensemble of monuments in styles from Romanesque to Renaissance. It seems a happy place, serene and quiet as the olive groves that surround it.

The prettiest corner of the town is **Plaza del Pópulo**. It is enclosed by decorative pointed arches and Renaissance buildings, and contains a fountain with four half-effaced lions; the fountain was patched together with the help of pieces taken from the Roman remains at Castulo, and the centrepiece, the fearless lady on the pedestal, is traditionally considered to be Imilce, the wife of Hannibal.

Heading north on the Cuesta de San Felipe, which can be reached by the steps leading off the Plaza del Pópulo, you pass the 15th-century **Palacio de Jabalquinto** (*open 10–2 and 4–6; closed Wed*), with an eccentric façade covered with coats of arms and pyramidal stone studs (a Spanish fancy of that age; you can see others like it in Guadalajara and Salamanca). The *palacio* was built in the 15th century by the Benavides family, and is now a seminary. Its patio is open to the public (*open Mon–Fri 9–2*) and boasts a beautiful two-tiered arcade around a central fountain, as well as a fine carved Baroque staircase. Adjoining the *palacio*, the 16th-century **Antigua Universidad** was a renowned centre of learning for three hundred years, until its charter was withdrawn during the reign of Fernando VII. It has since been used as a school; its indoor patio, like that of the Jabalquinto, is open to the public (*open daily 10–2 and 4–6, closed Wed*). The school has found latterday fame through Antonio Machado (Juan de Mairena), the *sevillano* poet who taught there (1913–19). His most famous prose work, *Sentencias, donaires, apuntes y recuerdos* (1936), follows the career of a fictional schoolmaster and draws heavily on his experiences in Baeza.

Getting Around

By Train

Come to Baeza by train at your own risk. The nearest station, officially named Linares-Baeza, t 95 365 02 02, is far off in the open countryside, 14km away. A bus to Baeza usually meets the train, but if you turn up at night or on a Sunday you may be stranded.

By Bus

Baeza's bus station, t 95 74 04 68, is a little way from the centre on Avda Alcalde Puche Pardo. Baeza is a stop on the Úbeda–Cordoba bus route, with 12 a day running to Jaén (1½hrs); eight to Granada (2hrs); two to Cazorla and one to Malaga (4–5hrs).

Tourist Information

Pza del Pópulo (also known as the Plaza de los Leones), t 95 374 04 44. *Open Mon–Fri 9–2.30, Sat 10–1; closed Sun.*

Internet: Speed Informática, Pso de la Constitución (next to the employment office), t 95 374 70 05.

Where to Stay and Eat

Baeza ✉ 23440

***Hotel Palacete Santa Ana**, C/Santa Ana Vieja 9, t 95 374 07 65, f 95 374 16 57 (*moderate*). A lavishly restored noble palace where politicians and leading *toreros* seek privacy – the closest thing you'll get to stepping back into the 18th century. There are just 14 bedrooms, reached by a marble staircase, all of them different and stuffed full of original mirrors, paintings and sculptures, but with all mod cons. There are two dining rooms, two living rooms, an indoor and outdoor patio, a *terraza* on the roof and a cellar below where *dueña* Ana Maria Rodriguez organizes private flamenco shows. The attention to detail here is extraordinary and the price for such splendour a giveaway. There is also a nearby restaurant connected to the hotel.

***Hotel Confortel Baeza**, C/Concepción 3, t 95 374 81 30, f 95 374 25 19, comerbaeza@

ctv.es (*moderate*). The second-best choice in Baeza, situated behind the Iglesia del Hospital de la Purísima Concepción, near the Plaza de España. The hotel is set in a monasterial building which used to be a religious school. The rooms open on to a peaceful arched quadrangle.

***Complejo Turistico Hacienda La Laguna**, on the Ctra Jaén–Puente del Obispo, t 95 312 71 72, f 95 312 71 74 (*moderate*). A delightful rural hotel in an old *cortijo* with lots of activities and amenities for kids and adults.

***Juanito**, Pso Arca del Agua s/n, t 95 374 00 40, f 95 374 23 24, *juanito.baeza@ via.goya.es* (*inexpensive*). Has rooms with bath plus its own pool, but the hotel is rather run down; situated on the road leaving Baeza in the direction of Úbeda.

***Hospederia Fuentenueva**, Pso Arca del Agua s/n, t 95 374 31 00, f 95 374 32 00, *www.rgo.net/fuentenueva* (*moderate*). On the same road, this is a more upmarket place set in its own grounds and with a pool attached.

Comercio, C/San Pablo 21, t 95 374 01 00 (*cheap*). A comfortable lodging where Machado stayed, and perhaps even penned a few poems.

Pensión El Patio, C/Conde Romanones 13, t 95 374 02 00 (*cheap*). This Renaissance mansion set around a courtyard is a good budget bet.

Andrés de Vandelvira, C/San Francisco 14, t 95 374 43 61 (*expensive*). A restaurant inside the San Francisco convent with tables filling the arched quadrangle; for more intimacy, dine upstairs. *Closed Sun afternoons.*

Juanito, Pso Arca del Agua s/n, t 95 374 00 40, f 95 374 23 24, *juanito.baeza@via.goya.es* (*expensive*). This hotel's restaurant is worth trying – it's in the Michelin guide.

La Gondola, Portales Carbonería 13, t 95 374 29 84 (*moderate*). Set back from the main Paseo, with an emphasis on heavy meats and *churrascos*.

Sali, C/Cardenal Benavides 15, t 95 374 13 65 (*moderate*). Fish and shellfish feature with game dishes like partridge in brine; situated opposite the town hall. *Closed Wed.*

Casa Pedro, C/Cardenal Benavides, t 95 374 80 87 (*inexpensive*). Next door to Sali; has a menu for 1,200pts.

A right turn at the next corner leads to the 16th-century Santa Iglesia **cathedral** (*open winter 10.30–1 and 4–6; summer 10.30–1 and 5–7; closed Wed*) on Plaza Santa María, a work of Andrés de Vandelvira. This replaced a 13th-century Gothic church (the chancel and portal survive), which in turn took the place of a mosque; a colonnade from this can be seen in the cloister. For the best show in town, drop a coin in the box marked *custodia* in one of the side chapels; this will reveal, with a noisy dose of mechanical *duende*, a rich and ornate 18th-century silver tabernacle. The fountain in front of the cathedral, the **Fuente de Santa María**, with a little triumphal arch at its centre (1564), is Baeza's landmark and symbol. Behind it is the Isabelline Gothic **Casas Consistoriales**, formerly the town hall, while opposite stands the 16th-century seminary of **San Felipe Neri** (also known as the Antonio Machado International University), its walls adorned with student graffiti – recording their names and dates in bull's blood. It's curiously reminiscent of the rowing eights' hieroglyphics which cover the quadrangle walls of the sportier Oxford and Cambridge colleges.

The Paseo de la Constitución, at the bottom of the hill, is Baeza's main, albeit quiet, thoroughfare, an elegant rectangle lined with crumbling shops and bars. Two buildings are worthy of note: **La Alhóndiga**, the 16th-century, porticoed corn exchange and, almost opposite, the **Casa Consistorial**, the 18th-century town hall. Just behind the Paseo, in Plaza Cardinal Benavides, the façade of the **Ayuntamiento** (1599) is a classic example of Andalucían Plateresque, and one of the last. From here it's a short walk to the 16th-century **Convento de San Francisco**, which now houses an excellent restaurant (*see* above). At the end of the Paseo, the inelegant Plaza de España marks the northern boundary of historic Baeza and houses yet more bars.

Úbeda

Even with Baeza for an introduction, the presence of this nearly perfect little city comes as a surprise. If the 16th century did well by Baeza, it was a golden age here, leaving Úbeda a 'town built for gentlemen' as the Spanish used to say, endowed with one of the finest collections of Renaissance architecture in all of Spain. Two men can take much of the credit: Andrés de Vandelvira, an Andalucían architect who created most of Úbeda's best buildings, and Francisco de los Cobos, imperial secretary to Charles V, who paid for them. Cobos is a forgotten hero of Spanish history. While Charles was off campaigning in Germany, Cobos had the job of running Castile. By the most delicate management, he kept the kingdom afloat while meeting Charles's ever more exorbitant demands for money and men. He could postpone the inevitable disaster, but not prevent it. Like most public officials in the Spanish Age of Rapacity, though, he also managed to salt away a few hundred thousand ducats for himself, and he spent most of them embellishing his home town.

Like Baeza, Úbeda is a peaceful and happy place; it wears its Renaissance heritage gracefully, and is always glad to have visitors. Slowly, it's gearing up for them. Tourism is less of a novelty here than it was even a couple of years ago, and a tour bus of camera-wielding Japanese trying to negotiate the delicate Renaissance plazas is

Getting Around

Úbeda's **bus** station, C/San José, **t** 95 375 21 57, is at the western end of town, and various lines connect the city directly to Madrid, Valencia and Barcelona, at least once daily, and more frequently to Baeza (16 daily, 20mins), Cordoba (3 daily, 2½hrs), Jaén (8 daily, 1½hrs) Granada (2 daily, 2½hrs) and Seville (3 daily). Cazorla and other villages in the region can easily be reached from Úbeda.

Tourist Information

Palacio Marques de Contadero, C/Baja del Marqués 4 (off the Plaza del Ayuntamiento), **t** 95 375 08 97. *Open Mon–Sat 8–3.*

Where to Stay and Eat

Úbeda ✉ 23400

****Parador Condestable Dávalos, Pza de Vázquez de Molina s/n, **t** 95 375 03 45, **f** 95 375 12 59, *ubeda@parador.es* (*expensive*). In a 16th-century palace with a glassed-in courtyard, one of the loveliest and most popular of the chain, it has recently been completely refurbished. All the beamed ceil-ings and fireplaces have been preserved and the restaurant is the best in town (which isn't saying a lot), featuring local specialities for around 3,500 pts for a full dinner. Ask to see the ancient wine cellar.

Palacio de la Rambla, Pza del Marqués 1, **t 95 375 01 96, **f** 95 375 02 67 (*expensive*). A romantic and slightly less expensive choice in the historic heart of the town, set in a magnificent ivy-clad Renaissance mansion with rooms surrounding an ivy-clad court-yard where the Marquesa de la Rambla lets out beautiful double rooms (ask for 106).

****Álvar Fáñez, C/Juan Pasquau 5 (just off the Plaza San Pedro), **t/f** 95 379 60 43 (*expen-sive*). Another recently converted ducal palace, with 11 tastefully decorated (albeit slightly austere) rooms, and a lovely *terraza* with views over the rooftops to the olive groves and the hills. The delightful old patio looks as it did 400 years ago. There is also a café serving excellent tapas and a good restaurant in the cellar. The hotels organizes cultural and environmental excursions. Rates include breakfast.

***María de Molina, Plaza del Ayuntamiento, s/n, **t** 95 379 53 56, **f** 95 379 36 94, *www.hotel-maria-de-molina.com* (*expensive–moderate*). Probably has the edge over the others in

not an uncommon sight. But it's still easy to understand the Spanish expression *'irse por los cerros de Úbeda'* ('take the Úbeda hill routes'). It basically equates to getting off the subject or wasting time and arose many years ago after Úbeda gradu-ally lost traffic to more commercial routes. Legend has it that a Christian knight fell in love with a Moorish girl and was reproached for his absence by King Fernando III. When questioned about his whereabouts during the battle the knight idly replied, 'Lost in those hills, sire'.

Úbeda today leaves no doubt how its local politics are going. In the **Plaza de Andalucía**, joining the old and new districts, there is an old metal statue of a fascist Civil War general named Sero glaring down from his pedestal. The townspeople have put so many bullets into it, it looks like a Swiss cheese. They've left it here as a joke, and have merrily renamed another square, from Plaza del Generalíssimo to Plaza 1 de Mayo.

The Torre de Reloj, in the Plaza de Andalucía, is a 14th-century defensive tower now adorned with a clock. The plaque near the base, under a painting of the Virgin, records a visit of Charles V. From here, Calle Real takes you into the heart of the old town. Nearly every corner has at least one lovely palace or church on it. Two of the best can be seen on this street: the early 17th-century **Palacio de Condé Guadiana** has an terms of position, just behind the main square. The patio has been modernized, and is a little too prettified, but the 20 rooms have some original furniture and paintings, all with lovely bathrooms. Also with café and very good restaurant: try the roasted kid leg or the deer loin.

★**Hostal Los Cerros**, Peñarroya 1, t 95 375 16 21 (*cheap*). A spotless *hostal* in the new town.

★★**Sevilla**, Avda/ Ramón y Cajal 9, t 95 375 06 12 (*cheap*). You can get a clean and pleasant double with bath for very good rates here – air conditioning is extra.

Castillo, Avda/ Ramón y Cajal 20, t 95 375 06 12 (*cheap*). With a café attached, satellite TV and air conditioning.

★**San Miguel**, Avda Libertad 69, t 95 375 20 49 (*cheap*). Another cheapie, where you can get a double without bath.

★★**Hotel Consuelo**, Avda/ Ramón y Cajal 12, t 95 375 08 40, f 95 375 68 34 (*inexpensive*). Rooms here are a bit fancier.

Apart from the *parador*, there are few good restaurants in Úbeda.

Cuzco, Parque Vandelvira 8, t 95 375 34 13 (*inexpensive*). Serves local dishes and standard *andaluz* fish and meat menus. It has a 950 pts menu of the day which includes two courses and wine.

El Seco, C/Corazón de Jesús 8 (near the Plaza Ayuntamiento), t 95 379 14 72 (*inexpensive*). A small dining room with reasonable food, if little atmosphere.

Mesón Navarro, Plaza Ayuntamiento, t 95 379 06 38. Pricier but has more atmosphere.

El Gallo Rojo, Plaza Torrenueva (at the top of Calle Trinidad), t 95 375 20 38 (*inexpensive*). During the daytime you'll find plenty of characters at the bar, and it's a lively place in the evening with excellent tapas and a restaurant.

Mesón Gabino, Fuenteseca s/n, t 95 375 42 07. Also good for tapas and light meals.

El Olivo, Avda Ramón y Cajal 2, t 95 375 20 92 (*inexpensive*). Has average fare at the expected prices.

Hostal Sevilla, Avda Ramón y Cajal 20, t 95 375 0612. The restaurant at this *hostal* is good value and worth a try.

The bar scene is fairly advanced in Úbeda.

Lupo, Plaza de San Pedro. This bar boasts a state-of-the-art interior.

Siglo XV, Calle de Muñoz García (Úbeda's liveliest street after dark). Set in a Gothic building which used to be a brothel.

Bar Palacio, Calle Trinidad (in the courtyard of the Palacio de los Bussianos). Stop off here for pre-dinner drinks.

ornate tower and distinctive windows cut out of the corners of the building, a common conceit in Úbeda's palaces. Two blocks down, the **Palacio Vela de los Cobos** (*ask at the tourist office for opening hours*) is in the same style, with a loggia on the top storey. Northeast of here, on C/Cervantes, lies a small **museum** (*open Tues–Sun 11–12.45 and 5–6.30*) with the tiny monastic cell where San Juan de la Cruz (St John of the Cross) died of cancer and ulceration of the flesh in 1591. Friar John, much persecuted in his lifetime because of his unorthodox teachings, is one of Spain's most illustrious poets and mystics.

The home of Francisco de los Cobos's nephew, another royal counsellor, was the great **Palacio de las Cadenas**, now serving as Úbeda's *ayuntamiento* and a small ceramics **museum** (*open Tues–Sat 10.30–2 and 5–7; adm*), on a quiet plaza at the end of Calle Real. The side facing the plaza is simple and dignified but the main façade, facing the **Plaza Vázquez de Molina**, is a stately Renaissance creation, the work of Vandelvira.

Plaza Vázquez de Molina

This is the only place in Andalucía where you can look around and not regret the passing of the Moors, for it is one of the few truly beautiful things in all this great

Úbeda's Pottery

Traditional dark green pottery, fired in kilns over wood and olive stones, is literally Úbeda's trademark. You'll see it all over town – try to pick up some authentic pieces before they become available in Habitat. Tito, on the Plaza Ayuntamiento, is a class establishment that produces and fires pieces on the premises. The designs are exquisite and are packed and shipped all over the world.

Highly recommended is a visit to the potters' quarter around the Calle Valencía, a 15-minute stroll from the Plaza Ayuntamiento. Heading northeast to the Plaza 1 de Mayo, cross the square diagonally and leave again by the northeast corner, along the Calle Losal to the Puerta de Losal, a 13th-century *mudéjar* gate. Continue downhill along the Calle de Merced, passing the Plaza Olleros on your left, and you come to Calle Valencia. Nearly every house is a potter's workshop; all are open to the public and you will soon find your own favourite. Ours is at No.36, where Juan José Almarza runs his family business, handed down through several generations. Juan spent two years in Edinburgh and is possibly the only potter in the province of Jaén with a Scottish accent.

region that was not built either by the Moors or under their influence. The Renaissance buildings around the Palacio de las Cadenas make a wonderful ensemble, and the austere landscaping, old cobbles and plain six-sided fountain create the same effect of contemplative serendipity as any chamber of the Alhambra. Buildings on the plaza include: the church of **Santa María de los Reales Alcázares** (which is currently being restored); a Renaissance façade on an older building with a fine Gothic cloister around the back; the *parador*; two sedate palaces from the 16th century, one of which, the **Palacio del Marqués de Mancera**, can be visited (*open daily 10am–11am*); and Vandelvira's **Sacra Capilla del Salvador** (*open 10.30–2 and 4.30–6; adm*), begun in 1540, the finest of Úbeda's churches, where Francisco de los Cobos is buried.

All the sculpture on the façades of Úbeda is first-class, especially the west front of the Salvador. This is a monument of the time when Spain was in the mainstream of Renaissance ideas, and humanist classicism was still respectable. Note the mythological subjects on the west front and inside the church, and be sure to look under the arch of the main door. Instead of Biblical scenes, it has carved panels of the ancient gods representing the five planets; Phoebus and Diana with the sun and moon; and Hercules, Aeolus, Vulcan and Neptune to represent the four elements. The interior, with its great dome, is worth a look despite a thorough sacking in 1936 (the sacristan lives on the first door on the left of Calle Francisco Cobos, on the north side of the church). Behind El Salvador, the **Hospital de los Honrados** has a delightful open patio – but only because the other half of the building was never completed. South of the plaza, the end of town is only a few blocks away, encompassed by a street called the **Redonda de Miradores**, a quiet spot favoured by small children and goats, with remnants of Úbeda's wall and exceptional views over the Sierra de Cazorla to the east.

Beyond Plaza Vázquez de Molina

Northeast of El Salvador, along **Calle Horno Contado**, there are a few more fine palaces. At the top of the street, on Plaza 1 de Mayo, is the 13th-century **San Pablo** church (*open 7–9pm*), much renovated in the 16th century; inside is an elegant chapel of 1536, the Capilla del Camarero Vago. On the same square is the elegant town hall, dating from the 16th century. North from here along C/Cervantes is the Casa de Mudéjar, with a pretty courtyard containing the town's small **archaeological museum** (*open Tues–Sun 10–2 and 5–9*). **San Nicolás de Bari** (*open daily 8.30–9.30*), further north, was originally a synagogue, though nothing now bears witness to this. It was confiscated in 1492, which has left it with one Gothic door and the other by Vandelvira, who oversaw the reconstruction.

Take the road west from here, C/Condesa, and you will pass yet more fine palaces, Casa del Caballerizo Ortega, Palacio de los Bussianos, on C/Trinidad, and near it **Trinity Church** (*open daily, 7.20pm–8.30pm*). On the western outskirts of town, near the bus station on Calle Nueva is Vandelvira's most remarkable building, the **Hospital de Santiago** (*open 8–3 and 3.30–10*). This huge edifice, recently restored, has been called the 'Escorial of Andalucía'. It has the same plan as San Nicolás de Bari, a grid of quad-rangles with a church inside. Oddly, both were begun at about the same time, though this one seems to have been started a year earlier, in 1568. Both are supreme examples of the *estilo desornamentado*. The façade here is not as plain as Herrera's; its quirky decoration and clean, angular lines are unique, more like a product of the 20th century than the 16th century.

Around Úbeda: the Sierra de Cazorla

If you go east out of Úbeda, you'll be entering a zone few visitors ever reach. Your first stop might be the village of **Torreperogil**, where the Misericordia growers' co-operative in the Calle España produces first-class red and white wines, such as their *tinto El Torreño*, at a modest price. The **Sierra de Cazorla**, a jumble of ragged peaks, pine forests and olive-covered lowlands, offers some memorable mountain scenery, especially around **Cazorla**, a lovely, undiscovered white village of narrow alleys hung at alarming angles down the hillsides, with a strangely alpine feel to it. Cazorla's landmarks are a ruined Renaissance church (again, by Vandelvira) half-open to the sky, and its castle. But there's an even better castle, possibly built by the Templars, just east of town. **La Iruela** is a romantic ruin even by Spanish standards, with a tower on a dizzying height behind. Beyond La Iruela is the pass into the Sierra, the wild territory of hiking, hunting and fishing.

All of this area is poorly served by public transport and you will need a car to explore far-flung villages such as **Hornos** and **Segura de la Sierra**, both topped with Moorish castles. The latter is a pretty little town, untouched by tourism, with a number of monuments on show, including some Moorish baths and a pretty Renaissance fountain. The road from here heads north to **Siles**, surrounded by embattlements and a lookout tower, before leaving the park via **Torres de Albánchez**, with more Moorish castle remains.

The mountain ranges of Cazorla and Segura make up one of the 10 national parks in Spain. The **Cazorla National Park** covers over half a million acres, and teems with wild boar, deer, mountain goat, buck and moufflon, while rainbow trout do their best to outwit the patient but determined anglers. The park abounds with mountain streams and is the source of the mighty Guadalquivir, nothing more than a trickle over a couple of stones at this point. A hike in search of the source of Andalucía's greatest river is desperately romantic (a good map will direct you). Visitors interested in flora and fauna will find the area one of the richest in Europe, with a variety of small birdlife that's hard to match – as well as larger species such as eagles, ospreys and vultures.

Tourist Information

Cazorla: Pso del Santo Cristo 17, t 95 371 01 02; and a Natural Park Tourist Office at C/Martinez Falero 11, t 95 372 01 25.
Segura de la Sierra: C/Regidor J. Isla 1, t 95 338 02 80.
Torres de Albánchez: Pza de la Constitución 2, t 95 349 41 00.

Where to Stay and Eat

Cazorla ✉ 23470
Cazorla has a surprising number of hotels, both in town and up in the mountains.
★★★Parador El Adelantado, t 95 372 70 75, f 95 372 70 77, cazorla@parador.es (*expensive*). Tucked about five miles inside the park, the *parador* is a mountain chalet with 33 rooms, a pool set right on the cliff edge and a cosy log fire. It is agreeably remote and has an appealing, if slightly institutional, feel to it. Its setting, however, is without equal; if budget allows, this is the obvious choice as a base for exploring the National Park. The restaurant is one of the best in the area, serving up lots of game dishes.
Hotel Ciudad de Cazorla, Plaza de la Corredera 9 (right on the main square), t 95 372 17 00, f 95 372 04 20 (*moderate*). The best hotel in town, with the sheer cliffs as a dramatic backdrop. The rooms are functional but undistinguished; swimming pool.
★★Hotel Guadalquivir, C/Nueva, 6, t/f 95 372 02 68 (*inexpensive*). The next best option, with 12 comfortable rooms in a good spot near the centre.

★★Parque, C/Hilario Marcos 46, t/f 95 372 18 06 (*inexpensive*). One of a number of options along C/Hilario Marcos, with mod cons like phones and TV; all rooms en suite.
★Don Diego, C/Hilario Marcos 163, t 95 372 05 31, f 95 372 05 45 (*inexpensive*). A comfortable little hotel.
Pension Limas, C/Hilario Marcos 175, t 95 372 09 09, f 95 372 19 09 (*inexpensive*). Similar, with a café attached.
★Mirasierra, Santiago de la Espada, Ctra del Tranco, km 20, t 95 371 30 44 (*cheap*). In a beautiful setting 20km north of Cazorla, on the road to the dam and reservoir at El Tranco; with a restaurant.

La Iruela, a small village 1km from Cazorla along the Ctra de la Sierra, also has a couple of possibilities.
★★★Peña de las Halcones, Travesía Camino La Iruela s/n, t 95 372 02 11, f 95 372 13 35 (*moderate*). A relatively sophisticated place with wonderful views and minibars in all of the rooms.
★★La Finca, Ctra de la Sierra, t 95 372 10 87 (*inexpensive*). Offers modest rooms, some with tremendous views. Its small dining room has the best kitchen in the area.

There are a few rural hotels near Segura where you can get away from it all.
★Hospedería de Montaña Rio Madera, t/f 95 312 62 04 (*inexpensive*). In a lovely setting, this place offers all the mod cons, including a pool, at a very reasonable price.
Hospedería Morceguillinas, along the road to Beas, t 95 312 61 52, f 95 349 62 84 (*inexpensive*). Offers similar facilities in another pretty setting.

Language

Castellano, as Spanish is properly called, was the first modern language to have a grammar written for it. When a copy was presented to Queen Isabel in 1492, she understandably asked what it was for. 'Your majesty', replied a perceptive bishop, 'language is the perfect instrument of empire'. In the centuries to come, this concise, flexible and expressive language would prove just that: an instrument that would contribute more to Spanish unity than any laws or institutions, while spreading itself effortlessly over much of the New World.

Among other European languages, Spanish is closest to Portuguese and Italian – and of course, Catalan and Gallego. Spanish, however, may have the simplest grammar of any Romance language, and if you know a little of any one of these, you will find much of the vocabulary looks familiar. It's quite easy to pick up a working knowledge of Spanish; but Spaniards speak colloquially and fast, and in Andalucía they leave out half the consonants and add some strange sounds all of their own. Expressing yourself may prove a little easier than understanding the replies. Spaniards will appreciate your efforts, and when they correct you, they aren't being snooty; they simply feel it's their duty to help you learn.

There are dozens of language books and tapes on the market; one particularly good one is *Teach Yourself Spanish*, by Juan Kattán-Ibarra (Hodder & Stoughton, 1984). Note that the Spaniards increasingly use the familiar *tú* instead of *usted* when addressing even complete strangers.

For food and drink vocabulary, *see* 'Menu Reader', pp.66–9.

Pronunciation

Pronunciation is phonetic but somewhat difficult for English speakers.

Vowels
a short *a* as in 'pat'
e short *e* as in 'set'
i as *e* in 'be'
o between long *o* of 'note' and short *o* of 'hot'
u silent after *q* and gue- and gui-; otherwise long *u* as in 'flute'
ü *w* sound, as in 'dwell'
y at end of word or meaning *and*, as i

Diphthongs
ai, ay as *i* in 'side'
au as *ou* in 'sound'
ei, ey as *ey* in 'they'
oi, oy as *oy* of 'boy'

Consonants
c before the vowels *i* and *e*, it's a *castellano* tradition to pronounce it as *th*; many Spaniards and all Latin Americans pronounce it in this case as an *s*
ch like *ch* in 'church'
d often becomes *th*, or is almost silent, at end of word
g before *i* or *e*, pronounced as *j* (see below)
h silent
j the *ch* in loch – a guttural, throat-clearing *h*
ll *y* or *ly* as in million
ñ *ny* as in canyon (the ~ is called a tilde)
q *k*
r usually rolled, which takes practice
v often pronounced as *b*
z *th*, but *s* in parts of Andalucía

Stress
If the word ends in a vowel, an *n* or an *s*, then the stress falls on the penultimate syllable, otherwise stress falls on the last syllable; exceptions are marked with an accent.

If all this seems difficult, remember that English pronunciation is even more difficult for Spaniards; if your Spanish friends giggle at your pronunciation, get them to try to say *squirrel*.

Practise on some of Spanish place names:

Madrid ma-DREED
León lay-OHN
Sevilla se-BEE-ah
Cáceres CAH-ther-es
Cuenca KWAYN-ka
Jaén ha-AIN
Sigüenza sig-WAYN-thah
Trujillo troo-HEE-oh
Jerez her-ETH
Badajóz ba-da-HOTH
Málaga MAHL-ah-gah
Alcázar ahl-CATH-ar
Valladolid ba-yah-dol-EED
Arévalo ahr-EB-bah-lo

Useful Words and Phrases

yes *sí*
no *no*
I don't know *No sé*
I don't understand Spanish *No entiendo español*
Do you speak English? *¿Habla usted inglés?*
Does someone here speak English? *¿Hay alguien que hable inglés?*
Speak slowly *Hable despacio*
Can you help me? *¿Puede usted ayudarme?*
Help! *¡Socorro!*
please *por favor*
thank you (very much) *(muchas) gracias*
you're welcome *de nada*
It doesn't matter *No importa/Es igual*
all right *está bien*
ok *vale*
excuse me *perdóneme*
Be careful! *¡Tenga cuidado!*
maybe *quizá(s)*
nothing *nada*
It is urgent! *¡Es urgente!*
How do you do? *¿Cómo está usted?*
    or more familiarly *¿Cómo estás? ¿Qué tal?*
Well, and you? *¿Bien, y usted?*
    or more familiarly *¿Bien, y tú?*
What is your name? *¿Cómo se llama?*
    or more familiarly *¿Cómo te llamas?*
My name is ... *Me llamo es...*
My number is ... *Mi nombre es...*
Hello *¡Hola!*
Goodbye *Adios/Hasta luego*
Good morning *Buenos días*
Good afternoon *Buenas tardes*

Good evening *Buenas noches*
What is that? *¿Qué es eso?*
What ...? *¿Qué ...?*
Who ...? *¿Quién ...?*
Where ...? *¿Dónde ...?*
When ...? *¿Cuándo ...?*
Why ...? *¿Por qué ...?*
How ...? *¿Cómo ...?*
How much? *¿Cuánto/Cuánta?*
How many? *¿Cuántos/Cuántas?*
I am lost *Me he perdido*
I am hungry *Tengo hambre*
I am thirsty *Tengo sed*
I am sorry *Lo siento*
I am tired (man/woman) *Estoy cansado/a*
I am sleepy *Tengo sueño*
I am ill *No siento bien*
Leave me alone *Déjeme en paz*
good *bueno/buena*
bad *malo/mala*
slow *despacio*
fast *rápido/rápida*
big *grande*
small *pequeño/pequeña*
hot *caliente*
cold *frío/fría*

Numbers

one *uno/una*
two *dos*
three *tres*
four *cuatro*
five *cinco*
six *seis*
seven *siete*
eight *ocho*
nine *nueve*
ten *diez*
eleven *once*
twelve *doce*
thirteen *trece*
fourteen *catorce*
fifteen *quince*
sixteen *dieciséis*
seventeen *diecisiete*
eighteen *dieciocho*
nineteen *diecinueve*
twenty *veinte*
twenty-one *veintiuno*
thirty *treinta*
thirty-one *treinta y uno*

forty *cuarenta*
forty-one *cuarenta y uno*
fifty *cincuenta*
sixty *sesenta*
seventy *setenta*
eighty *ochenta*
ninety *noventa*
one hundred *cien*
one hundred and one *ciento-uno*
five hundred *quinientos*
one thousand *mil*
first *primero*
second *segundo*
third *tercero*
fourth *cuarto*
fifth *quinto*
tenth *décimo*

Time

What time is it? *¿Qué hora es?*
It is two o'clock *Son las dos*
... half past two *... las dos y media*
... a quarter past two *... las dos y cuarto*
... a quarter to three *... las tres menos cuarto*
noon *mediodía*
midnight *medianoche*
month *mes*
week *semana*
day *día*
morning *mañana*
afternoon *tarde*
evening *noche*
today *hoy*
yesterday *ayer*
soon *pronto*
tomorrow *mañana*
now *ahora*
later *después*
it is early *está temprano*
it is late *está tarde*

Days

Monday *lunes*
Tuesday *martes*
Wednesday *miércoles*
Thursday *jueves*
Friday *viernes*
Saturday *sábado*
Sunday *domingo*

Months

January *enero*
February *febrero*
March *marzo*
April *abril*
May *mayo*
June *junio*
July *julio*
August *agosto*
September *septiembre*
October *octubre*
November *noviembre*
December *diciembre*

Colours

red *rojo*
blue *azul*
green *verde*
yellow *amarillo*
orange *anaranjado*
pink *rosado*
purple *púrpura, morado*
brown *marrón, pardo*
black *negro*
grey *gris*
white *blanco*

Shopping and Sightseeing

I would like... *Quisiera...*
Where is/are...? *¿Dónde está/están...?*
How much is it? *¿Cuánto vale eso?*
open *abierto*
closed *cerrado*
cheap *barato*
expensive *caro*
bank *banco*
beach *playa*
booking/box office *taquilla*
church *iglesia*
hospital *hospital*
money *dinero*
museum *museo*
theatre *teatro*
newspaper (foreign) *periódico (extrajero)*
pharmacy *farmacia*
police station *comisaria*
policeman *policía*
post office *correos*
postage stamp *sello*

sea *mar*
shop *tienda*
antique shop *anticuario*
bakery *panadería*
butcher's *carnicería*
confectioner's *confitería*
department store *almacén*
pharmacy *farmacia*
hairdresser's *pelaquería*
hardware shop *ferretería*
jeweller's *joyería*
kiosk *quiosco*
market *mercado*
stationer's *papelería*
winery *bodega*
Do you have any change? *¿Tiene cambio?*
telephone *teléfono*
telephone call *conferencia*
tobacconist's *estanco*
supermarket *supermercado*
toilet/toilets *servicios/aseos*
men *señores/hombres/caballeros*
women *señoras/damas*

Accommodation

Where is the hotel? *¿Dónde está el hotel?*
Do you have a room? *¿Tiene usted
una habitación?*
Can I look at the room? *¿Podría ver
la habitación?*
How much is the room per day/week?
*¿Cuánto cuesta la habitación por
día/semana?*
... with two beds *con dos camas*
... with double bed *con una cama grande*
... with a shower/bath *con ducha/baño*
... for one person/two people *para una
persona/ dos personas*
... for one night/ one week *una noche/
una semana*

Driving

rent *alquiler*
car *coche*
motorbike/moped *moto/ciclomotor*
bicycle *bicicleta*
petrol *gasolina*
garage *garaje*
This doesn't work *Este no funciona*
road *carretera*

motorway *autopista*
Is the road good? *¿Es buena la carretera?*
breakdown *avería*
(international) driving licence *carnet de
conducir (internacional)*
driver *conductor, chófer*
speed *velocidad*
exit *salida*
entrance *entrada*
danger *peligro*
dangerous *peligroso*
no parking *estacionament prohibido*
narrow *estrecha*
give way/yield *ceda el paso*
road works *obras*

Note: Most road signs will be in international pictographs

Transport

aeroplane *avión*
airport *aeropuerto*
bus/coach *autobús/autocar*
bus/railway station *estación*
bus stop *parada*
car/automobile *coche*
customs *aduana*
platform *andén*
port *puerto*
seat *asiento*
ship *buque/barco/ embarcadero*
ticket *billete*
train *tren*

Directions

I want to go to... *Deseo ir a...*
How can I get to...? *¿Cómo puedo llegar a...?*
Where is...? *¿Dónde está...?*
When is the next...? *¿Cuándo sale
el próximo...?*
What time does it leave (arrive)? *¿Parte (llega)
a qué hora?*
From where does it leave? *¿De dónde sale?*
Do you stop at ...? *¿Para en...?*
How long does the trip take? *¿Cuánto tiempo
dura el viaje?*
I want a (return) ticket to... *Quiero un billete
(de ida y vuelta) a...*
How much is the fare? *¿Cuánto cuesta
el billete?*

Have a good trip! *¡Buen viaje!*
here *aquí*
there *allí*
close *cerca*
far *lejos*
left *izquierda*
right *derecha*
straight on *todo recto*
forwards *adelante*
backwards *hacia atrás*
up *arriba*
down *abajo*
north (n./adj.) *norte/septentrional*
south (n./adj.) *sur/meridional*
east (n./adj.) *este/oriental*
west (n./adj.) *oeste/occidental*
corner *esquina*
square *plaza*
street *calle*

The Beach

sand *arena*
sea *mar*
wave *ola*
seaweed *alga*
dune *duna*
high/low tide *marea alta/baja*
cove *cala*
bay *bahía*
lifeguard *vigilante*
lifeboat *lancha de socorro*
swimsuit *traje de baño*
sunbathe *tomar el sol*
sun cream *crema bronceadora*
tan *bronceado*
sunburn *quemadura*
sunglasses *gafas del sol*
parasol *sombrilla*
towel *toalla*

Clothing

clothing *ropa*
belt *cinturón*
blouse *blusa*
coat *abrigo*
raincoat *impermeable*
dress *vestido*
suit *traje*
jacket *chaqueta*
trousers *pantalone*
jeans *vaqueros*
T-shirt *camiseta*
skirt *falda*
shoes *zapatos*
socks *calcetines*
boots *botas*
underwear *ropa interior*
shorts *pantalón corto*
tennis shoes *zapatillas*
sweater *suéter*
tie *corbata*
handkerchief *pañuelo*
hat *sombrero*
scarf *bufanda*
vest *chaleco*
swimsuit *traje de baño*
gloves *guantes*
wallet *cartera*
purse *bolsa*

Glossary

Corregidor: chief magistrate.
Corrida de toros: bullfight.
Cortijo: Andalucían country house.
Cúpula: cupola; dome or rounded vault forming a roof or ceiling.
Custodia: tabernacle, where sacramental vessels are kept.
Diputación: seat of provincial government.
Embalse: reservoir.
Ermita: hermitage.
Esgrafiado: style of painting, or etching designs in stucco, on a façade.
Estilo desornamentado: austere, heavy Renaissance style inaugurated by Philip II's architect, Juan de Herrera; sometimes described as Herreran.
Fandango: traditional dance and song, greatly influenced by the gypsies of Andalucía.
Feria: major festival or market, often an occasion for bullfights.
Finca: farm, country house or estate.
Fonda: modest hotel, from the Arabic *funduq*, or inn.
Fuero: exemption or privilege of a town or region under medieval Spanish law.
Grandee: select member of Spain's highest nobility.
Hammam: Moorish bath.
Herreran: see *estilo desornamentado*.
Hidalgo: literally 'son of somebody' – the lowest level of the nobility, just good enough for a coat of arms.
Homage tower: the tallest tower of fortification, sometimes detached from the wall.
Humilladero: calvary, or stations of the Cross along a road outside town.
Isabelline Gothic: late 15th-century style, roughly corresponding to English perpendicular.
Judería: Jewish quarter.
Junta: council, or specifically, the regional government.
Khan: inn for merchants.

Kufic: angular style of Arabic calligraphy originating in the city of Kufa in Mesopotamia, often used as architectural ornamentation.
Lonja: merchants' exchange.
Madrasa: Muslim theological school, usually located near a mosque.
Majolica: type of porous pottery glazed with bright metallic oxides.
Mantilla: silk or lace scarf or shawl, worn by women to cover their head and shoulders.
Maqsura: elevated platform usually with grills.
Matador: the principal bullfighter, who finally kills the bull.
Medina: walled centre of a Moorish city.
Mercado: market.
Mezquita: mosque.
Mihrab: prayer niche facing Mecca, often elaborately decorated in a mosque.
Mirador: scenic viewpoint or belvedere.
Monterías: hunting scenes (in art).
Moriscos: Muslims who submitted to Christianization to remain in al-Andalus after the Reconquista.
Mozárabes: Christians under Muslim rule in Moorish Spain.
Mudéjar: Moorish-influenced architecture, characterized by decorative use of bricks and ceramics; Spain's 'national style' in 12th to 16th centuries.
Moufflon: wild, short-fleeced mountain sheep.
Muqarnas: hanging masonry effect created through multiple use of support elements.
Ogival: pointed (arches).
Parador: state-owned hotel, often a converted historic building.
Paseo: promenade, or an evening walk along a promenade.
Patio: central courtyard of a house or public building.
Picador: bullfighter on horseback, who goads and wounds the bull with a *pica* or short lance in the early stages of a bullfight in order to weaken the animal.

Plateresque: heavily ornamented 16th-century Gothic style.

Plaza: town square.

Plaza de toros: bullring.

Plaza mayor: main square at the centre of many Spanish cities, often almost totally enclosed and arcaded.

Posada: inn or lodging house.

Pronunciamiento: military coup.

Pueblo: village.

Puente: bridge.

Puerta: gate or portal.

Reconquista: the Christian Reconquest of Moorish Spain beginning in 718 and completed in 1492 by the Catholic Kings.

Reja: iron grille, either decorative inside a church or covering the exterior window of a building

Retablo: carved or painted altarpiece.

Los Reyes Católicos: The Catholic Kings, Isabella and Ferdinand.

Romería: pilgrimage, usually on a saint's feast day.

Sagrario: reliquary chapel.

Sala capitular: chapterhouse.

Sillería: choir stall.

Souk: open-air marketplace found in Muslim countries.

Stele: stone slab marking a grave or displaying an inscription.

Taifa: small Moorish kingdom; especially one of the so-called Party Kingdoms which sprang up in Spain following the 1031 fall of the caliph of Cordoba.

Taracea: inlaid wood in geometric patterns.

Torero: bullfighter, especially one on foot.

Torre: tower.

Vega: cultivated plain or fertile river valley.

Chronology

BC

c. 50,000 Earliest traces of man in Andalucía.

c. 25,000 Palaeolithic Proto-Spaniards occupy and decorate region's caves.

c. 7000 Arrival of Iberians, probably from North Africa.

c. 2300 Bronze-Age settlement at Los Millares, largest in Europe.

c. 1100 Phoenicians found Cádiz.

c. 800 Celts from over the Pyrenees join the Iberians; period of the kingdom of Tartessos in Andalucía.

c. 636 Greeks found trading colony near Malaga.

c. 500 Carthage conquers Tartessos.

241 Carthage loses First Punic War to Rome.

227 Rome and Carthage sign treaty, assigning lands south of the Ebro to Carthage.

219 Second Punic War breaks out when Hannibal besieges Roman ally Sagonte.

218 Hannibal takes his elephants and the war to Italy.

211–206 Romans under Proconsul Scipio Africanus take the war back to Spain, defeating Carthage.

206 Founding of Itálica, a Roman veterans' colony, near Seville.

55 The elder Seneca born in Cordoba.

46 During the ups and downs of the wars and colonizations of Spain, Caesar intervenes, riding from Rome to Obulco (60km from Cordoba) in 27 days; founds veterans' colony at Osuna.

27 Octavian divides Iberian peninsula into Interior Spain, Lusitania (Portugal) and Further Spain, soon better known as Bætica (Andalucía).

AD

39 Roman poet Lucan born in Cordoba.

50 All of Spain finally conquered by Romans, who lay out the first road network.

54 Trajan, future Roman emperor, born at Itálica.

70 Romans under Titus destroy the Temple in Jerusalem; in the subsequent diaspora thousands of Jews end up in Spain.

76 Hadrian, Trajan's successor in 117, born at Itálica.

306 Council of Iliberis (Elvira, near Granada) consolidates the Christianization of Spain, votes for the celibacy of priests and also bans Christians from marrying pagans.

409–28 Vandals vandalize Bætica and (probably) change its name to Vandalusia.

478 Visigoths, followers of the Arian heresy, control most of Spain, including Andalucía.

554 Byzantine Emperor Justinian sends troops to take sides in Visigoth civil war, and overstays his welcome.

573 King Leovigild of the Visigoths chases the Greeks out of their last footholds.

589 Leovigild's son, Reccared, converts to Catholicism.

602–35 Writings of St Isidore, Bishop of Seville, which provide main link between the ancient and medieval worlds.

711 Arabs and Berbers under Tariq ibn-Ziyad defeat Roderick, the last Visigoth king.

718 Pelayo, in Asturias, defeats Muslims at Covadonga, marking the official beginning of the Reconquista.

756 Abd ar-Rahman, of the Ummayyad dynasty, first emir of al-Andalus begins the Great Mosque of Cordoba.

844 Abd ar-Rahman II begins the Alcázar in Seville.

880–917 Revolt against the Ummayyads by Ibn-Hafsun, at Bobastro.

912–76 Abd ar-Rahman III declares himself caliph of Cordoba and begins the magnificent palace-city of Medinat az-Zahra.

977 Last enlargements of the Great Mosque by al-Mansur.

994 Birth of Ibn-Hazm of Cordoba (Abernhazam; d. 1064), greatest scholar of century and author of the famous treatise on love, *The Ring of the Dove*.

1003 Birth of the love poet Ibn-Zaydun in Cordoba (d. 1070).

1008 Caliphate starts to unravel.

1013 Berbers destroy Medinat az-Zahra.

1031 Caliphate abolished as al-Andalus dissolves into factions of the Party Kings.

1085 Alfonso VI of Castile and El Cid capture Toledo from the Muslims.

1086 Taifa kings summon aid of the Berber Almoravids.

1105 Birth of philosopher Ibn-Tufayl (Abubacer) in Guadix, author of the charming narrative romance Hayy ibn-Yaqzan (*The Awakening of the Soul*), one of the masterworks of al-Andalus.

1110 Almoravids gobble up the taifa kingdoms.

1126 Birth of Ibn-Rushd in Cordoba, philosopher and commentator on Aristotle, better known in the west as Averroës (d. 1198).

1135 Alfonso VII of Castile and León takes the title of Emperor of Spain.

1145 Uprisings against the Almoravids.

1172 Almohads conquer Seville, rounding off the defeat of the Almoravids.

1195 Completion of La Giralda in Seville.

1212 Alfonso VII's victory at Las Navas de Tolosa opens the gate to al-Andalus.

1231 Muhammad ibn-Yusuf ibn-Nasr carves out a small realm around Jaén.

1236 Fernando III ('the Saint') captures Cordoba.

1238 Muhammad ibn-Yusuf ibn-Nasr takes Granada, founding the Nasrid dynasty, and begins construction of the Alhambra.

1248 Fernando III takes Seville with the help of his vassal, Muhammad ibn-Yusef ibn-Nasr.

1262 Alfonso X ('the Wise') picks up Cádiz.

1292 Sancho IV takes Tarifa.

1309 Guzmán el Bueno seizes Gibraltar.

1333 Alfonso XI loses Gibraltar to the king of Granada.

1350–69 Reign of Pedro the Cruel of Castile.

1415 Ceuta is captured by Portuguese, though it remains in Spanish hands after the division of the two kingdoms.

1462 Enrico IV gets Gibraltar back for Castile.

1479 Isabella and Ferdinand (Isabel and fernando) unite their kingdoms of Castile and Aragon.

1480 Spanish Inquisition sets up a branch office in Seville.

1492 Ferdinand and Isabella complete the Reconquista with the capture of Granada and expel Jews from Spain; Columbus sets off from Seville to discover the New World.

1500 First Revolt of the Alpujarras.

1516 Birth of lyric poet Luis de Góngora in Cordoba.

1516–56 Isabella and Ferdinand's grandson becomes King Carlos I.

1519 Carlos is promoted and becomes Holy Roman Emperor Charles V.

1528 Sculptor Pietro Torrigiano dies in the Inquisition's prison in Seville.

1556–98 Reign of Carlos's bureaucratic son, Philip (Felipe) II.

1568 Philip II's intolerance leads to the Second Revolt of the Alpujarras.

1580 Seville largest city in Spain, with population of 85,000.

1578–1621 Reign of Felipe's rapacious son, Felipe III.

1599 Diego Velázquez born in Seville (d. 1660).

1609–14 Felipe III forces half a million Muslims to move to North Africa.

1617 Murillo born in Seville (d. 1682).

1621–65 Reign of Felipe IV, chiefly remembered through Velázquez's portraits.

1627 Birth of *sevillano* libertine Don Miguel de Mañara, believed to be the original Don Juan Tenorio of Tirso de Molina (the Don Giovanni of Mozart).

1630 Madrid becomes the largest city in Spain.

1649 Plague leaves one out of three people dead in Seville.

1665–1700 Reign of the weak and deformed Carlos II, last of the Spanish Habsburgs.

1700–46 Louis XIV exports his brand of Bourbon to Spain, in the form of his grandson Felipe V. The danger of Spain and France becoming united under a single ruler leads to the War of the Spanish Succession.

1704 Anglo-Dutch fleet, under the auspices of Charles of Austria, captures Gibraltar.

1713 The Spanish cede Gibraltar to Britain under the Treaty of Utrecht.

1726 Spain tries in vain to regain the Rock.

1746–59 Reign of Fernando VI.

1757 Completion of Seville's tobacco factory, where Carmen would work.

1759–88 Reign of Carlos III.

1779–83 The Great Siege of Gibraltar.

1783 Treaty of Versailles confirms British possession of Gibraltar.

1788–1808 Reign of the pathetic Carlos IV, caricatured by Goya.

1808–13 The installation by Napoleon of his brother, Joseph Bonaparte, as king leads to war with France.

1814–33 End of Peninsular War and reinstatement of the Bourbon king, Fernando VII; his repeal of the Salic law and the succession of his daughter as Isabel II (1833–70) leads to the Carlist wars during her troubled reign.

1830 So many English winter in Málaga that they need their own cemetery.

1832 Washington Irving publishes *Tales of the Alhambra*.

1870–85 Reign of Alfonso XII.

1876 Manuel de Falla born in Cádiz (d. 1946).

1881 Pablo Picasso born in Malaga; Nobel-prize winning poet Juan Ramón Jiménez born in Moguer de la Frontera (d. 1958).

1886–1931 Reign of Alfonso XIII, who abdicated in favour of a successor who was to become king 'when Spain judges it opportune'.

1893 Andres Segovia born near Jaén.

1898 Birth of Federico García Lorca near Granada (d. 1936).

1920 Ibero-American Exhibition in Seville gets a disappointing turnout.

1936–9 Spanish Civil War.

1940 Hitler tries to get Spain to join Axis by promising to help Spain conquer Gibraltar, but Franco says no.

1953 First economic–military cooperation between Spain and the USA.

1956 Spain ends its protectorate in Morocco, but keeps Ceuta and Melilla.

1962 Franco's Minister of Tourism gives go ahead for development of the Costa del Sol.

1966 An American bomber over Palomares collides with another plane and drops four nuclear bombs.

1975 Death of Franco; Juan Carlos, grandson of Alfonso XIII crowned king of Spain.

1982 Felipe González of Seville elected prime minister.

1983 Andalucía becomes an autonomous province.

1985 Frontier between Gibraltar and Spain opens.

1986 Spain and Portugal join the EC.

1992 International Exhibition in Seville to commemorate the 500th anniversary of Columbus's departure from Huelva to the New World.

1997 The political troubles of the north reach southern Spain, with a car bomb in Granada, blamed on the Basque Eta group.

1998 In January, a councillor and his wife are shot dead in Seville. Five Eta members are arrested in Seville in March in a safe house where 600kg of explosives are also found.

Further Reading

General and Travel

Baird, David, *Inside Andalusia* (Lookout Publications). Background reading. Glossy, full of history and anecdote.

Borrow, George, *The Bible in Spain*. One of the best-known travel books about Spain, opinionated and amusing; first published in 1842.

Brenan, Gerald, *The Face of Spain* (Penguin, 1987). An account of his journey through central and southern Spain in the spring of 1949.

Chetwode, Penelope, *Two Middle-Aged Ladies in Andalusia*. A delightful bosom-heaving *burro*-back look at the region.

Elms, Robert, *Spain: A Portrait After the General* (Heinemann, 1992). Incisive, witty, honest look at the new Spain from one of Britain's foremost young travel writers.

Ford, Richard, *Gatherings from Spain* (Everyman). A boiled-down version of the all-time classic travel book *A Handbook for Travellers in Spain*, written in 1845. Hard to find but worth the trouble.

Hooper, John, *The Spaniards* (Penguin, 1987). A comprehensive account of contemporary Spanish life and politics. Well done.

Jacobs, Michael, *A Guide to Andalusia* (Viking). Informative and well-researched volume on history, culture and sights.

Josephs, Allen, *White Wall of Spain* (Iowa State UP, USA). An interesting collection of essays on Andalucían folklore, with a particular focus on religious festivals, flamenco and bullfights.

Lee, Laurie, *As I Walked Out One Midsummer Morning* and *A Rose for Winter*. Very well written adventures of a young man in Spain in 1936, and his return 20 years later.

Stewart, Chris, *Driving Over Lemons* (Sort of Books, UK, 1999). A witty account of an Englishman and his wife setting up home in a farmhouse in Las Alpujarras, Granada.

History

Brenan, Gerald, *The Spanish Labyrinth* (Cambridge, 1943). Origins of the Civil War.

Castro, Américo, *The Structure of Spanish History* (E L King, 1954). A remarkable interpretation of Spain's history, published in exile during the Franco years.

Cohen, J M (editor), *The Four Voyages of Christopher Columbus* (Penguin Classics). Accounts of all four of Columbus's voyages to the Indies, including passages from the explorer's own log entries.

Elliott, J H, *Imperial Spain 1469–1714* (Pelican, 1983). Elegant proof that much of the best writing these days is in the field of history.

Gibson, Ian, *The Assassination of Federico García Lorca* (Penguin, 1983).

Mitchell, David, *The Spanish Civil War* (Granada, 1982). Anecdotal; wonderful photographs.

O'Callaghan, J F, *History of Medieval Spain* (Cornell University, 1983).

Thomas, Hugh, *The Spanish Civil War* (Penguin, 1977). The best general work.

Watt, W H, and **Cachia, P,** *A History of Islamic Spain* (Edinburgh University Press, 1977).

Art and Literature

Brenan, Gerald, *The Literature of the Spanish People* (Cambridge, 1951).

Burckhardt, Titus, *Moorish Culture in Spain* (Allen and Unwin). Indispensable for understanding the world of al-Andalus.

Cervantes, Miguel de, *Don Quixote* (Penguin/Signet). The early 17th-century Spanish classic.

García Lorca, Federico, *Three Tragedies* (Penguin); *Five Plays: Comedies and Tragicomedies* (Penguin); *Selected Poems* (Bloodaxe Books, UK); *Poem of the Deep Song* (City Lights, USA). Works by the great Andalucían playwright and poet, who was murdered by fascists in Granada.

Goodwin, Godfrey, *Islamic Spain* (Penguin, 1991). From the informative 'Architectural Guides for Travellers' series. Covers all the significant Islamic buildings in Spain

Hemingway, Ernest, *For Whom the Bell Tolls* (Cape/Scribner). Set in Andalucía during the Civil War. A young American volunteer experiences the dangers of war behind the lines, and discovers Maria.

Irving, Washington, *Tales of the Alhambra* and *The Conquest of Granada* (London, 1986).

Jimenéz, Juan Ramón, *Platero and I* and *Pepita Jimenéz*. Noble Prize-winning poet from Andalucía. The former of his works evokes the people and landscape of Andalucía through conversions with Platero, the poet's donkey.

Rice, David Talbot, *Islamic Art* (Thames & Hudson, UK). A renowned introduction to the whole subject of Islamic art and architecture.

Index

Main page references are in **bold**. Page references to maps are in *italics*.
C = Cordoba; G = Granada; S = Seville

Acknowledgements

The updater, Adam Coulter, would like to thank his mother and James, Ed and Lucy, Harry, Denise and Kai, Rob and his father, Liz, John and Val Howard, Raquel and Jonathan, Alan and Jenny, Julie Hetherington, Pati, Ana Serrano and Juan Peiro at the Paradores press office, Terri Palmer at P&O, Lisa Donohue at Hertz, Doug Goodman, Jason Nicholls at GB Airways, Bienvenido at Turarche car hire, Albert and Carmel Parody, James Gaggero of Bland Travel, Marcello Sanguinetti at the Gibraltar Tourist Office, Claire Turner and Patricia Ibarrola at the Spanish Tourist Office, and all the many helpful tourist offices and officers in Andalucía, especially Dolores Lopéz Sánchez and Francisco Miguel Alaminos in Granada, Israel Huertas Salazar in Lucena, and all those in Córdoba and Torremolinos. A special thanks to Kelly, for her love and support and sharing so much of this with me.

Also available from Cadogan Guides in our European series...

The Italy Series

Italy
Italy: The Bay of Naples and Southern Italy
Italy: Lombardy and the Italian Lakes
Italy: Tuscany, Umbria and the Marches
Italy: Tuscany
Italy: Umbria
Italy: Northeast Italy
Italy: Italian Riviera
Italy: Bologna and Emilia Romagna
Italy: Rome and the Heart of Italy
Sardinia
Sicily
Rome, Florence, Venice
Florence, Siena, Pisa & Lucca
Rome
Venice

The France Series

France
France: Dordogne & the Lot
France: Gascony & the Pyrenees
France: Brittany
France: The Loire
France: The South of France
France: Provence
France: Corsica
France: Côte d'Azur
Corsica
Paris
Short Breaks in Northern France

The Spain Series

Spain
Spain: Andalucía
Spain: Northern Spain
Spain: Bilbao and the Basque Lands
Granada, Seville, Cordoba
Madrid, Barcelona, Seville
Madrid
Barcelona

The Greece Series

Greece: The Peloponnese
Greek Islands
Greek Islands By Air
Corfu & the Ionian Islands
Mykonos, Santorini & the Cyclades
Rhodes & the Dodecanese
Crete

The UK and Ireland Series

London
London–Amsterdam
London–Edinburgh
London–Paris
London–Brussels

Scotland
Scotland: Highlands and Islands
Edinburgh

Ireland
Ireland: Southwest Ireland
Ireland: Northern Ireland

Other Europe Titles

Portugal
Portugal: The Algarve
Madeira & Porto Santo

Malta

Germany: Bavaria

Holland
Holland: Amsterdam & the Randstad
Amsterdam

Brussels, Bruges, Ghent & Antwerp
Bruges

Cadogan Guides are available from good bookshops, or via **Grantham Book Services,** Isaac Newton Way, Alma Park Industrial Estate, Grantham NG31 9SD, **t** (01476) 541 080, **f** (01476) 541 061; and **The Globe Pequot Press**, 246 Goose Lane, PO Box 480, Guilford, Connecticut 06437–0480, **t** (203) 458 4500, **f** (203) 458 4600.